THE BIG6™ COLLECTION: The Best of the Big6™ Newsletter

By Michael B. Eisenberg and Robert E. Berkowitz

Linworth

PUBLISHING, INC.

Linworth Publishing, Inc.
Worthington, Ohio

Library of Congress Cataloging-in-Publication Data

Published by Linworth Publishing, Inc.
480 East Wilson Bridge Road, Suite L
Worthington, Ohio 43085

Copyright © 2000 by Michael B. Eisenberg and Robert E. Berkowitz

ISBN 0-938865-97-8

5 4 3 2 1

Table of Contents

Table of Contents *continued*

Table of Contents *continued*

Table of Contents continued

Introduction:
Notes from Mike and Bob

Greetings Big6ers and Future Big6ers!

We are pleased to offer this compilation of the best of *The Big6 Newsletter*. This extensive collection includes in-depth articles, practical tips and explanations, and guidance in implementing the Big6 across educational environments and situations.

In typical Eisenberg and Berkowitz fashion, we approached the task of pulling all this together from a Big6 perspective. Focusing on the task, we recognized the overwhelming demands on educators to do it all—to teach academic content and life skills, improve students' social skills as well as watch over the students' nutritional, hygiene, and mental health needs. We also know that living in the "information age" only adds to the stresses of modern day teaching and learning. Therefore, we knew that we needed to provide meaningful information that directly addressed the needs of classrooms, libraries, and special educational environments. For us, that meant an extensive synthesis task in order to minimize your time and effort for location and access. We sought to facilitate ease of use by careful clustering of related material and, of course, providing an extensive table of contents and index.

The Big6

"The Big6 approach can be used whenever students are faced with an information problem or with making a decision that is based on information." *(Eisenberg and Berkowitz, 1990)*

We've each written this statement hundreds of times. We do so again here because we want to emphasize that one of the strengths of the Big6 is its wide applicability across situation. But what exactly is the Big6? First and foremost, the Big6 is a process model of information problem-solving that encom-passes six stages and 2 sub-stages under each:

From experience and study, we've found that the Big6 stages are necessary and sufficient. That is, the stages are necessary because successful information problem-solving requires successful completion of each of these stages at some point in time. And, they do not have to be done in order. For example, a person can jump right into location and access or use of information, and later loop back to task definition and figure out exactly what he or she is trying to accomplish (Eisenberg and Lowe, 1997).

The Big6 stages are also sufficient because the Big6 stages and sub-stages encompass the range of skills needed to complete an information task. More specific activities, processes, and skills are easily grouped under one or more of the Big6 stages. That is why the Big6 is often used as the structure for developing an information literacy or information and technology skills curriculum.

But the Big6 is more than just the six-stage process or the curricula built around it. The Big6 is a complete approach to implementing meaningful learning and teaching information and technology skills. We continually emphasize that the Big6 Skills must be taught in the context of classroom curriculum, activities, and assignments. Students "get it" when they learn the Big6 skills as they are working through projects, reports, worksheets, and other assignments in the subject areas. In our numerous writings, productions, and presentations, we've shared systematic strategies for fully integrating Big6. Therefore, the Big6 represents a unified program for information and technology literacy across educational settings.

Lastly, the Big6 can be thought of as a movement. We—Big6ers—believe that the Big6 skills represent critical and essential skills for living in our society.

Components of the Big6 Skills

1 Task Definition

1.1 Define the problem.

1.2 Identify the information needed.

2 Information Seeking Strategies

2.1 Determine all possible sources.

2.2 Select the best sources.

3 Location & Access

3.1 Locate sources.

3.2 Find information within sources.

4 Use of Information

4.1 Engage (e.g., read, hear, view).

4.2 Extract relevant information.

5 Synthesis

5.1 Organize information from multiple sources.

5.2 Present the result.

6 Evaluation

6.1 Judge the result (effectiveness).

6.2 Judge the process (efficiency).

Learning the Big6 is not optional! Information and technology skills are basic to a 21st century education and it is our responsibility to see that students gain them. To paraphrase from the mission statement of the American Association of School Librarians, our job is "to ensure that students are effective users of ideas and information" (AASL/AECT 1999). This is a worthy mission for all educators, and the writings in this compilation provide substantive ideas on how to achieve it.

This Book: Contents

This book offers an incredibly rich and varied range of material about students and teachers, the Big6, curriculum, and learning and teaching. As stated above, we worked hard to present the material in a way that makes sense and that's easy to use. This resulted in ten sections—each with a different focus or scope of concern or style of presentation.

PART I provides a comprehensive and scholarly treatment of the concept of information literacy through substantial excerpts from the definitive book on the topic: *Information Literacy: Essential Skills for the Information Age*. Written by Big6ers Kathy Spitzer, Mike Eisenberg, and Carrie Lowe, the book has received worldwide attention—in K-12, higher education, and various training programs. Part I also provides a research perspectives with Carrie Lowe's research reports on Stephen Krashen's work on reading, Carol Kuhlthau's extensive studies of information skills and behavior, and others.

PART II provides specific guidance on a point made earlier—the importance of implementing the Big6 through integration with the real, classroom curriculum. The first article by Mike Eisenberg, "Implementing the Big6: Context, Context, Context," drives this point home and the follow-up article, "Plans and Planning" explains how and provides tools to help do so.

PART III digs into practical approaches for teaching and learning the Big6. This part of the book is organized into six sub-sections starting with working with young children and the Super3, and then focusing on middle and upper grades. Also included are sections on working with special needs and using sports as the context for Big6 learning. This part of the book ends with an in-depth treatment of the relationship of technology and the Internet to the information problem-solving process. Technology is not an add-on or enhancement; it is integral to every Big6 stage, and the articles here show exactly what that means.

PART IV is a compilation of "TIPS" for teaching every Big6 stage. These short targeted, explanations were one of the most popular sections of the newsletter. Here, they are compiled for the first time—and it's an impressive collection!

PART V focuses on one of the most asked about aspects of the Big6: assessment. Bob Berkowitz has done extensive work using Big6 scoring guides to determine students' Big6 abilities within the context of the subject area curriculum and assignments. In addition, there are two "must reads" in this part of the book. These are the articles describing the impact of the Big6 on student performance in Scott Hopsicker's classroom. Scott worked with Bob Berkowitz for one year and it transformed his approach to teaching and the performance of his students on standardized tests.

PART VI offers some creative and fun ways to present the whole Big6 process—especially to new audiences of elementary and middle school students. Included here is the famous Banana Split Lesson developed by Tami Little. There's also Big6 poetry and a Big6 song.

PART VII presents a case study implementation of the Big6 across the state of Utah. The articles span K-12 and are impressive for the scope of the project as well as the energy and enthusiasm of participants. The second section in this part brings together Carrie Lowe's newsletter columns, "Reports from the Front Lines" which described a range of Big6 implementations in libraries and other classrooms.

PART VIII turns to cutting edge technology as Virtual Dave Lankes and others relate the latest in technology developments to the Big6. Included are explanations of various technologies (e.g., AskA services, interactive documents, intranets, real time messaging, various technology tools, and web portals) as well as discussions of the implications of these technologies on learning and teaching.

PART IX is a short but important section encompassing material from our Helping With Homework book as well as some new ideas. Parents quickly relate to the Big6. They see its value and applicability and are eager to learn ways to help their children through **the Big6.**

PART X closes the book with a final word: some interesting questions about the Big6 and our answers to them.

Whew—that's quite a lineup! Looking at it as a whole, it's an impressive collection of material about the Big6skills, approach, curriculum, and relationship to all aspects of learning and teaching. We are pleased to be able to offer these to you in one place.

Think Big – 6!

Mike Eisenberg and Bob Berkowitz
October 7, 1999

Bibliography

AASL/AECT (1998). *Information Power: Building Partnerships for Learning*. Chicago: American Library Association.

Eisenberg, M. and Berkowitz R. (1990). *Information Problem-Solving: The Big Six Skills Approach to Library & Information Skills Instruction.* Ablex Publishing, 1990.

Eisenberg, M. and Lowe, C. (1997). "The Big6™ Skills: Looking at the World through Information Problem-Solving Glasses." In: Callison, McGregor, and Small, Instructional Interventions for Information Use. Proceedings of the Treasure Mountain Research Retreat VI, Troutdale, OR, March 31-April 1, 1997, 1997.

Spitzer, K., Eisenberg, M., and Lowe, C. (1998). *Information Literacy: Essential Skills for the Information Age.* Syracuse: ERIC Clearinghouse on Information & Technology. IR-140.

For more information, please check the website: **www.Big6.com.**

Dedication

Dedicated to those who made *The Big6 Newsletter* and this book possible—
Kathy Spitzer, Sue Wurster, Carrie Lowe, Dave Lankes, Beth Mahoney,
Marlene Woo-Lun, and Blythe Bennett.

The BIG 6

Teaching Technology & Information Skills

PART I

Information Literacy

CHAPTER 1

The BIG 6

What Every Educator Should Know about Information Literacy

What Every Educator Should Know About Information Literacy – Part I

v2 n2, p4-5, 10-11, 14

By Kathleen L. Spitzer

In the past, educational philosophy placed an emphasis on the acquisition and retention of prescribed content and encouraged students to work individually to achieve those ends. Unfortunately, this type of learning didn't always prepare students to transfer and apply knowledge. Educational philosophies are shifting towards a process approach to learning. Costa (1993) states "As we abandon traditional views of education, the skills of thinking and problem solving will replace discrete subject areas as the core of the curriculum and will lead to changes in instruction and assessment" (p. 50). These changes will require students to take an active part in their own learning, to reflect on what they have learned, to connect new concepts to their knowledge of the world, and to demonstrate their learning through authentic assessment. Rather than depend on an outdated textbook, teachers will require students to select information from a range of sources such as the Internet, periodicals, books, or videos. Students will need to locate,

> *Rather than depend on an outdated textbook, teachers will require students to select information from a range of sources such as the Internet, periodicals, books, or videos.*

analyze, interpret, evaluate, use, organize, and present information. In other words, students will need to be information literate.

This article will examine the development of the concept of information literacy and determine how the National Education Goals and Secretary's Commission on Achieving Necessary Skills (SCANS) report imply the importance of that concept to economic success. Efforts to implement information literacy standards and competencies in K-12 and higher education will be explored. Finally, we will provide and examine how information literacy skills can be taught.

The Concept Develops

The concept of "information literacy" was introduced in 1974 by Paul Zurkowski, President of the Information Industry Association, in a report to the National Commission on Libraries and Information Science. Zurkowski stated, "People trained in the application of information resources to their work can be called information literates. They have learned techniques and skills for utilizing the wide range of information tools as well as primary sources in molding information-solutions to their problems" (p.6). Since its first use, the concept has received much attention by those in the field of library science and by those in K-12 and higher education.

The seminal event in the development of the concept of information literacy was the establishment of the American Library Association (ALA)

Presidential Committee on Information Literacy in 1987. The committee, established by ALA President Margaret Chisholm, consisted of seven national leaders from education and six from librarianship. Their final report, released in January 1989, asserted that information literacy was a necessary skill for everyday life, for the business world and for democracy:

How our country deals with the realities of the Information Age will have enormous impact on our democratic way of life and on our nation's ability to compete internationally. Within America's information society, there also exists the potential of addressing many long-standing social and economic inequities. To reap such benefits, people—as individuals and as a nation—must be information literate. To be information literate, a person must be able to recognize when information is needed and have the ability to locate, evaluate, and use effectively the needed information. Producing such a citizenry will require that schools and colleges appreciate and integrate the concept of information literacy into their learning programs and that they play a leadership role in equipping individuals and institutions to take advantage of the opportunities inherent within the information society. Ultimately, information literate people are those who have learned how to learn. They know how to learn because they know how knowledge is organized, how to find information, and how to use information in such a way that others can learn from them. They are people prepared for lifelong learning, because they can always find the information needed for any task or decision at hand (American Library Association Presidential Committee on Information Literacy, 1989, p.1).

This section of the final report contains the definition of information literacy to which many scholars and educators have referred: "To be information literate, a person must be able to recognize when information is needed and have the ability to locate, evaluate, and use effectively the needed information" (1989).

A 1992 Delphi study expanded this definition by identifying the attributes of an information literate person. According to Doyle, an information literate person is one who:

- **Recognizes that accurate and complete information is the basis for intelligent decision making**
- **Recognizes the need for information**
- **Formulates questions based on information needs**
- **Identifies potential sources of information**

> *To be information literate, a person must be able to recognize when information is needed and have the ability to locate, evaluate, and use effectively the needed information.*

- **Develops successful search strategies**
- **Accesses sources of information including computer-based and other technologies**
- **Evaluates information**
- **Organizes information for practical application**
- **Integrates new information into an existing body of knowledge**
- **Uses information in critical thinking and problem solving (1992, p.8).**

Throughout the '90s, the concept of information literacy has been the topic of scores of journal articles and publications and has been examined by educational institutions, professional organizations and scholarly individuals. Many higher education institutions have formed campus-wide committees to work toward including information literacy as a graduation outcome. Some are even calling it a new liberal art. As each group or individual has explored information literacy, new definitions have been offered:

- Information literate students are competent, independent learners. They know their information needs and actively engage in the world of ideas. They display confidence in their ability to solve problems and know what is relevant information. They manage technology tools to access information and to communicate. They operate comfortably in situations where there are multiple answers, as well as those with no answers. They hold high standards for their work and create quality products. Information literate students are flexible, can adapt to change and are able to function independently and in groups (Colorado Department of Education, 1994).

- (Information literacy is) a new liberal art that extends from knowing how to use computers and access information to critical reflection on the nature of information itself, its technical infrastructure, and its social, cultural and even philosophical context and impact (Shapiro & Hughes, 1996, online).

- Information competence is the fusing or the integration of library literacy, computer literacy, media literacy, technological literacy, ethics, critical thinking, and communication skills (Work Group on Information Competence, Commission on Learning Resources and Instructional Technology, 1995, p. 5).

- (Information literacy is) the ability to find, evaluate, use, and communicate information in all of its various formats (Work Group on Information Competence, Commission on Learning Resources and Instructional

Technology, 1995, p. 4).

- (Information literacy is) the ability to effectively identify, access, evaluate, and make use of information in its various formats, and to choose the appropriate medium for communication. It also encompasses knowledge and attitudes related to the ethical and social issues surrounding information and information technology (California Academic and Research Libraries Task Force, 1997, online).

Whether information comes from a computer, a book, a government agency, a film, a conversation, a poster, or any number of other possible sources, inherent in the concept of information literacy is the ability to dissect and understand what you see as well as what you hear. If we are to teach information literacy, we must teach students to sort, to discriminate, to select, and to analyze the array of messages that are presented (Lenox & Walker, 1992, p.4-5).

The last four definitions demonstrate that information may be presented in a number of formats, from the simple to the complex, and may include printed words, illustrations, photographs, charts, graphs, tables, multimedia, sound recordings, computer graphics, or animation. The concept of information literacy is evolving to include all of these forms of information.

Information Literacy: Key to Economic Success

The nature of the world's economy is changing. Information and knowledge are replacing capital and energy as the primary wealth-creating assets, just as capital and energy replaced land and labor 200 years ago (Haeckel & Nolan, 1993). The effect of this transformation is that physical laborers are being replaced by knowledge workers—workers who are information literate.

An economy based on information requires workers who will know how to locate, analyze, manage, interpret, use, and present information in all of its formats. In identifying the skills necessary for the work place of the future, the Secretary's Commission on Achieving Necessary Skills (SCANS) report published in 1991 notes that workers will need to be lifelong learners who possess skills beyond those of reading, writing, and arithmetic. The Commission concluded that due to the global nature of the economy, and the impact of technology, "good jobs will increasingly depend on people who can put knowledge to work" (SCANS, 1991, p. xv).

The SCANS report suggests and recommends skills that all Americans will need for entry level employment. These recommendations are phrased as outcome measures, and include both foundation skills and practical competencies. The three-part skills foundation includes basic skills, thinking skills, and personal qualities. The five competencies relate to the management of resources, interpersonal skills, information, systems, and technology.

While information literacy is not explicitly mentioned in the SCANS Report, the five competencies identified in the report fit well with the comprehensive definition of information literacy

---

Figure 1 *Correlation of Scans Report Competency 3 with the Expanded Definition of Information Literacy*

COMPETENCY 3:

Information:

- Acquires and evaluates information

- Organizes and maintains information

- Interperts and communicates information

- Uses computers to process information

(SCANS, p.xvii)

INFORMATION LITERACY—EXPANDED DEFINITION

- recognizes that accurate and complete information is the basis for intelligent decision making
- recognizes the need for information
- formulates questions based on information needs
- identifies potential sources of information
- develops successful search strategies
- accesses sources of information including computer-based and other technologies
- evaluates information
- organizes information for practical application
- integrates new information into an exisiting body of knowledge
- uses information in critical thinking and problem solving.

(Doyle, 1992)

(Doyle, 1994). The report recognizes that workers must not only be able to read, write, and do arithmetic but also be skilled at listening and speaking, thinking critically, and knowing how to learn. This implies skills that are included in the process of information literacy. A direct comparison of the third competency with Doyle's expanded definition of information literacy emphasizes the importance of information literate workers (see Figure 1).

National Education Goals

The Goals 2000: Educate America Act, which specifies our National Education Goals, acknowledges the connection between education and the economy. The adoption of National Education Goals was set into motion in 1989 when President Bush met with the nation's governors at an Education Summit. As a result of the summit, six goals for the improvement of education were outlined. The aim of the National Education Goals was expressed as: "individually, to promote higher levels of individual student achievement, and collectively, to build a globally competitive American work force" (U. S. Department of Education, 1991, p. 2). The National Education Goals were incorporated in the America 2000 Excellence in Education Act which President Bush submitted to Congress in May, 1991. However, Congress failed to pass this act.

During the Clinton administration, two additional goals focusing on teacher education and parental participation were added to the six goals that had been announced by President Bush and the Nation's governors. The Goals 2000: Educate America Act. was signed into law on March 31, 1994 by President Clinton. The eight goals as they were incorporated into law are:

- Goal 1: School Readiness
- Goal 2: School Completion
- Goal 3: Student Achievement and Citizenship
- Goal 4: Teacher Education and Professional Development
- Goal 5: Mathematics and Science
- Goal 6: Adult Literacy and Lifelong Learning
- Goal 7: Safe, Disciplined, and Alcohol- and Drug-free Schools
- Goal 8: Parental Participation

The original six goals as proposed by President Bush's administration formed the basis of a 1992 Delphi study that involved a national panel of experts from the organizational memberships comprising the National Forum for Information Literacy (NFIL). As a preliminary task, the group rated those education goals that members thought could be attained through information literacy skills. Goals 1, 3, and 6 were rated well above the others, and were the subjects for further consideration. The common theme of all three

goals was lifelong learning:

- Children starting school ready to learn (Goal 1)
- Students leaving grades 4, 8, and 12 demonstrating competency with subject matter and able to use their minds well (Goal 3), and
- All adults being literate and equipped with skills necessary to survive in the global economy (Goal 6) (Doyle, 1994).

The panelists' comments show that information literacy is implicit in achieving these three goals (see Figure 2). Both the SCANS report and the National Education Goals recognize that our nation's economic success will depend on highly skilled workers. Such workers must be able to find and interpret information and turn data into knowledge. [End Part I].

Note: Part II will appear in The Big6 Newsletter, v 2.3; Part III will appear in v 2.5.

Bibliography

American Library Association Presidential Committee on Information Literacy. Final Report. (1989). Chicago: Author. (ED 315 074)

California Academic and Research Libraries Task Force. (1997, September 29). Draft recommendations to WASC on an information literacy standard. [Online]. Available: **http:// www.carl-acrl.org/ Reports/rectoWASC.html** [1998, January 18].

Colorado Department of Education. (1994, September). Model information literacy guidelines. Denver, CO: Author.

Costa, A. L. (1993, February). How world-class standards will change us. Educational Leadership, 50(5), 50-51. (EJ 457 363)

Doyle, C. S. (1992). Outcome measures for information literacy within the National Education Goals 1990. Final report to National Forum on Information Literacy. Syracuse, NY: ERIC Clearinghouse on Information Resources. (ED 351 033)

Doyle, C. S. (1994). Information literacy in an information society: A concept for the information age. Syracuse, NY: ERIC Clearinghouse on Information & Technology. (ED 372 763)

Haeckel, S. H., & Nolan, R. L. (1993). The role of technology in an information age. In Annual Review of the Institute for Information Studies, The Knowledge Economy (pp. 1-24). Queenstown, MD: Aspen Institute.

Delphi Study Panelists' Comments Relating to the National Education Goals

GOAL 1: SCHOOL READINESS

By the year 2000, all children in America will start school ready to learn.

The panelists agreed that children starting school ready to learn might be interpreted as: acquiring skills such as knowing how to learn, valuing information, and having a positive and enthusiastic attitude.

Preschool children learn to value information by watching their parents—their first teachers. Other adults, including preschool teachers, are also role models. Childrens' motivation to read and access information begins with these first role models. Parents need to value information, and need to be able to demonstrate to their children effective strategies for accessing, evaluating, and using information. Many parents have yet to acquire these skills, so Goal 5, adult literacy, applies to them as learners.

GOAL 3: STUDENT ACHIEVEMENT AND CITIZENSHIP

By the year 2000, all students will leave grades 4, 8, and 12 having demonstrated competency over challenging subject matter including English, mathematics, science, foreign languages, civics and government, economics, arts, history and geography, and every school in America will ensure that all students learn to use their minds well, so they may be prepared for responsible citizenship, further learning, and productive employment in our Nation's modern economy.

Goal 3 is concerned with the way students learn how to use their minds to make informed decisions. During their years of general education (K-12), all students need to learn how to process information as they apply problem-solving and critical thinking skills to their school and personal lives. Learning these skills requires an active learning format where students can process information to meet specific needs at a level that is developmentally appropriate for them.

GOAL 6: ADULT LITERACY AND LIFELONG LEARNING

By the year 2000, every adult American will be literate and will possess the knowledge and skills necessary to compete in a global economy and exercise the rights and responsibilities of citizenship.

Goal 6 focuses on adult literacy and the skills necessary for gainful employment and good citizenship. In terms of information literacy, all Americans need to be lifelong learners, able to access a variety of resources, proficient with various types of technologies, and able to evaluate and use information to meet personal and job-related needs. With over 80 percent of American jobs somehow related to services, information has become the most important commodity in the marketplace. Those who can access information will be empowered with the skills necessary to be successful as employees and citizens.

Panelists' comments were excerpted from: Doyle, C. S. (1992). Final report to National Forum on Information Literacy. Syracuse, NY: ERIC Clearinghouse on Information Resources. (ED 351 033).

Lenox, M. F. & Walker, M. L. (1992). Information literacy: Challenge for the future. International Journal of Information and Library Research, 4(1), 1-18.

Secretary's Commission on Achieving Necessary Skills. (1991). What work requires of schools: A SCANS report for America 2000. Washington, DC: U.S. Government Printing Office. (ED 332 054)

Shapiro, J. J., & Hughes, S. K. (1996, March/April). Information literacy as a liberal art. Educom Review [Online], 3(2). Available: **http://www.educause.edu/pub/er/review/reviewarticles/31231.html** [1998, February 16].

United States Department of Education. (1991). America 2000: An educational strategy. Sourcebook. Washington, DC: Author. (ED 327 985)

Work Group on Information Competence. Commission on Learning Resources and Instructional Technology Task 6.1. (1995, December). Information competence in the CSU: A report.[Online]. Available: **http://www.calstate.edu/ITPA/Docs/html/info_comp_report.html** [1998, January 23].

Zurkowski, P. G. (1974). The information service environment relationships and priorities. Related paper no. 5. Washington, DC: National Commission on Libraries and Information Science. (ED 100 391)

What Every Educator Should Know About Information Literacy – Part II

v2 n3 p12-13

By Kathleen L. Spitzer

In the last issue of The Big6 Newsletter, we presented the first part of this excerpt from Kathy Spitzer's new book on information literacy. We expect this book to stand as a seminal piece on the state of information literacy thinking and programs in the late 1990s. This part of the article explores information literacy within the new standards for school library media programs.

Information Literacy in K-12

Education must change to meet the needs of an economy based on knowledge and information. As the SCANS report points out, the skills required by the work place of the future are very different from the skills required to participate in the work place of the past. Instead of performing the routine tasks of mass production, workers will participate in multi-skilled work teams to envision and carry out flexible and customized production. To prepare our children for these changes, educators must shift from requiring the rote memorization of facts to placing an emphasis on lifelong learning, on process as well as content, and on cooperative learning.

Standards prepared by the national content area disciplines show that this shift is underway. The various national content area standards documents recommend that students be able to locate, analyze, interpret, evaluate, use, organize and present information (Spitzer, Eisenberg, & Lowe, 1998). As teachers implement these new standards, students will increasingly use information from a variety of sources to construct knowledge. These students must possess the essential skills of information literacy.

Information Power

Information literacy has long been a concern of the American Association of School Librarians (AASL) and the Association for Educational Communications and Technology (AECT). The 1988 publication, *Information Power: Guidelines for School Library Media Programs*, stated that the mission of the library media program was "to ensure that students and staff are effective users of ideas and information" (ALA, 1988, p.1). This mis-sion is restated in *Information Power: Building Partnerships for Learning*, the revised national guidelines for library media programs published in 1998. However, the achievement of that mission depends on school library media programs and services focused on information literacy. To this end, the publication includes the "Information Literacy Standards for Students Learning."

These standards are articulated in three categories: information literacy, independent learning, and social responsibility. Within the three categories are nine standards and twenty-nine indicators to describe the content and processes students need to achieve to be information literate. The nine standards are:

Category I: Information Literacy:

- **STANDARD 1:** The student who is information literate accesses information efficiently and effectively.
- **STANDARD 2:** The student who is information literate evaluates information critically and competently.
- **STANDARD 3:** The student who is information literate uses information accurately and creatively.

Category II: Independent Learning:

- **STANDARD 4:** The student who is an independent learner is information literate and pursues information related to personal interests.
- **STANDARD 5:** The student who is an independent learner is information literate and appreciates and enjoys literature and other creative expressions of information.
- **STANDARD 6:** The student who is an independent learner is information literate and strives for excellence in information seeking and knowledge generation.

Category III: Social Responsibility:

- **STANDARD 7:** The student who contributes positively to the learning community and to society is information literate and recognizes the importance of information to a democratic society.
- **STANDARD 8:** The student who contributes positively to the learning community and to society is information literate and practices ethical behavior in regard to information and information technology.
- **STANDARD 9:** The student who contributes positively to the learning community and to society is information literate and participates effectively in groups to pursue and generate information. (abridged, ALA, 1998)

Information Power: Building Partnerships for Learning provides library media specialists and teachers with excellent examples of how to implement a program that will help students achieve information literacy.

The next, and last, installment of this article will focus on information literacy in the states and in higher education. The article concludes with a discussion of approaches and efforts to implement and teach information literacy in all settings. Note: Part III will appear in v 2.5. For price availability of *Information Literacy: Essential Skills for the Information Age*, by Spitzer, Eisenberg and Lowe, call 1-800-464-9107.

Bibliography

American Association of School Librarians and Association for Educational Communications and Technology. (1988). *Information power: Guidelines for school library media programs*. Chicago: Author. (ED 315 028)

American Library Association. (1998). *Information power: Building partnerships for learning*. Chicago: Author.

Spitzer, K. L., Eisenberg, M. E., Lowe, C. A. (1998). *Information literacy: Essential skills for the information age*. Syracuse, NY: ERIC Clearinghouse on Information and Technology IR-104.

What Every Educator Should Know About Information Literacy – Part III

v2 n5 p4-7

By Kathleen L. Spitzer

This article is the final installment of a three-part series (see Big6 Newsletter issues 2.2 and 2.3) based on the new book, Information Literacy: Essential Skills for the Information Age by three Big6 Newsletter editors— Kathy Spitzer, Mike Eisenberg, and Carrie Lowe. The book is available from Linworth Publishing, Inc. 800-786-5017 or send an e-mail to newslin@aol.com.

States Recognize Information Literacy

Individual states are now creating initiatives to ensure that students attain information literacy skills by the time they graduate high school. For example, Kentucky's information literacy initiative, titled Online II: Essentials of a Model Library Media Program, was developed in recognition of the impor-

tance of information literacy skills in the marketplace of an information-based society. The program underscores the vital collaboration among library media specialists and teachers in developing students' thinking skills. As the Kentucky Department of Education (1995) writes in the handbook to the program:

> One of the national education goals is for all adult Americans to be literate and to possess the knowledge and skills to compete in a global economy. Library media specialists promote information literacy as they help students access, synthesize, produce, and communicate information. This goal is accomplished more effectively when teachers and library media specialists collaborate in providing opportunities for students to think critically (Foreword).

The Utah State Department of Education has developed an information literacy curriculum for secondary schools based on the Big6 Skills approach to information problem-solving. The mission of the Library Media/Information Literacy Core Curriculum for Utah Secondary Skills is, to ensure that all students are effective users of ideas and information in all formats (1996). This is enacted through the program's inter-disciplinary approach, which places an emphasis on process and promotes confidence in students' problem solving abilities.

The California Media and Library Educators Association has created a resource for educators seeking to integrate the goals of information literacy into their curriculum. From Library Skills to Information Literacy: A Handbook for the 21st Century is based on the idea that it is the responsibility of educators to prepare students for the challenges that they will face in the Information Age. The handbook stresses the idea of information literacy as a process as viewed from three perspectives: the searcher's thinking process, the stages of the research process, and instructional strategies. These three interdependent components must be addressed in an information literacy curriculum to ensure that students will be properly prepared for success in the information age.

These efforts and others that are currently underway demonstrate that information literacy is a concept that has been established in the K–12 educational community.

Information Literacy in Higher Education

The development of information literacy in higher education can be traced to a symposium co-sponsored by Columbia University and the University of Colorado in

March 1987. The symposium, "Libraries and the Search for Academic Excellence," brought together academic leaders and leaders in the field of librarianship to examine the role of libraries in academia. The outcomes and action recommendations resulting from the symposium established the importance of information literacy skills and form the basis for current information literacy efforts in higher education:

Reports on undergraduate education identify the need for more active learning whereby students become self-directed independent learners who are prepared for lifelong learning. To accomplish this, students need to become information literate whereby they understand the process and systems for acquiring current and retrospective information, e.g., systems and services for information identification and delivery; are able to evaluate the effectiveness and reliability of various information channels and sources, including libraries, for various kinds of needs; master certain basic skills in acquiring and storing their own information, e.g., database skills, spreadsheet skills, word and information processing skills, books, journals, and report literature; are articulate and responsible citizens in considering current and future public policy issues relating to information, e.g., copyright, privacy, privatization of government information, and those issues yet to emerge.

To make possible the above, information gathering and evaluation skills need to be mastered at the undergraduate level, and learning opportunities should be integrated within the existing departments, analogous, to "writing across the curriculum," rather than as standalone bibliographic instruction programs. Administrators, faculty and librarians should be engaged in creative new partnerships which transmit to students the value and reward of research in their lives as students and beyond. Information literacy should be a demonstrable outcome of undergraduate education (Breivik & Wedgeworth, 1988, pp. 187-188).

Since the publication of these outcomes and action recommendations, institutions of higher education have been working toward this goal. For example, the California State University system, the State University of New York system, the University of Massachusetts system, and the University of Arizona are all engaging in information competence efforts.

Accreditation Agencies

Accreditation agencies deem information literacy important as well. For example, the Commission on

Information literacy should be a demonstrable outcome of undergraduate education

Higher Education (CHE), Middle States Association of Colleges and Schools, which accredits institutions of higher education in Delaware, the District of Columbia, Maryland, New Jersey, New York, Pennsylvania, Puerto Rico, The Republic of Panama, and the U.S. Virgin Islands developed the following standard on information literacy in 1994:

Each institution should foster optimal use of its learning resources through strategies designed to help students develop information literacy–the ability to locate, evaluate, and use information in order to become independent learners. It should encourage the use of a wide range of non-classroom resources for teaching and learning. It is essential to have an active and continuing program of library orientation and instruction in accessing information, developed collaboratively and supported actively by faculty, librarians, academic deans, and other information providers (in Commission on Higher Education, 1995, p. v).

In 1997, the California Academic and Research Libraries (CARL) established a Task Force to Recommend Information Literacy Standards to the Western Association of Schools and Colleges, an accreditation agency. A draft version of the task force's recommendations include a Statement of Principles for Information Literacy Criteria that focuses on institutions' roles in developing information literate graduates:

An institution ensures that all graduating students are information literate through a systematic and course-integrated campuswide information literacy program. Information literacy learning opportunities are part of general education, academic majors, and graduate/professional programs. Educational program requirements or goals include statements about students' use of libraries, computing, information and learning resources and how course assignments contribute to their becoming information literate. Professional staffs with appropriate expertise are available to teach information literacy skills and develop collections, learning resources and information literacy curricula and learning experiences. The institution provides support for maintaining and improving the quality of information literacy instruction (1998, Online).

The Western Association of Schools and Colleges is currently reviewing its standards for accreditation, and will consider the inclusion of such a standard on information competence.

Establishment of a National Information Literacy Institute

The ability to initiate, develop, and teach information skills in higher education depends on academic librarians and administrators who are knowledgeable in the theory and practice of information literacy. To meet this need, the Association of College and Research Libraries (ACRL) has established the Institute for Information Literacy (IIL). In the summer of 1999, IIL will sponsor its first immersion program; an intensive four and a half day education and training workshop. Additional information about the Institute for Information Literacy may be obtained by visiting the IIL web site at **http://www.ala.org/acrl/nili/nilihp.html.**

Teaching Information Literacy Skills

A number of approaches may be used to teach information literacy skills; however, these skills should never be taught in isolation. They must always be integral to learning for a real purpose. That purpose may be related to a student's educational explorations or to real life. Information literacy skills should not be confused with what some refer to as "library skills." Information literacy skills are not taught out of context. They are taught as a process used to solve an information problem.

One such process is the Big6 Skills Approach to Information Problem-Solving (Eisenberg & Berkowitz, 1990). As the name implies, the Big6 involves six basic processes that are negotiated each time there is an information problem: Task Definition, Information Seeking Strategies, Location & Access, Use of Information, Synthesis, and Evaluation. These six basic steps encompass twelve other processes that lead students to success in tackling an information problem (see Big6 Skills on page viii).

An information problem might take the form of a homework assignment. For example, part of Karen's math homework contained this problem: 1) Evaluate each of the following proportions and identify which ones are true: A. 8/10 = 6/16 B. 3/4 = 13/36 C. 2/3 = 8/12

As Karen began her homework in class, her teacher noticed that she seemed frustrated with this problem. He approached Karen and offered to help by identifying the information problem to be solved. Together they determined that Karen didn't know what a proportion was; nor did she know how to determine if a proportion was a true proportion. The teacher demonstrated that Karen had three possibilities for finding the information: she could browse back through the chapter to find the explanation, she could use the index at the end of the book to locate a definition, or she could use the definitions in the glossary. After Karen found the information she needed, she read it and learned what proportions were. She applied the information to solve the homework problem. As she checked her work, she found out that she had been successful in determining what a proportion was and confirming whether proportions were true.

Certainly, not all information problems are this simple. Writing a term paper, confirming a hypothesis, or completing a research project would require a student to solve a number of information problems.

Educators may wonder how the Big6 and information literacy relate to each other. Figure 3, on page 12, demonstrates that the Big6 process encompasses the information literacy skills as specified by the Information Literacy Standards for Students Learning. By using the Big6 process each time there is an information problem, students will develop these essential information literacy skills.

Conclusion

Patricia Senn Breivik, noted educator, author, and information literacy proponent states, "In this next century, an 'educated' graduate will no longer be defined as one who has absorbed a certain body of factual information, but as one who knows how to find, evaluate, and apply needed information" (1998, p. 2). Breivik points to the importance of an education that imparts process as well as content. Those in the K-12 educational community and those in the academic community have identified information literacy competence as an essential component of such an education. It is incumbent on us, as educators, to provide the resources necessary for our students to achieve information literacy.

Figure 3 The Big6 Process Encompasses Information Literacy Skills

Information Literacy Standards for Student Learning	The Big6 Skills Approach to Information Problem-Solving
CATEGORY I: INFORMATION LITERACY	
Standard 1: The student who is information literate accesses information efficiently and effectively. 1. Recognizes the need for information 2. Recognizes that accurate and comprehensive information is the basis for intelligent decision making 3. Formulates questions based on information needs 4. Identifies a variety of potential sources of information 5. Develops and uses successful strategies for locating information.	Recognizing the need for information, recognizing that accurate and comprehensive information is the basis for intelligent decision making, and formulating questions based on information needs all relate directly to **Big6 Skill #1-Task Definition**, as students define the problem and identify the information needed. Identifying a variety of potential sources of information is **Big6 Skill #2-Information Seeking Strategies.** Students use **Big6 Skill #3-Location & Access** to develop successful strategies for locating information.
Standard 2: The student who is information literate evaluates information critically and competently. 1. Determines accuracy, relevance, and comprehensiveness 2. Distinguishes among fact, point of view, and opinion 3. Identifies inaccurate and misleading information 4. Selects information appropriate to the problem or question at hand.	As students read, hear or view information, then evaluate it critically and extract relevant information, they are using **Big6 Skill #4-Use of Information.**
Standard 3: The student who is information literate uses information accurately and creatively. 1. Organizes information for practical application 2. Integrates new information into one's own knowledge 3. Applies information in critical thinking and problem solving 4. Produces and communicates information and ideas in appropriate formats.	Using information effectively and creatively related to **Big6 Skill #5-Synthesis** as students organize information from multiple sources and present the results.
CATEGORY II: INDEPENDENT LEARNING	
Standard 4: The student who is an independent learner is information literate and pursues information related to personal interests. 1. Seeks information related to various dimensions of personal well-being, such as career interests, community involvement, health matters, and recreational pursuits 2. Designs, develops, and evaluates information products and solutions related to personal interests.	Standard 4 implies the ability to use the **entire Big6 process** as students seek and use information related to their own interests.
Standard 5: The student who is an independent learner is information literate and appreciates and enjoys literature and other creative expressions of information. 1. Is a competent and self-motivating reader 2. Derives meaning from information presented creatively in a variety of formats.	Students use **Big6 Skill #4-Use of Information** as they derive meaning from information presented in a variety of formats. To develop creative products in a variety of formats, students would need to use the **entire Big6 process.**
Standard 6: The student who is an independent learner is information literate and strives for excellence in information seeking and knowledge generation. 1. Assesses the quality of the process and products of personal information seeking 2. Devises strategies for revising, improving, and updating self-generated knowledge.	Striving for excellence in information seeking and knowledge generation clearly relates to **Big6 Skill #6-Evaluation** as students judge their effectiveness and efficiency.
CATEGORY III: SOCIAL RESPONSIBILITY	
Standard 7: The student who contributes positively to the learning community and to society is information literate and recognizes the importance of information to a democratic society. 1. Seeks information from diverse sources, contexts, disciplines, and cultures 2 Respects the principle of equitable access to information.	Students would use **Big6 Skill #2-Information Seeking Strategies** to brainstorm all possible sources and select the best sources.
Standard 8: The student who contributes positively to the learning community and to society is information literate and practices ethical behavior in regard to information and information technology 1. Respects the principles of intellectual freedom 2. Respects intellectual property rights 3. Uses information technology responsibly.	Respecting the principles of intellectual freedom and intellectual property rights, and using information technology responsibly relates to **Big6 Skill #4-Use of Information** as students read, hear, or view information and also to **Big6 Skill #5-Synthesis** as students avoid plagiarizing and use proper citations to identify their sources.
Standard 9: The student who contributes positively to the learning community and to society is information literate and participates effectively in groups to pursue and generate information. 1. Shares knowledge and information with others 2. Respects others' ideas and backgrounds and acknowledges their contributions 3. Collaborates with others, both in person and through technologies, to identify information problems and to seek their solutions 4. Collaborates with others, both in person and through technologies, to design, develop, and evaluate information products and solutions.	The ability to collaborate with others to identify information problems and seek their solutions (Big6 #3), and the ability to design, develop, and evaluate information products and solutions (Big6 #4), imply the ability to use the **entire Big6 process.**

Bibliography

Breivik, P. S. (1998). Student learning in the information age. Phoenix, AZ: Oryx Press.

Breivik, P. S. & Wedgeworth, R. (1988). Libraries and the search for academic excellence. Metuchen, NJ: Scarecrow Press.

California Academic and Research Libraries Task Force. (1997, September 29). Draft recommendations to WASC on an information literacy standard. [Online]. Available: **http://www.carl-acrl.org/Reports/rectoWASC.html** [1998, January 18].

California Media and Library Educators Association. (1994). From library skills to information literacy: A handbook for the 21st century. Castle Rock, CO: Hi Willow Research and Publishing.

Commission on Higher Education. Middle States Association of Colleges and Schools (1995). Information literacy, lifelong learning in the middle states region. A summary of two symposia. Philadelphia, PA: Middle States Association.

Eisenberg, M. B., & Berkowitz, R. E. (1990). Information problem solving: The Big Six skills approach to library & information skills instruction. Norwood, NJ: Ablex.

Kentucky Department of Education. (1995). Online II: Essentials of a model library media program. Louisville, KY: Author.

Spitzer, K. L., Eisenberg, M.E., & Lowe, C.A. (1998). Information literacy: Essential skills for the information age. Syracuse, NY: ERIC Clearinghouse on Information and Technology. IR-104.

Utah State Office of Education. (1996). Library media/information literacy core curriculum for Utah secondary schools. Salt Lake City, UT: Author.

CHAPTER 2

The BIG 6

Research Reports

Models of Information Literacy

v1 n5 p10-11

By Carrie Lowe

This issue of "Research Reports" discusses the features of different models of information literacy and skills instruction. Each model adds to our understanding of how people look for and use information. The main commonality across these models—and with the Big6—is the emphasis on "process." People engage in a series of stages to resolve information problems and needs.

The specific stages and descriptions in the models vary due to differences in approach, emphasis, context, and level of analysis. Overall, however, the models share striking similarities. These similarities were first presented in a chart by Eisenberg and Brown (1992), updated here as Figure 1.

The findings presented below—the commonalities across models, the non-linearity of the process, the changing emotions that students go through, and the transferability and applicability beyond school settings—offer valuable insights for anyone interested in helping students to learn and apply the Big6 Skills.

Carol Kuhlthau, Information Seeking

As we learned in the first "Research Reports" (September/October 1997), Carol Kuhlthau has done extensive research in the area of information problem-solving. Her model of information problem-solving, which she calls "information seeking," is unique in several ways. Kuhlthau has identified seven steps in the information-seeking process. They are: initiation, selection, formulation, exploration, collection, presentation, and assessment.

Kuhlthau's approach identifies how the affective domain relates to the information seeking process. Kuhlthau learned that as students begin a task, they may experience feelings of uncertainty. Through the research process, uncertainty gives way to clarity, and finally (with the satisfactory resolution of the research problem), relief.

Ann Irving, Information Skills

Ann Irving (1985) was one of the first researchers to note the importance of information skills. Irving notes that such skills are not just for completing school assignments, but are essential skills for all aspects of life—academic, professional, and personal. She believes that the information retrieval and processing skills practiced and acquired through the completion of classroom assignments will transfer to the other areas of a student's life.

Although Irving's process is outlined as steps, it is not intended to be negotiated in lockstep fashion. Irving acknowledges that some steps in the process may be taken more than once, while some may be skipped altogether.

Barbara Stripling and Judy Pitts, Research Process

Stripling and Pitts observed that students doing research always seem to choose the same topics, use the same resources, and turn in the same term paper copied out of an encyclopedia. Stripling and Pitts determined that students were not engaging in the research project or the process. They created a 10-step process, outlined in Brainstorms and Blueprints (1988), that defines various points at which students pause and reflect. They emphasize the research process as a thinking process requiring learner to be actively engaged.

Since most students are not experienced researchers, the first steps of the Stripling and Pitts research process cover selecting a topic, gaining an initial overview through research and reading, narrowing the topic, and researching this narrower topic in depth. These steps build in the recursiveness that Eisenberg and Berkowitz refer to in the Big6 Skills.

New South Wales Department of Education—The Information Process

There are many information literacy models, but the one that most closely matches the Big6 Skills model is the New South Wales (NSW) Information Process model. The six steps of the Information Process model are:

1. Defining,
2. Locating,
3. Selecting,
4. Organising,
5. Presenting, and
6. Assessing.

The New South Wales Department of Education presents the information process as "a philosophical basis and working tool" for planning and teaching information problem-solving skills. The authors believe that this process involves parents and administrators as well as teachers and library media specialists.

The goal of the NSW information process is to develop "successful information users." This goal is achieved through teaching students information skills and teaching positive information attitudes and values. Information skills are taught in school and reinforced in family and community settings. The authors place

Figure 1 Comparison of Information Skills Process Models

Eisenberg/Berkowitz Information Problem-Solving	Kuhlthau Information Seeking (The Big6 Skills)		Irving Information Skills	Pitts/Stripling Research Process	New South Wales Information Process
1. Task Definition 1.1 Define the problem 1.2 Identify info requirements	1. Initiation 2. Selection		1. Formulation/analysis of information need	1. Choose a broad topic 2. Get an overview of the topic 3. Narrow the topic 4. Develop thesis/ purpose statement	Defining
	1. Formulation (of focus)				
2. Information Seeking Strategies 2.1 Determine range sources 2.2 Prioritize sources	3. Exploration (investig. info on the general topic)	5. Collection (gather info on the focused topic)	2. Identification/appraisal of likely sources	5. Formulate questions to guide research 6. Plan for research & production	Locating
3. Location & Access 3.1 Locate sources 3.2 Find info			3. Tracing/locating indiv. resources 4. Examining, selecting, & rejecting indiv. resources	7. Find, analyze, evaluate resources	Selecting
4. Information Use 4.1 Engage (read, view, etc.) 4.2 Extract info			5. Interrogating/using individual resources 6. Recording/storing info	8. Evaluate evidence take notes/compile bib.	Organizing
5. Information Use 5.1 Organize 5.2 Present	6. Presentation		7. Interpretation, analysis, synthesis and eval. of info. 8. Shape, presentation, and communication of info	9. Formulate questions to guide research 10. Create and present final product	Presenting
6. Evaluation 6.1 Judge the product 6.2 Judge the process	7. Assessment (of outcome/process)		9. Evaluation of the assignment	(Reflection point—is the paper/project satisfactory)	Assessing

information skills into two categories: skills concerned with locating information (for instance, finding information in a variety of forms and sources, and then finding information within sources), and skills concerned with understanding and using information (including evaluating information found, synthesizing information, presenting relevant information, among others). Both skills are necessary for successful information problem-solving. The Information Process model promotes a positive attitude and sends the message that schools should strive to produce well-rounded citizens of the information age.

Findings:

Figure 1 (on page 16) displays a number of commonalities among the four processes and with the Big6:

- Solving an information problem involves a process comprising a number of steps.
- Regardless of the terminology, all the processes require users to identify an information problem, determine possible information sources, locate and engage sources, synthesize the results of their search, and evaluate the results.
- It may be necessary to repeat some of the steps in the information problem solving process.
- Information skills are transferable beyond the educational setting.
- The information problem-solving process evokes an emotional response.

Implications:

Resolving the question about which of these models is "right" is unlikely. Moreover, the question is not important. No matter which model you consult, solving an information problem is a process. Students need to realize that information problem-solving involves a number of steps, some of which might be repeated. Teachers, library media specialists, and technology teachers are preparing students to apply the process to life's information problems.

Sources consulted:

Eisenberg, M., & Berkowitz, R. (1988). *Curriculum initiative: An agenda and strategy for library media programs.* Greenwich, CT: Ablex Publishing.

Eisenberg, M., & Brown, D. (1992). *Current themes regarding library and information skills instruction: Research supporting and research lack*ing. School Library Media Quarterly, 20(2), 103-109.

Kuhlthau, C. (1993). *Seeking meaning: A process approach to library and information services.* Greenwich, CT: Ablex Publishing.

Irving, A. (1985). *Study and information skills across the curriculum.* London: Heinemann Educational Books.

New South Wales Department of Education. (1988) *Information skills in the school.* New South Wales: NSW Department of Education.

Stripling, B., & Pitts, J. (1988). *Brainstorms and blueprints: Teaching library research as a thinking process.* Littleton, CO: Libraries Unlimited.

The Work of Stephen Krashen

v1 n6 p 3,5

By Carrie Lowe

This column focuses on research related to the importance of reading in all aspects of student performance. When addressing this topic, there is no one better qualified than **Stephen Krashen** *of the* **University of Southern California**, *author of* The Power of Reading: Insights from the Research. *In this book, as well as in his other works, Krashen explores the vital role reading plays in vocabulary acquisition and language development and how educators can best promote reading.*

Finding

Free voluntary reading (FVR) is an essential component of successful instruction. In the introduction to The Power of Reading, Krashen defines FVR as "reading because you want to, with no book report and no questions at the end of the chapter." Students' performances on standardized tests demonstrate that FVR programs raise reading comprehension levels. Studies have found that readers are better students than non-readers. This is particularly true in the areas of language arts and social studies. FVR also improves students' vocabularies and their writing ability. Students show the most improvement in their reading through involvement in long-term (longer than seven months) FVR programs.

Implication

Free voluntary reading can be an extremely important educational tool. Reading improvement is the result of long term involvement. Teachers who wish to create a free voluntary reading program need to be willing to make FVR a regular commitment (e.g. set aside time each day during the entire school year). The teacher should also read during FVR time to provide a model for students.

Teachers can evaluate students' participation in the FVR program by arranging brief individual student-teacher conferences and by holding group discussions with the entire class about the books that both the students and the teacher are reading.

Finding

Free voluntary reading is the best tool that teachers have for developing students' literacy skills. Research has shown that FVR is more successful in developing literacy than the alternative approach—direct instruction featuring a combination of skill-building activities and error correction. Typically, the effect of direct instruction on student skill-building is small or non-existent. Experts believe the English language is far too complex to learn by drill and practice alone. To learn to read, students must read.

Implication

It is not necessary to completely overhaul a school's language arts program based on the finding that FVR is the best tool for developing literacy. Free reading can be viewed as a necessary component of a skills-based curriculum and can be implemented on either a formal or informal basis. Students who read a book of their own choosing for fifteen minutes a day show significant improvement in reading comprehension skills.

Finding

Having a good library makes better readers. Krashen's research shows that there is a positive relationship between student performance on the reading comprehension sections of standardized tests and high quality, frequently used libraries. Krashen's research also suggests embracing the "cafeteria-bookstore" model to attract people to the library media center—allowing, even supplying, food and beverages.

Krashen's research shows that there is a positive relationship between student performance on the reading comprehension sections of standardized tests and high quality, frequently used libraries.

Implication

The importance of a strong library media program in terms of student achievement cannot be ignored. By supporting a strong, vibrant library media program, administrators can create tangible benefits for students. Library media programs can market themselves by creating a warm, comfortable atmosphere where students are encouraged to browse, read quietly, and relax while enjoying their lunch or a snack. In doing so, the library promotes reading and supports the students' overall educational achievements.

Sources

Krashen, S. (1994). An answer to the literacy crisis: Free voluntary reading. In Carol Kuhlthau, (Ed.), *School Library Media Annual.* Englewood, CO: Libraries Unlimited. (pp. 113-122).

Krashen, S. (1996). Eating and reading in the library. *Emergency Librarian, 23*(5), 27.

Krashen, S. (1993). *The power of reading: Insights from the research.* Englewood, CO: Libraries Unlimited, Inc.

Krashen, S. (1995). School libraries, public libraries, and the NAEP reading scores." *School Library Media Quarterly, 23*(4), 235-237.

The Work of Carol A. Kuhlthau

v1 n1 p11,14

By Carrie A. Lowe

This regular feature, Research Reports, focuses on research related to information and technology literacy. While it is important for us to have a solid understanding of the research base, it can be difficult to keep up with such a quickly-changing field. That is why we are presenting the work of key researchers in this format—what they are finding and how the findings apply to the work you do as an educator. For this very first column, we are reporting on the important work of Carol Kuhlthau from Rutgers University. Carol has conducted some of the most extensive studies of information processes and skills instruction in the field. Her studies—over a period of more than 10 years—provide a solid foundation for all efforts to develop information skills.

Finding

As students go through the research process, they are actively involved in sense-making. New information is assimilated into the framework of what they already know. This means that an individual determination of the relevance of information is highly personal, and may not match the system's relevance rating. Information is transformed into meaning when the information is synthesized and presented.

Implication

When working with students on Use of Information, it is important for teachers and library media specialists to remember that each student has his or her own idea of what information is relevant to their problem. Teachers should encourage students to think critically about their research problem and the information that they might need to solve it, rather than expecting them to rely on the system.

Finding

There is a set of affective experiences that mirror the information-seeking behavior of the student. An important feeling that occurs early in the information-seeking process is uncertainty. Uncertainty is a state that causes anxiety and lack of confidence. Uncertainty and anxiety can be exacerbated by a lack of focus in the search process and by the lack of knowledge of technology and resources. As students work through the information problem-solving process, they become more clear and focused, gain confidence, and their anxiety lessens.

Implication

While uncertainty and anxiety are uncomfortable for the student, they are a necessary part of the information problem-solving process. When working with students, educators (classroom teachers, library media specialists, technology teachers) should be aware that students will be uncertain and anxious.

In our work with the Big6™, we often find that students are insecure at the beginning of each stage of the process but gain confidence and feel more positive as they complete the stage. For example, some students panic when they first get an assignment. But, they get more comfortable once they've thought about the assignment and selected a topic. Once the information problem-solving process is under way and they start searching for information, feelings of anxiety may return. Again, as they work through developing a search plan and start locating resources, their uncertainty gives way to confidence. This process can repeat at each stage of the Big6™. Educators and parents can help students to recognize that feeling anxious is a natural part of the information problem-solving experience and help them work through each stage.

Finding

During their search, students identify both formal and informal mediators as possible resources. Interviews with students in the information problem-solving process have found that students tend to rely more on informal mediators, such as friends, family and peers, than on formal mediators like teachers and school library media specialists, who they view more as a last resort.

Implication

This is a cue for teachers and library media specialists; by taking a process approach to information problem solving and assisting students in each stage, you can be an active helper rather than a passive mediator. While many informal mediators have valuable advice to share with students, it is important that students also recognize teachers and librarians as valuable and approachable sources of information.

Sources

Kuhlthau, C. (1993). "Implementing a Process Approach to Information Skills: A Study Identifying Indicators of Success in Library Media Programs." *School Library Media Quarterly, 22,* (1), 11-18.

Kuhlthau, C. (1989). "Information Search Process: A Summary of Research and Implications for School Library Media Programs." *School Library Media Quarterly, 18,* (1), 19-24.

Kuhlthau, C. (1991). "Inside the Search Process: Information Seeking from the User's Perspective." *Journal of the American Society for Information Science, 42,* (5), 361-371.

Kuhlthau, C. (1993). *Seeking Meaning: A Process Approach to Library and Information Services.* Greenwich, CT: Ablex Publishing Corporation.

> *"As students work through the information problem-solving process, they become more clear and focused, gain confidence, and their anxiety lessens."*

The Work of Seymour Papert

v2 n2 p3,15

By Carrie Lowe

Many people are familiar with the work of Seymour Papert—the inventor of the LOGO programming language, which was a very popular tool for teaching children the basics of computing in the 1980s. LOGO also taught children about mathematics by providing them with an easy way to communicate commands to a computer to draw pictures, create simple programs, or do anything else they could imagine. There is an entire generation of people (including me!) who grew up with a different perspective on computers, thanks to having learned LOGO as a child.

The fact that Papert developed the LOGO programming language for children is not surprising since his research on the ways children interact with computers is well-known. His interest in the cognitive development of children and on the ways that development is impacted by computer use was heavily influenced by his early work with the developmental psychologist Jean Piaget. When asked which of Piaget's concepts most influences LOGO, Papert replied, "Constructivism." The constructivism view is that children create their own knowledge by interacting with the environment. This is oppositional to the view that knowledge must be poured forth from the teacher to the student (Reinhold, 1986).

Although LOGO has been an important tool in teaching many students the basics of computing, limiting this column to a discussion of LOGO does not do justice to Papert's entire body of research. Seymour Papert provides us with valuable insights into the ways that students incorporate new information, such as technology skills, into the knowledge they already possess. Since the Big6 information problem-solving process helps students construct knowledge and since technology skills instruction is vital to our goal of preparing our students for the information age, Papert's ideas are important for us to consider.

Finding

The best learning children do is through discovery. The learning that takes place when children interact with their environment prior to formal schooling is an example of discovery learning. This same kind of learning can occur in school if children are given the proper tools for learning.

Implication

As instructors, we must take advantage of students' natural curiosity and willingness to learn. Rather than thinking of students as vessels to fill with knowledge—think of them as junior detectives, and assist them in their search for information. Teach students that technology can help them in their search, and show them how to use technology in context. The Big6 provides an excellent framework for teaching students how to be in charge of their own learning without losing sight of their goal.

Finding

Students learn technology best in a classroom with a "computer culture" where knowledge about computers is shared by everyone, making it easier to find and acquire information about computers and their capabilities (Papert, 1985). This means that the culture of the classroom encourages students to dis-

cuss and brainstorm solutions to their problems.

Implication

A good starting point for fostering a computer culture in your classroom is to establish a rule that encourages students to work together to solve their problems prior to asking the teacher. For example, the rule could state: "Before asking the teacher a question about a computer function, students must ask three other classmates to see if they know the answer." Students can learn to use one another to solve simple problems, such as which HTML tag to use to create a heading, leaving the teacher free to deal with more complex, higher level problems.

Finding

Children are natural theorists. When exploring the world around them, they try to make sense of new information by comparing it to information that they already know. They then produce theories; however, theories must be tested. Children test theories by consulting a source such as a knowledgeable person or an information resource. If children are not able to test their theory for some reason, they can become frustrated and lose interest.

Rather than thinking of students as vessels to fill with knowledge— think of them as junior detectives, and assist them in their search for information.

Implication

It is important to provide a learning environment rich in the information sources that students can use to verify their theories. For example, through the Internet students can use Ask-A services to contact an expert (see Virtual Wisdom in Vol. 1, No. 3 of The Big6 Newsletter). The Internet provides students with a wonderful resource for discovery learning. Teachers who use the Big6 information problem-solving process provide their students with a framework for accomplishing discovery learning. Very young students (kindergarten-second grade) can learn the Super 3, plan-do-review. This teaches students to approach information problems logically and systematically, so that even if they can't read yet, they can find the answer to their question.

Sources Consulted:

Papert, S. (1993). *The children's machine: Rethinking school in the age of the computer.* New York: Basic Books.

Papert, S. (1985). Different visions of LOGO. *Computers in the Schools*, 2(2), 3-8.

Papert, S. (1980). *Mindstorms.* New York: Basic Books.

Papert, S. (1986). New views on LOGO. *Electronic Learning, 6*(5), 33-35.

Reinhold, F. (1986). *An interview with Seymour Papert.* Electronic Learning, 6(5), 35-36, 63.

The Work of Ross Todd

v1 n3 p7,13

By Carrie Lowe

This regular feature presents the findings of researchers in the fields of library/information science and education related to information and technology literacy. The format—research finding and implications—is intended to provide insights into the research as well as practical application of the findings for teaching and learning.

The column for this issue reports on the work of Ross Todd, lecturer in the School of Information Studies of the University of Technology, Sydney, Australia. Ross focuses his research efforts on creating ties within the curricula between information literacy and classroom curriculum. His studies provide proof of the importance of teaching information literacy skills to improve student success.

Finding: Integrated Information Skills Instruction Leads To Student Success

The benefits of integrated information skills in the classroom cannot be overemphasized. In a study of the effect of integrated information skills instruction on Australian high school students, Todd found that such instruction has a significant impact both on the students' abilities to grasp the subject matter of the class and their ability to effectively solve information problems. In this study, the method of information problem-solving taught was the New South Wales model which is similar in approach to the Big6 (see Big6 sidebar on page 22).

Implication

This study provides evidence of the significant impact that teaching information problem-solving skills (such as the Big6) can have on the learning experiences of students. Although this study was based on the experiences of high school students, integrated information problem-solving curriculum benefits students of all ages. This study is an important argument for the administrative support of cooperative teaching and integrated curriculum. It is important that teachers and library media specialists have the freedom (in terms of scheduling and workload) to combine their strengths in the classroom.

Finding: Information Literacy-Based Instruction and Student Achievement

The concept of information literacy focuses on the ability to use information purposefully and effectively. Rather than being passive receptacles of information, the information-literate are actively involved in their own learning; they approach learning and information problem-solving as a process. An information literacy-based curriculum can have a positive impact on students' self-perception, learning processes, view of information, learning outcomes, and learning environment.

Implication

Integrating information literacy concepts into classroom curriculum has a positive effect on students' abilities and attitudes. Through information literacy instruction, teachers and library media specialists help students gain the skills they will need to succeed in the information society. There is an immediate impact in the classroom, and students also develop confidence in their ability to find and use information in any situation.

Finding: Information Overload and Accuracy

"Information overload" is a serious concern throughout society. It might be expected that, as individuals are given increasingly large amounts of information to process, their ability to make accurate and efficient choices decreases. Todd studied one possible overload effect by presenting students with differing amounts of information on catalog cards. Contrary to speculation about information overload, Todd found that students' accuracy was not adversely affected by increasing the amount of information on the cards. However, increasing the number of information items on the catalog cards did affect the time taken to make a selection.

Implication

The results of this study indicate that it is not wise to assume that by simply increasing the amount of information available to students, information overload will necessarily occur. While students may not be able to make a choice as quickly when provided with more information, it seems that providing students with increased amounts of information decreases their confusion when making choices.

Therefore, teachers should provide students with as much information as they deem necessary, without worrying about causing students to experience information overload.

Finding: Concept Mapping and Teaching Theoretical Content

A major challenge that teachers of college students face (particularly those in education for professional practice, such as librarianship) is helping students to understand not only the practice-based knowledge important to the profession, but also the research-based theoretical foundations supporting the profession. One excellent way to help students learn the theories behind practice (and their interconnectedness) is through the use of concept mapping. By having students create concept maps and use them as the basis for discussion, students can see a picture of their own level of understanding, as well as have a model of difficult-to-grasp theories.

Implication

Although this study was directed at university-level teachers in professional programs, the idea of concept mapping is appropriate for any grade level. Concept maps help students separate trivial information from important information and, in this way, fosters critical-thinking skills. It can also lead to changes in the way students select, organize, and use information for understanding. Since critical thinking skills are a vital part of information literacy and information problem-solving, concept mapping can be an extremely valuable exercise.

NSW–Big 6 Comparison	
The Information Process New South Wales	**The Big6 Eisenberg & Berkowitz**
Defining	Task Definition
Locating	Information Seeking Strategies
	Location & Access
Selecting	Use of Information
Organizing	Synthesis
Presenting	
Assessing	Evaluation

Sources

Todd, R. (1992). "Bibliographic Information and Book Selection: An Experimental Study of Information Load on Choice Behavior in a School Library." *Library and Information Science Research* 14, 447-464.

Todd, R. and Kirk, J. (1995). "Concept Mapping in Information Science." *Education for Information* 13, 333-347.

Todd, R. (1995). "Integrated Information Skills Instruction: Does it Make a Difference?" School Library Media Quarterly 23 (2), 133-138.

Todd, R., and others (1992). "The Power of Information Literacy: Unity of Education and Resources for the 21st Century." Conference paper. ERIC Document 354916.

The Work of Marjorie Pappas

v2 n6 p12-13

By Carrie A. Lowe

"The process of gathering and using information has become another basic skill in today's Information Age. The skills and processes of an information-skills model should be developed across all areas of a curriculum."—Marjorie Pappas, from "Information Skills for Electronic Resources."

Marjorie Pappas represents an important voice in the field of information literacy instruction. Pappas is an associate professor at the University of Northern Iowa, where she also serves as the Coordinator for the Division of Library Media Studies. She is probably best known for developing the Pathways to Knowledge: Follett Software Company's Information Skills Model with her co-author, Ann Tepe.

The Pathways to Knowledge includes six steps. These steps are:

- **APPRECIATION:** Affinity for a topic which can spark interest leading to research. Appreciation will grow throughout the information seeking activity. Although appreciation doesn't need to be present, it makes for a more rewarding information problem-solving experience.
- **RESEARCH:** In this stage, searchers begin to make connections between their topic and what they already know. They should do some initial exploratory research and begin to narrow and focus their topic.

- **SEARCH:** At this point, searchers plan and implement their search strategy.
- **INTERPRETATION:** Searchers analyze the information that they have found and begin to draw connections between topics. This is a key critical thinking exercise.
- **COMMUNICATION:** In this stage, searchers choose the appropriate format for the information they have found, and then organize and present it.
- **EVALUATION:** Like appreciation, evaluation is present in every stage of the Pathways to Knowledge Information Skills Model. Evaluation gives students a basis to make revisions and improvements. This concept includes both self and peer evaluation.

It is easy to see some connections between the Pathways to Knowledge Information Skills Model and the Big6. Research corresponds to Big6 #1, Task Definition, while Search encompasses Big6 #2, Information Seeking Strategies, and #3, Location & Access. Interpretation is closely related to Big6 #4, Use of Information, and Communication corresponds to #5, Synthesis. The element of Evaluation is present in both information skills models. What really separates the two is Pappas and Tepe's idea of a growing appreciation for a topic.

Pappas's research and writing goes far beyond the Pathways to Knowledge. She writes frequently about information literacy, authentic learning, and technology integration. Her findings are extremely useful for the practitioner.

Finding

Pappas is a great advocate of visual organizers to teach students the research process. Organizers, or visual representations which can help students make sense of a cognitive process, come in many different forms. There are webs, mind maps, Venn diagrams, timelines, and many more. Educators should work with students to make sure they know how to use the organizer.

Different steps in the research process call for different tools. For example, in Pappas and Tepe's Communication step, the authors suggest that flow charts, story boards, timelines, graphs, and presentation software can be helpful. In the Search step, students can use flow charts, Venn diagrams, and hierarchical charts to visually display their search strategies.

Implication

Visual organizers can help students keep track of research they have done, as well as help them to figure out the relationship between topics. In develop-

ing organizers, be creative. Getting students in the habit of organizing their thoughts visually will prepare them to tackle more complex information problems in the future.

Finding

Pappas strongly believes that in order to evaluate a student's performance on a project completely, a teacher must consider all aspects of the student's work, including their information problem solving strategies. When evaluating these strategies, it is key that instructors focus on process rather than content.

Evaluation can pose a special challenge for educators committed to teaching good information problem solving practices. It is key to remember that the student's process must be evaluated; the product does not always give a complete picture of the student's work.

When evaluating these strategies, it is key that instructors focus on process rather than content.

Implication

Just as it is important not evaluate students' information problem-solving processes by focusing on what they produce, library media specialists and teachers must be careful not to focus entirely on students' mastery of discrete skill sets. Information skills must be taught in context, Therefore, they must also be evaluated in context. For instance, a pop quiz on the Readers' Guide to Periodical Literature may not lend as much insight into students' work as asking them to keep a log as they research their topic. Although it is important that students are familiar with the tools that they use in the library, they must know when and in what way to use the tools.

A great tool for evaluation is a rubric. Rubrics allow you to map criteria and expectations along with possible student outcomes. When establishing these criteria, students' input is extremely valuable. Seeking students' input serves two purposes; it ensures that students know and are comfortable with what is expected of them, and it demonstrates to students that library media specialists and teachers value their judgment.

Finding

Pappas feels that another key to evaluation is to get several different opinions on the same project. In other words, when it comes time to evaluate, cooperate.

Implication

Cooperative teaching provides a rich, complete learning experience for students and cooperative evaluation can give a more complete picture of a student's work. One great team member for evaluation is the library media specialist. Teachers and media specialists can divide the components of a project between them; for instance, the teacher might evaluate the quality of a student's research question, and the LMS the appropriateness of the resources the student consulted.

Student self-evaluation is another great way to get a different perspective on a students' work. Pappas particularly encourages self-evaluation across projects. A great end-of-the-semester (or unit, or year) reflective thinking exercise would be to have students compare their information problem-solving strategies on several different projects. What have they improved upon? What still needs improvement?

After completing a project, students often know the assignment more intimately than the teacher. Teachers and library media specialists can use this to their advantage by having students peer evaluate their projects. After students evaluate a partner's work, have them do a little reflective writing about their own project. Peer evaluation gives students a basis for comparing their own work with the work of others.

Any evaluation should work toward Pappas's goal of developing independent learners. Independent learning means that students are information literate and are effective information problem-solvers. Reflective thinking, such as through self-evaluation and the use of visual organizers, encourage students to be independent learners.

Sources

Pappas, M. (1998). "Designing Authentic Learning." *School Library Media Activities Monthly*, 14(6), 29-31, 42.

Pappas, M. (1998). "Evaluating the Inquiry Process." *School Library Media Activities Monthly,* 14(8), 24-26.

Pappas, M. (1995). "Information Skills for Electronic Resources." *School Library Media Activities Monthly*, 11(8), 39-40.

Pappas, M. "Introduction to the Pathways to Knowledge: Follett's Information Skills Model." Available: **http://www.fsc.follett.com/ products/pathwaysmodel/**

Pappas, M. (1997). "Organizing Research." S*chool Library Media Activities Monthly,* 14(4), 30-32.

CHAPTER 3

The Big6 Skills Approach to Information and Technology Literacy
v1 n1 p8-9

Context

We live in an increasingly complex and information-rich world. Information and information technologies are central to just about every aspect of our lives. If students are to thrive in our information society, they must learn and be able to apply a comprehensive, unified set of information and technology skills. That's the purpose of the Big6™ approach: to provide students with the understandings and skills they need to succeed.

The Big6 Skills™ can be considered from a number of perspectives—as an information and technology literacy curriculum, an information problem-solving process, a set of skills which provide a strategy for effectively and efficiently meeting information needs, and an overall approach for developing programs to help students learn essential information and technology skills. With the Big6 Skills™, students learn how to recognize their information needs and how to progress through a series of steps to solve information problems effectively and efficiently.

Themes of the Big6™

A number of basic themes characterize the Big6 Skills™:

1 The Big6 Skills™ is a general approach to information problem-solving that can be applied to any information situation.

The Big6 Skills™ approach can be used whenever students are in an academic or personal situation that requires information to solve a problem, make a decision, or complete a task. This model is transferable to school, personal, and work applications, as well as all content areas and the full range of grade levels, pre-K through higher education. One of the major differences between the Big6 Skills™ approach and other information skills models is its broad applicability. In addition to school projects, reports, research papers, and assignments, the Big6™ can be applied to such diverse situations as deciding what movie to go to on Saturday night, selecting an appropriate birthday gift, or analyzing stock market picks.

2 The Big6 Skills™ is an ideal curriculum for integrating information and technology literacy instruction with all subject area curricula at all grade levels,

All students have information problems to solve, whether it is in a kindergarten lesson about community helpers, a 7th grade unit on igneous, metamorphic and sedimentary rocks, or a 12th grade economics class. The Big6™ is easily adapted to meet the unique requirements of students at alt age and ability levels, and is easily adapted to all instructional situations.

3 The Big6 Skills™ approach is not always a linear, step-by-step process.

While the Big6 Skills'™ process is usually presented in a step-by-step fashion (from Task

Definition through Evaluation), people do not always work in this way. It seems that successful information problem-solving requires successful completion of each of the Big6™ stages at some point in time. However in a given situation, individuals may jump around, branch off, or loop back. Therefore, the Big6 Skills" approach advocates developing competence in each of the Big6 Skills™ areas, but not a prescriptive linear application of the skills.

4 The Big6 Skills™ provides a broad, top-down structure for information and technology literacy curriculum.

While information and technology literacy is receiving significant national attention (e.g., President Clinton's call for the need to make children technologically literate by the 21st Century), many information or technology curricula are little more than laundry lists of isolated skills. The Big6 Skills'™ approach avoids this. With the Big6™ the process is used as a framework for an entire information and technology skills curriculum. Individual skills can be developed as part of the appropriate broader skill areas (e.g., selecting a topic is part of Task Definition, learning word processing is part of Synthesis, communicating via e-mail facilitates Evaluation, and considering the accuracy of an information source relates to Information Seeking Strategies or Use of Information). The scope of the Big6 Skills™ curriculum includes the entire set of skills and sub-skills; the sequence is the overall information problem-solving process.

5 The Big6 Skills™ incorporates a critical thinking hierarchy.

Inherent to the Big6™ approach is its concern with students' cognitive development. Thinking and reasoning skills are important skills that are central to the Big6 Skills™ approach. Through its attention to a process approach, the Big6 Skills™

- helps students learn to ask good questions.
- teaches students to independently organize and assess information.
- teaches creative, higher order thinking processes such as analysis, synthesis and evaluation.
- allows teachers, library, information, and technology specialists to set challenging performance.
- provides students with a strategy to logically and systematically solve information problems and evaluate solutions

The BIG 6

Teaching Technology & Information Skills

PART II

Big6 Skills

Implementing the Big6: Context, Context, Context

v1 n4 p8-9, 14-15

By Mike Eisenberg

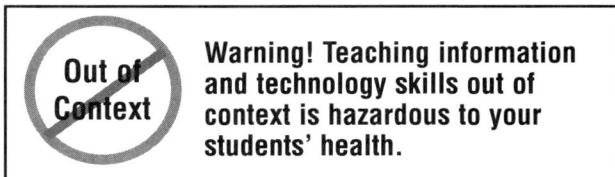

> **Out of Context** Warning! Teaching information and technology skills out of context is hazardous to your students' health.

Introduction: Contexts

In real estate, agents talk about the three key elements: location, location, and location. We consider the key elements to implementing a meaningful information and technology literacy program in a similar way: context, context, and context.

Information and technology skills—the Big6—are best taught in the context of real needs. Students today, more than ever before, want to see the connection between what they are learning and their lives. They want to know why something is relevant. This is no problem for the Big6 approach since it emphasizes applicability across environments and situations.

There are actually two contexts that are essential for effective implementation of a Big6 program:

- the Big6 process itself, and
- the classroom curriculum.

By the process itself, we mean the six stages of the Big6 process. When working on an assignment, project, report, or even an information problem of personal interest, students should be able to identify where they are in the process. For example, are they reading an article related to current events? That's Use of Information (Big6 #4). Are they searching for sources using a CD-ROM index? That's Location and Access (Big6 #3).

Similarly, teachers should frame instructional and learning experiences related to information and technology skills instruction within the Big6 process. Are they teaching PowerPoint for a multimedia presentation? That's Synthesis (Big6 #5). Are students working with the library media specialist to brainstorm possible sources for a project? That's Information Seeking Strategies (Big6 #2).

Anchoring instruction in individual skills within the overall Big6 process provides students with a familiar reference point. They see the connections among seemingly separate skills and are able to reflect on what came before and anticipate what comes after.

The second context for implementing effective information and technology skills instruction is the actual classroom curriculum. This includes the subject area units and lessons of study, and most importantly, the assignments on which students will be evaluated. Throughout the school year, teachers and students engage in a rich range of curriculum subjects and topics. In fact, one of the current problems we face in education is "curriculum information overload"—there's just too much to cover in a limited time.

That's why, in implementing Big6 instruction, we do not promote adding new curriculum content, units, or topics. There's plenty going on in the curriculum already. The last thing that classroom teachers and students need is more content. Therefore, from a Big6 perspective, the challenge is to determine good opportunities for learning and teaching Big6 Skills within the existing curriculum. This involves:

1 Gathering reliable information about the curriculum.

2 Analyzing the curriculum to a) select units and assignments that are well suited to Big6 skills instruction and b) determine which Big6 skills are particularly relevant to the selected curriculum units and assignments,

3 Developing plans that lay out the integrated Big6-subject curriculum instructional program.

This is analysis and planning on a broad or "macro" level. Once completed, classroom teachers, library media specialists, technology teachers, and others will work together to design specific, "micro" level units and lesson plans in context to fulfill the integrated Big6-curriculum plan. And ultimately after implementation, both the macro and micro must be evaluated and revised as necessary.

Gathering and Displaying Curriculum Information: Curriculum Mapping

In K-12 education, the building block of curriculum is the curriculum unit. Even when curriculum guidelines are presented as a series of standards—statements of expected learning outcomes and competencies—teachers, curriculum committees, and even state education departments expect that the actual subject area curricula will be implemented as a series of instructional units. Therefore, gathering reliable curriculum information means focusing on detailed information about curriculum units.

Of course, there are many sources of curriculum information—state and local curriculum guides, subject textbooks, building or district handbooks, and course syllabi. However, these guides don't really report on the actual curriculum taught in the classroom. For example, guides generally do not include specific information about the actual timeframe, numbers of students involved, and assessments employed. Fenwick English, the founder of curriculum mapping, called curriculum guides the "fictional" curriculum. It's what we want the curriculum to be, but not what the curriculum actually is.

Figure 1 Curriculum Mapping: Data Collection Worksheet

School:	

Grade:	
Teacher	
Subject:	
Unit:	

Date:	

Number of Sections:	
Number of Students:	
Total Teaching Time:	
Marking Period:	

Level of instruction:
☐ introduced
☐ reinforced
☐ expanded
comment:

Resources:
☐ text
☐ one source
☐ multiple sources
  ☐ reference (print/electr.)
  ☐ periodicals
  ☐ WWW
  ☐ book (nonfiction)
  ☐ book (fiction)
  ☐ human
  ☐ other:

Organization of instruction
☐ large group
☐ small group
☐ individual
Comment:

Primary Teaching Method
☐ desk work
☐ lecture
☐ demonstration
☐ video, film, multimedia
☐ lab, hands-on
☐ discussion
☐ independent study
☐ multimedia project
☐ report
☐ other:

Assignment(s):
☐ test
☐ short written project
☐ report
☐ project/product
☐ observation
☐ other:

Technologies:
☐ tool (word processing, database, presentation, spreadsheet)
☐ communication (e-mail, listserv, chat, video conferencing)
☐ Information (web, database, electronic resources, Q & A)
☐ other:

Big6
☐ task definition
☐ information seeking strategies
☐ location & access
☐ use of information
☐ synthesis
☐ evaluation

Library & Information Services:
☐ resources provision
☐ facilities provision
☐ reading guidance
☐ information service
☐ skills instruction (direct, indirect)
☐ consultation

Comments:

Figure 2 — Sample Elementary Curriculum Map

GR	TCHR	SUBJ	UNIT	#SEC	#STUD	TIME	MAR_PER	LEV	RES	ORG	METHODS	ASSIGN	TECH
00-00	LIE	LA	Colors	1	24	40	1234	I	multi	lg	disc/hands-on	worksheet	none
01-01	REB	LA	ABC Book	1	25	15	x2xx	R/E	multi	lg/ind	demo/ind study	product	none
01-01	MAB	Math	Whole Parts	1	32	10	x2xx	I	text/multi	lg	lect/desk work	worksheet	none
03-03	RDY	Sci	Planets	1	33	15	xx3x	I	multi	sg/lg	lect/group	project	WWW
03-03	RDY	Sci	Endangered Animals	1	33	15	xxx4	I	multi	lg/ind	lect/disc/ind	project	Hyperstudio/WWW
03-03	RDY	SS	Community	1	33	20	x2xx	R/E	multi	sy/lg	lect/disc/trip	project	Hyperstudio
03-04	CAL	LA	Letter Writing	1	27	8	x2xx	I	multi	ind	lect/desk work	product	w proc
03-04	CAL	Math	Graphs	1	27	15	xxx4	I	text	lg/ind	lect/desk work	product	none
03-04	CAL	Sci	Simple Machines	1	27	40	1xxx	I/R	text/multi	sg	lab/ind study	products	none
03-04	CAL	Sci	Work & Energy	1	27	8	xxx4	I	text	lg	lect	text	none
05-05	MBE	Library	Biography	5	120	2	xx3x	R/E	multi	lg	lect/disc	none	online catalog
06-06	SEW	LA	Folktales and Legends	1	29	20	x23x	R/E	multi	lg	lect/disc/desk work	homework/test	none
06-06	SEW	Sci	Vocabulary	1	29	3	1xxx	R/E	text	lg/ind	lect/desk work	homework	none
06-06	SEW	SS	Current Events	1	29	40	1234	IR/E	multi	lg/ind	disc/ind study	report	WWW
06-06	SEW	SS	Native American-Iroquois	1	29	10	x2xx	I	text	lg	lect/desk work	test	none

Figure 3 — Sample Secondary Curriculum Map

GR	TCHR	SUBJ	UNIT	#SEC	#STUD	TIME	MAR_PER	LEV	RES	ORG	METHODS	ASSIGN	TECH
07-07	MBE	Library	Dictionary Sill	6	150	2	1xxx	R/E	one	lg	lect/desk work	swa	none
07-07	TMJ	Sci	Weather	3	87	15	xx3x	R/E	text	lg	lect/disc	test	none
07-07	TCH	SS	Recycling	3	87	15	x23x	R/E	multi	lg/ind	lect/ind	product	none
08-08	TMU	Sci	Noise	2	45	40	x2xx	R-E	multi	sg/lg/ind	demo/disc	written report	WWW/w proc/present/elec res
08-08	HJW	SS	Map Skills	4	111	10	1xxx	R/E	multi	lg	worksheet	worksheet	none
09-12	CER	Health	Diet & Nutrition	10	250	20	1x3x	R/E	multi	lg/sg	lect/disc/prod	posters	WWW/present
09-12	CER	Health	Tobacco & Smoking	10	250	10	1x3x	R/E	multi	lg/sg	lect/disc	test	none
09-12	CER	Health	Drugs	10	250	10	x2x4	R/E	multi	lg/sg	lect/disc/prod	product	WWW/present/w proc
10-10	MBE	Library	Web Authoring	9	20	10	x2xx	I	multi	ind	demo/prod/ind/study	product (web page)	Front Page/HTML/scanner
10-10	BAB	Math	Probability	4	104	20	xx3x	R/E	text	lg/ing	lect/desk work	homework	none
10-12	RBW	Physics	Light Lab	1	17	4	xx3x	I/R/E	laser, lab apparatus, text	lg-pairs	lect/lab	lab report	none
10-12	RBW	Physics	Light	1	17	15	xx3x	I/R/E	text	lg	lect/disc	test	none
11-12	CJC	LA	Catcher in the Rye	3	86	10	xx3x	I	multi	lg	lect/disc	report	none
11-12	MAB	Spanish 4	Spanish Cooking	1	14	10	xxx4	E	multi	ind	ind	product	WWW
11-12	BDE	SS	Supply & Demand	3	68	20	xx3x	I/R	multi	lect/disc	lect/disc	obs/swa	none

Curriculum mapping is an alternative approach to relying on curriculum guides and syllabi. Curriculum mapping is the process of systematically gathering information about curriculum units on a number of variables (see Figure 1), and then combining that information into a series of charts and tables that describe the curriculum of a particular teacher, department, school, or district (see Figures 2 and 3).

Figure 1, on page 30, represents the latest version of a continually revised "curriculum mapping data collection worksheet." It accommodates data gathering on a range of variables. Information about numbers of students, time, resources, teaching methods, and assignments are particularly important for the next step—analysis.

Completing a data collection worksheet is a relatively simple and quick process. Explaining the purpose and some of the terms and filling out two worksheets can take 10-15 minutes at faculty, department, or subject area meetings. Some library media specialists and technology teachers fill out the forms when working with teachers one-on-one. Still others find that after an initial explanation of the purpose and process, faculty are willing to complete and turn in the forms on a monthly or quarterly basis.

Combining data from the worksheets is also relatively easy. Charts can be created manually, however it is generally easier to use some form of database management software (Microsoft Access, Filemaker), electronic spreadsheet (Lotus 1-2-3, Excel), or the database or spreadsheet functions within a more general package (Claris Works or Microsoft Works).

Analyzing Curriculum Maps from a Big6 Perspective

As noted, the purpose of curriculum mapping is to systematically review the curriculum to select the units and assignments best suited to integrated information and technology skills instruction. I refer to these units as "big juicies"—those information-rich curriculum units that are filled and dripping with information potential.

For example, we might select units that involve a report, project, or product rather than those that rely on a test for assessment. And, we probably wish to focus on units that require a range of multiple resources rather than large number of students and span a reasonable timeframe. In Figure 2, on page 31, there are a number of units that meet both these criteria, including the grade 3 units on planets, endangered animals, and community. How do we select among these units or do we just integrate the Big6 with all three?

I refer to these units as "big juicies"— those information-rich curriculum units that are filled and dripping with information potential.

Deciding may also depend on other factors, including the time available for Big6 instruction. What else is going on during that time of the year? The community unit comes earliest in the year and includes 20 periods, the most time, so it might be a good choice. But the endangered animals unit relies on both HyperStudio software and the World Wide Web, so we could teach lessons on both.

Looking at the Figure 3 map on page 31 as a whole, the health unit on diet and nutrition certainly stands out. It reaches the most students, is repeated twice during the year, covers 20 periods each time, uses technology, and results in an interesting assessment, a poster. In grade 7, the recycling unit certainly seems more appropriate than the weather unit because it is assessed by a product, and the eighth-grade map skills unit reaches more students than the noise unit.

So, which units should we choose? That really depends upon the specific situation and needs. Are individual teachers looking at their units across the school year for Big6 opportunities? Is the technology program trying to move to an integrated Big6 approach and involve new subject areas and teachers? Is there an effort to ensure that all fifth- and sixth-grade students have at least two collaborative library media-classroom instructional events for each of the Big6 Skills?

Curriculum mapping can gather the necessary data to meet needs in these and other situations.

The next issue of *The Big6 Newsletter* will expand on the application of curriculum mapping and give examples of developing macro plans for a variety of curriculum situations.

Implementing the Big6 - Part II - Plans and Planning

v1 n5 p1, 6-7, 14-15

By Mike Eisenberg

The key to successfully teaching the Big6 Skills is context, context, context. Students find Big6 Skills instruction relevant when it is taught within the context of their regular curriculum. The planning process is essential when implementing a Big6 Skills instruction program. First, identify what actually occurs in the classroom and school throughout the academic year. Next, analyze the data and create plans.

Introduction

Systematic planning for integrated Big6 Skills instruction is essential if we are to make a difference in our classrooms and schools. If we truly believe that information and technology skills are critical for student success, then we must make sure that students have frequent opportunities to learn and practice these skills.

It's not enough to work with students on a one-to-one basis or to offer an isolated lesson on note-taking or Web search engines. Students need lessons in each Big6 Skill, delivered in the context of real, subject area assignments. Accomplishing comprehensive, integrated Big6 instruction requires classroom teachers, library media specialists, technology teachers, and administrators to make a concerted and systematic effort to plan and document their efforts.

As discussed in "Implementing the Big6—Part I" (see The Big6 Newsletter, March/April 1998), curriculum mapping is a useful procedure for gathering and presenting reliable curriculum information. Curriculum mapping involves two steps:

1. Systematically collecting curriculum information about actual classroom activities and

2. Combining this information into charts and tables to describe the curriculum in a particular setting.

Curriculum maps can be created for individual teachers, teams, subject areas, schools, or even districts. Planning integrated instruction involves reviewing the curriculum maps and selecting units that are best suited to integrated information and technology skills instruction. This planning process can be summarized and documented on any level—individual teacher through district—with a Big6 Skills by Unit Matrix (see Figures 1-4 on pages 34-37). The Matrix is a planning tool. It displays valuable information like when a unit is taught, the total time of instruction (noted in periods), the subject, assignments, and Big6 Skills slated for instruction. The Matrix can be a planning tool and serve as a record of what Big6 Skills instruction actually took place. At the end of the year, this record is examined and plans can be created for next year.

Plans for the Individual Teacher

We will illustrate the planning process by showing the example of a teacher using Big6 instruction for the first time. Mr. Hancock is a fourth grade teacher who is very excited about the Big6 and has decided that

The Big6 Skills by Unit Matrix becomes a blueprint for integrated Big6 Skills instruction.

this year he will integrate information skills instruction with his curriculum. To create a new plan, he looks at his lesson plans from the past year. He fills out curriculum mapping worksheets to detail a number of important instructional units. He uses Microsoft Access to organize the information from the curriculum worksheets into a curriculum map (see the Big6 Newsletter, March/April 1998, pp. 8-9 for an example of a curriculum worksheet and map). His next step is to identify units that seem like good candidates for integrating the Big6 skills. Mr. Hancock knows that long term projects that may include a report, project, or product provide good opportunities to integrate a range of information skills.

Mr. Hancock immediately identifies two major units: one on state history culminating in a written report, and one on food groups that requires students to produce a chart, posters, and advertisements. He chooses the state history unit first since it occurs during the first and second marking periods. The unit doesn't occur until a few weeks into the quarter, so he will have a chance to settle into the school year and get to know his students before taking on something new. Mr. Hancock meets with the library media specialist to design and deliver these first Big6 lessons. To document these plans, Mr. Hancock adds these lessons to the Big6 Skills by Unit Matrix (See Figure 1).

The other major unit that Mr. Hancock chooses is the food group unit in the third marking period. Since he will have six computers with Internet access in his classroom, he sees this unit as a great opportunity to emphasize using the Web in the Big6 context. Student can gather information and pictures for the charts, posters, and advertisements. He talks to the technology teacher to coordinate efforts on teaching content and technology within the Big6 framework.

Mr. Hancock is intrigued by the idea that the Big6 could improve students' test-taking strategies. He decides to identify a few minor and major tests to try this idea out. Students take tests every week throughout the school year. In the first quarter of the year, he intends to teach a lesson on Big6 #4, Use of Information, in conjunction with the spelling unit, focusing on strategies for learning and remembering correct spelling. Mr. Hancock will also mention Big6 #5, Synthesis, by reminding students how to present their answers on their spelling tests.

As the year progresses, Mr. Hancock will adjust the Skills by Unit Matrix to represent the Big6 Skills instruction that he actually delivers. At the end of the year, the Matrix will offer detailed documentation of what he actually accomplished. The plans will also serve as the basis for follow-up planning by teachers who will have the same students next year.

THE BIG6											
Unit	**Subject**	**Assignment**	**M_Per**	**Pers**	**1**	**2**	**3**	**4**	**5**	**6**	**Comments**
Spelling	Language Arts	Test	1234	40				X	–		strategies for learning/ remembering spelling
State History	Social Studies	Written	12xx	30	X	X	X	X	X	X	major unit—lessons on all Big6
Geography	Social Studies	Maps	1x3x	20	X			X			computer graphics to produce maps
Listening	Language Arts	Test	1xxx	10	X			X			note-taking, tape recording
Personal Hygiene	Health	Ads, Product	1xxx	15	X	–			–	X	evaluating ads, creating posters
Letter Writing	Language	Product	1xxx	15	X				X	X	what makes a good letter using word processing
Food	Health	Product (chart posters, ads)	x2xx	15	X	X	X	X			periodical indexes on CD and the web
Multiplication Tables-10	Math	Test	x2xx	20					–		just mention ways to memorize
Structure of Plants	Science	Experiment Test	xx34	20				X			lab reports—can computer generate
Rocks and Minerals	Science	Worksheet Test	xx3x	20		X	X				use sources for worksheet—focus on brainstorm, narrow and keywords
Metric Measurements	Math	Test	xx3x	20		X	X				test will include examples of the metric system in action—will need sources
Deserts/Life Weather	Social Studies/ Science	Written and Oral Report	xx3x	30	X	X	X				2 subjects, lots of electronic information seeking strategies, location & access
Mixed Numbers	Math	Worksheet	xx3x	20						X	self-evaluation

Planning for a Subject Area, Grade, or Team

While Big6 implementation through individual teachers is essential, it is also important to coordinate Big6 Skills instruction in broader contexts. This section explains how this can happen within a particular subject area, grade, or team.

Figure 2 is a sample of what a Big6 Skills by Unit Matrix might look like if it is created by a high school social studies department. The data included are similar to Figure 1, however, columns are added for Teacher and Grade. The subject is omitted since this plan includes only social studies. The depart-

ment meets and shares their intentions for Big6 instruction. They then fill out a rough draft of a plan using the Skills by Unit Matrix.

From Figure 2, we see that Ms. Sullivan, the ninth-grade teacher, plans to focus on the Big6 in three units. In the first marking period, the class studies Latin America, and the unit culminates in a test. Sullivan explains to the other teachers that since this is the beginning of the school year she will quickly review the overall Big6 process, but will also develop lessons that focus on:

■ Task Definition: understanding what is expected on her tests,

Figure 2: Sample Big6 Skills by Unit Matrix: Social Studies Department

												THE BIG6
GR	**Tchr**	**Unit**	**Subject**	**Assignment**	**QTR**	**1**	**2**	**3**	**4**	**5**	**6**	**Comments**
9	Sullivan	Latin America	World History	Test	1xxx	X	–	–	–	X	X	test taking strategies—task definition, synthesis
9	Sullivan	Northern Africa	World History	Test, Report	x2xx		X	X	X			sources—web searching, note-taking
9	Sullivan	India	World History	Test	1xxx	X				X		
10	Ryan	WWI	World History	Maps, Product	xx3x					X		
10	Ryan	Between the Wars	World History	Test, Short Written Assignment	12xx		X	X	–	–		essay writing strategies
10	Ryan	WWII	World History	Project, Test	x2xx		X	X	–	–		web-based information
10	Ryan	Cold War	World History	Test	xx3x						X	
10	Ryan	Vietnam	World History	Oral Report	xx34		–	–	X	X	–	presentation and graphics software
11	Rossini	Colonization of Western Hem.	World History	Test	1xxx	X				X		extracting relevant information from the textbook and notes
11	Rossini	Civil War Smoking	U.S. History	Report, Project	xx3x		X	X	X			using primary and secondary sources
11	Jackson	Constitution	U.S. History	Written and Report	x2xx					X	X	presentation software (PowerPoint)
11	Jackson	Civil War	U.S. History	Test	xx3x	X						nature of test
12	Petruso	Street Law	Government	Project	xxx4		X			X		community resources and law libraries
12	Valesky	Stock Market	Economics	Project	1234	X	X	X	–	–	X	full-year, competitive intelligence

- Synthesis: developing strategies for writing short essays on tests, and
- Evaluation: recognizing the criteria for success, including which topics and concepts are more or less important.

Sullivan also talks about wanting to work with the library media specialist and technology teacher to deliver other Big6 lessons during the school year. For example, the library media specialist could provide a lesson on selecting, locating, and using quality sources particularly in relation to the World Wide Web (Big6 #s 2,3,4) for the Northern Africa unit. The technology teacher could offer instruction on special software for creating computer-generated maps (Big6 #5) for the unit on India.

The other teachers then discuss what they might do to build on Sullivan's foundation. In grade 10,

Mr. Ryan plans to integrate Big6 instruction across five units. Like Sullivan, he will focus on one or two of the Big6 Skills within a given unit, but by the end of the year he will cover all six stages in depth. Ryan also coordinates with the technology teacher and library media specialist to bring technology into the process. Students complete an oral report about WWII and Vietnam by using graphics software to create visuals.

The two 11th grade teachers state that they each used the Big6 with only one unit in the past, but they are willing to expand to a second unit. Someone suggests that the Civil War unit in Rossini's class, culminating in a report, is good for developing Big6 #2 through #4, Information Seeking Strategies, Location & Access, and Use of Information. Jackson plans to teach the same topic, but he will assess with a test. He explains that he will teach a Big6 lesson that reminds students about test-taking in other grades and that he will focus on the task definition aspects.

The 12th grade teachers, Petruso and Valesky, teach senior elective courses. They are new to the Big6, but at the meeting indicate that they are willing to give it a try. Petruso and the library media specialist work together on a collaborative lesson introducing the students to resources in the community library and special law library. Valesky will compare the value of all types of information resources.

When looking at the complete draft Matrix, it is clear that the teachers are covering a full range of Big6 Skills. The heaviest emphasis is on Synthesis, which is probably appropriate for secondary school students. Evaluation is covered in only four units, so the department may consider adding lessons on evaluation. Of course, not every student will be enrolled in all classes, and there may be other social studies teachers who are not integrating Big6 instruction at this time. Therefore, the department, the library media specialist, and the technology teacher will need to coordinate efforts. All students need ample opportunities to develop the full range of Big6 Skills. This leads to the next section–planning on the school or district level.

Planning on the School or District Level

The goal for systematic planning at the school or district level is to ensure that students have a range of Big6 instructional experiences across grade levels and subjects. These experiences should build on each other. By the end of their K-12 education, each student should have many opportunities to develop competencies in specific technology and information skills within the overall Big6 context.

As noted, school-wide Big6 planning requires cooperation among classroom teachers, library media specialists, technology teachers, and administrators. From experience, we find that active, engaged library media specialists are in an ideal position to coordinate the school-wide Big6 Skills effort. First, information skills instruction is a major function of library media programs. In addition, library media specialists are involved with instruction across the curriculum. They are responsible for providing resources and services to all grades and subjects and generally have an excellent overview of the existing school curriculum. Therefore, we recommend, when possible, that library media specialists coordinate Big6 planning with technology teachers, classroom teachers, administrators, and support staff.

Figure 3 is a partially completed Big6 by Unit Matrix for a middle school, grades 6-8. At this point, the Matrix includes only some of the units slated for integrated Big6 instruction. The library media specialist is compiling this plan, and has worked on documenting integrated units across the grade levels and subject areas. For example, so far she has planned two units in grades 6-8 and two additional units in the health curriculum that include students in grades 7 and 8. The health units are particularly use-

Figure 3: Big6 Skills by Unit Matrix: Middle School   Sorted by Grade Level and Marking Period

THE BIG6												
GR	Tchr	Unit	Subject	Assignment	QTR	1	2	3	4	5	6	Comments
06–06	SEW	Current Events	SS	report	1234	X	X	X	X	X	X	*all year long—can hit all Big6*
06–06	ARB	Poetry	English	short written assignment	xxx4				X	X	X	*#4—reading poems, #5/6 — writing good poetry*
07–07	SLJ	Graphs	Math	product	x2xx					X	X	*types of graphs and spreadsheet software*
07–07	TCH	Recycling	SS/Sci	product	x23x	–	X	X	–	X	–	*lots of technology*
08–08	HJW	Map Skills	SS	worksheet	1xxx		X		X			*use of maps*
08–08	TMJ	Noise	Sci	written report	x2xx	–	X	X		X	–	*build on grade 7, technology*
07–08	CER	Diet & Nutririon	Health	posters	1x3x	X	X	–	–	X	–	*health reaches all students; repeats 2x year*
07–08	CER	Tobacco & Smoking	Health	test	1x3x	X			X	X	X	*cooperative teacher, test-taking strategies & the Big6*

THE BIG6												
GR	Tchr	Unit	Subject	Assignment	QTR	1	2	3	4	5	6	Comments

ful since they involve a range of resources, and all students must take health classes at some time. The sixth-grade current events unit is also important. Because it lasts all year, there is a good opportunity to offer lessons in each Big6 Skills.

While this middle school Matrix shows a range of integrated skills instruction, there is room for expansion. As the library media specialist contacts teachers, this plan will grow to document the full-school information and technology skills effort.

Conclusion

Figure 4 is a blank Big6 Skills by Unit Matrix to help you get started in planning for integrated Big6 Skills instruction. As noted earlier, a completed Skills by Unit Matrix can be used both as a planning tool and as documentation of what took place. Faculty can revise the plan as they progress during the year so that at the end of the year there is a full record of the integrated information and technology skills program. Finally, the Matrix can be the basis for reviewing the program and for making revisions for the next year.

There is one more planning tool that can help in planning at all levels: the Big6 and Curriculum Timeline. This tool will be included and explained in a future issue of The Big6 Newsletter.

The BIG6 Teaching Technology & Information Skills

PART III

Big6
Practical Approaches:
K-Adult

CHAPTER 4

The BIG 6

Little Kids

So What About Working with the Very Youngest?

v1 n1 p16

*We are often asked whether you can really teach Kindergarten and preschool students the Big6™. For example, **Audrey Daigneault, Pleasant Valley School Media Center, Groton, Connecticut,** e-mailed the following request:*

Request:

"Mike, I've been using Big6™ this year with great success with upper grades. The teachers I can't seem to crack are our first grade ones. They think the Big6™ is too difficult for their students. They won't agree to try flexible scheduling at all. Every other grade level will try it for at least once a year. I need some first grade examples of success stories from other schools. I heard Bob speak at AASL about a Super Three for primary grades. Did you two ever work on that?"

Response:

Well, Audrey, yes we did work on a "Super 3." In working with kindergarten children, we found that six steps are sometimes a little too much to remember. But, they can still think in terms of a process. The Super 3 focuses process as having three broad steps:

- a beginning,
- a middle, and
- an end.

Young kids can easily relate to this. We like to tell them that whenever they have a job to do—for example, making a picture of signs of Spring—they should do it as if they were living in a story. In a story, there are usually three parts (a beginning, middle, and end).

We like to tell them that whenever they have a job to do—they should do it as if they were living in a story.

We say, when you get an assignment or a task, BEFORE you start doing anything...at THE BEGINNING - you should think, "what am I supposed to do and what will it look like if I do a really good job?" Then, in THE MIDDLE, just do it—find the information, put it all together, make the picture, whatever. And finally, before you turn your work in, at the END, stop again and think, "did I do what I was supposed to do and do I feel o.k. about this? Should I do something else before I turn it in?" That's it—that's the Super 3:

THE BEGINNING:
- think about what I'm supposed to do

THE MIDDLE:
- do it

THE END:
- think about what I did.

Kids should be able to relate their story at any point in time—at the beginning, when they are starting out, in the middle, while they are doing it, or at the end, when they are done or about to finish. Kids can tell the story by making a picture about it, making a story book, telling each other or a number of other ways. So, try this with the little ones. And if you are a library media specialist or technology teacher working with reluctant or skeptical teachers, just start by talking to the kids when you see them about what they are doing in class. You can do this without flexible scheduling if necessary. By the way, when we explained about the Super 3 on the BigSix listserv, some contributors noted that it sounded a whole lot like the PLAN—DO—REVIEW model. Well, we agree—it sure does. In the beginning—PLAN, in the middle—DO; and in the end—REVIEW. We've tried to track down the origin of this model and find that it appears in a number of places including the Effective Schools movement.

Awareness and Fun with Information! Introducing Young Researchers to Information Problem-Solving with Big6™ Activities

v1 n2 p1,6-7

By Barbara A. Jansen,
Librarian, Forest Creek Elementary,
Round Rock, Texas

We've worked with Barbara Jansen for many years on implementing the Big6 approach in elementary schools. Barbara also helps to coordinate the Big6 listserv with us. This article is an excellent example of successfully integrating classroom content, library media activities, and the Big6.

Listening intently, the first-grade students never took their eyes off the "teacher." Not only was the "teacher" telling them about how to find information about the desert, but she had four legs and bumpy green skin! She was a puppet, who sang a song about the Big6 in a high, croaky voice, encouraging her audience to join in the refrain.

The toad's charming southern voice belonged to the library media specialist who used the puppet to introduce and teach the information problem-solving process. Over the next few weeks, as the children learned about deserts from their classroom teachers, the library media specialist's toad continued to join in—introducing each step of the process with song and fun. The result was a successful, collaborative classroom-library media center learning experience.

Even in the earliest primary grades, students can begin learning a process for seeking and using information if the teachers and library media specialist keep three factors in perspective:

1. Research in grades K-2 should be kept on a developmentally appropriate level.

2. Lessons focusing on information seeking and use should be fun and relevant.

3. Students should gain an awareness of and experience in using the skills; mastery should never be expected at the early grade levels.

After repeated lessons using the Big6 in question form (see questions below) young students begin to understand that when they need information to solve a task, they can use the Big6!

Usually in whole-group format, instruction based on the six stages is fairly easy to design and implement. Consider using puppets to help with the presentation; it is fun for you and the students. The puppet can have a content connection; for example, use a cow for a study on farm animals, a wolf for a lesson on mammals, or a toad for a unit on deserts. When the puppet sings to Kindergarten and first grade students, and recites poetry to second graders (even third!), it will secure and keep the attention of the students, so that you can explain each step of the lesson. (See song and poetry in sidebars on pages 7 and 11.)

The following unit gives you an idea of how the Big6 can be implemented with young students. The first-grade team and library media specialist at Live Oak Elementary school (Round Rock, Texas) worked together to develop an integrated unit on farm animals. The library media specialist and the teachers planned and taught each step of the unit together.

One of the lessons presented here employs the Big6 Song as the focus for the students. Also, for this unit, fifth-grade students assisted the first graders with Big6 stages #3 and #4 (location & access and use of information, specifically, note-taking). If you do not have older students to help, parent participation works nicely. Average primary students are cognitively unable to independently locate sources and to read and take notes.

Big6/Farm Animal Unit Sequence

DAY ONE:

In the classroom the teacher and the library media specialist introduce the project—to find out about caring for farm animals on a Texas farm.

Divide the first grade class into pairs. The students pretend that they are starting a farm. Have the class brainstorm a list of farm animals, and write them on a chart tablet. Discuss with the class what a farmer needs to know in order to take care of the animals on a farm in Texas (what do farm animals eat, what do they produce/how are they useful, how often and how many babies do they have, what is each family member called, where can they live on the farm). Each pair of students chooses a farm animal (e.g., hen, rooster, chick) for which they will locate the information that was determined during the discussion.

DAY TWO:

Group fifth graders with first-grade pairs at tables in the library media center.

The library media specialist introduces the Big6 using Maybelle the cow puppet. Maybelle talks about what she needs to know about moving to the farm. She needs to find out about what kind of food they serve, how the farmer will take care of her and her babies, and where she will live on the farm. The library media specialist and Maybelle have a conversation about what information is and how to find it. The library media specialist talks about the Big6, and displays the Big6 song (see page 145) on the transparency so that the fifth-grade students can sing it with her. Maybelle sings the introductory verse.

Big6 #1: Task Definition: What do I need to do?

Show the transparency with the question for Big6 #1. Maybelle reads the question and sings the verse that accompanies this stage. Instruct the students to sing the refrain. Tell the class that they already finished Big6 #1 in their classroom. Review the task (finding out what a farmer needs to know in order to take care of the animals on a farm in Texas). Review the questions they will find. (What does the farm animal eat? What does it produce/how is it useful to the farmer? How often and how many babies does it have? What is each family member called? Where can it live on the farm?)

Big6 #2: Information-Seeking Strategies: What can I use to find what I need?

Show the transparency with the question for Big6 #2. Maybelle again reads the question and sings the

Help the students realize that they can use encyclopedias, library books about farm animals, and the CD-ROM computer encyclopedia

verse that accompanies stage #2. The students will probably sing the refrain. Tell the students that in order to find the answers to the questions, they must decide which books or other sources contain the information. Brainstorm a list of sources with the class. Help the students realize that they can use encyclopedias, library books about farm animals, and the CD-ROM computer encyclopedia. (Of course, you will use what is available in your own school library media center, school, and community). Also try to use human sources as often as possible—for example, the music teacher who lives on a farm, someone's Uncle Charlie, a farmer, or an expert at the zoo.

Big6 #3: Location & Access: Where can I find what I need?

Maybelle reads the question on the transparency and sings the verse for Big6 #3. Discuss location and access. Tell students that you collected some of the books for them and put them on a cart. You can show the students how you found the books using the online catalog and where they are located in the library media center. Also discuss where they might locate their people sources, for example you might have Uncle Charlie or the farmer available to talk with them. Their Big6 Buddies (fifth grade helpers) will locate the appropriate encyclopedia from the book shelves and help younger students use the computer CD-ROM. Big6 #2 and #3 do not usually take too much time with the younger students.

DAYS THREE AND FOUR:

Big6 #4: Use of Information: What information can I use?

Maybelle performs for Big6 #4 as she did for the other stages. Show the children how they can look at pictures, read the books, or have their Big6 Buddies and their teachers read to them to find out the information they asked in their questions. The fifth grade students will record the answers to each question on prepared data charts. Fifth graders should use vocabulary that the first graders can understand. (For an explanation of data charts, see "TIPS#1: The Trash-n-Treasure Note-Taking Technique" on page 103-104). Instruct the fifth graders to explain to the first graders everything that they do to locate the answers to the questions. They should ask the first graders to listen for the answers as they read aloud from appropriate sections. Allow adequate time for finding and recording answers.

Big6 #5: Synthesis: How can I put my information together?

Maybelle and students sing the verse to Big6 #5. Discuss synthesis in terms a first grader can understand. Instruct the pairs of students to sketch a picture of their farm animal, including the information from the data chart. They do not need to include these questions, as they will record these into the computer: What does the farm animal produce/how is it useful to the farmer? What is each family member called? Have the pair of students share a computer and *show* their information by drawing it in Kid Pix. The teacher will save all pictures on one disk.

Pairs should print a draft of their picture and write in sentence form, the answers to the two questions not included in the picture.

The teacher and library media specialist will put the slide show together, allowing each pair to record their sentences with their accompanying picture. Present the slide show to the Big6 Buddies and other grade levels.

Big6 #6: Evaluation: How will I know if I did well?

Tell students that Big6 #6—evaluation is important because that's how we learn to improve. Maybelle and the students sing the last verse and refrain. Have each student answer the questions below by filling in answers on an evaluation sheet, providing written responses. The teacher or library media specialist should read each question, having students answer each, one at a time.

EVALUATION QUESTIONS:

- What did I learn?
- How well did I do on my picture?
- Did I include the things I found out about my farm animal?
- Did I work well with my partner?
- Did I cooperate with my Big6 Buddy?
- What did I do well this time?
- What could I do better next time?

You won't get perfection on the evaluation sheet. But as the students gain experience in self-evaluation and writing, you will gain insight into their thought processes and you may modify your instruction accordingly (For more on this see Jansen, Barbara A. "Self-Evaluation: The Forgotten Step to Achievement," School Library Media Activities Monthly, October 1995, 24-27.)

Conclusion

Guided research with young learners gives them an awareness that there is a process and specific skills to follow to seek and use information. Students begin understanding that they need to formulate appropriate questions to complete a task. Give young students opportunities to use human resources, survey and observation, too— not only traditional print or electronic materials. Big6 instruction integrates content learning and processes. Students learn how to approach tasks and how library media centers, technology, and information are used for a purpose. When they are developmentally ready to locate and use sources independently they should make the transition with ease. The foundation you set will start them on their way to becoming life-long learners, and you will have fun doing it!

A Home For Toad: Using Storytelling to Teach Big6 Skills

v1 n6 p1,6,11

By Barbara Jansen

Toad was hopping along the hot desert sand looking for a place to get out of the heat. She was looking for a home to stay in when the sun was too hot for her bumpy skin. She needed a home that was not too hot, not too hard, and not too prickly.

The first graders listen intently as the bumpy green toad puppet defines her task. As the story develops, the students sing along with Toad and learn about the homes of various desert animals. A picture of each animal and its home is placed on a flannel board. The children laugh and clap for Toad when she finally solves her problem. Using a poster showing the Big6 in question form, the librarian explains to the students how Toad uses the process to solve her information problem:

WHAT DO I NEED TO DO? (TASK DEFINITION):
Toad needs a new home that cannot be too hot, too hard, or too prickly.

WHAT CAN I USE TO FIND WHAT I NEED? (INFORMATION SEEKING STRATEGIES):
She can either look for a home herself, or ask one of the other desert animals. She decides to ask other desert animals.

WHERE CAN I FIND WHAT I NEED? (LOCATION & ACCESS):

She walks until she sees Javelina.
She walks until she sees Lizard.
She walks until she sees Pack Rat.
She keeps walking until she decides to dig a hole in the sand.

WHAT INFORMATION CAN I USE? (USE OF INFORMATION):

She asks Javelina about his home and decides that it is too hot. Javelina tells her to find a cooler place with more water. She asks Lizard about his home and decides that it is too hard. Lizard tells her to find a place that is softer. She asks Pack Rat about his home and decides that it is too prickly. Pack Rat tells her to find a smoother home.

HOW CAN I PUT MY INFORMATION TOGETHER? (SYNTHESIS):

Toad finds that the animals' homes are not suitable for her and she uses what they tell her to find a home deep in the sand under the yucca plant.

HOW WILL I KNOW IF I DID WELL? (EVALUATION):

She knows it is a good home because it is not too hot, not too hard, and not too prickly and she remembers the song.

Following this poster demonstration, the librarian provides story strips representing each story event to each group of three students. Groups then place the story strips onto chart paper in the Big6 sequence with the assistance of parent helpers. As they do so, they refer to the flannel board to check the order of the animals. In arranging the story strips, students easily understand how Toad had to revisit Big6 #3 and #4 several times before she found a place to live.

Help the students realize that they can use encyclopedias, library books about farm animals, and the CD-ROM computer encyclopedia

After students complete the story strip activity, the teacher and librarian use the Big6 as they discuss each step of the ensuing desert study with students and their parent helpers. Parents help their groups locate information about a specific desert animal (a physical description and where it lives in the desert). Groups draw a picture of the animal in its habitat for a class book and write a sentence explaining why their animal's home would or would not be suitable for Toad.

After the student groups and parent helpers complete their desert study, the teacher reads the completed class book to the class and the librarian administers a simple written evaluation instrument for each student to complete. The evaluation instrument requires students to focus on what they learned about the content and the Big6, how well they participated with their parent helper and partner, and their efforts in producing a page for the class book.

Using Stories to Teach the Big6

Children respond enthusiastically to stories. By using stories in relation to the Big6 research process, teachers and librarians can create meaningful instruction that captures students' interest. In choosing or creating stories to use, consider these factors:

■ The characters must have a problem to solve that requires information for the solution.

■ The storyteller should capture the audience's attention. This can be achieved through audience participation and/or by using puppets or other visuals.

■ The Big6 storytelling session should be integrated into a curriculum related project that requires students to use the Big6.

Strategies for Implementation

Teachers and librarians can use several strategies to successfully integrate stories into the Big6 process and subject area curriculum:

1. Read a children's picture book that has the appropriate curriculum connection.

For example, when studying the characteristics of amphibians, the lesson can be introduced by reading Ted Arnold's *Green Wilma* (Dial Books For Young Readers, 1993). In this story, a little girl turns into a frog and creates havoc in school as she tries to participate in routine activities, and catch a fly. The book can provide a 'jumping off point' for a conversation weaving the Big6 into the curricular activity. For example, after reading Green Wilma to the class, the librarian or teacher can capture the class' attention by using a hand puppet of a toad. The toad acts confused by the little girl who turned into a frog. This leads to a conversation between the puppet and the teacher or librarian, concluding with a problem to solve: find out about what makes one animal an amphibian and another one a human. What process can help us find the solution to our problem? The Big6! The puppet sings the "Big6 Song" (see *Big6 Newsletter*, Vol. 1 No. 2, page 145) when beginning an activity for each step. Of course, children's literature can be used without puppets and singing. The librarian and teacher will need to make the curriculum and Big6 connection, however, through discussion with the class.

2. Modify a story from a children's book.

The idea for "A Home for Toad," came from the lively story Lizard's Song by George Shannon

(Greenwillow Books, 1981). In the original story, a silly bear likes the song that Lizard sings but cannot remember the words until he finds a place of his own. The story and song were modified to create "A Home for Toad." In looking at potential ideas for adaptation, stories that feature a character with a problem to solve make good candidates. Use your imagination and modify the story to suit your needs.

3. Write a story based on the curriculum connection.

For example, when studying the lives of cowboys, the librarian made up a story about a little girl who wished to be a cowgirl but wasn't sure what she needed to know about cowboys/girls in order to get a job on a ranch. The story took her through the information finding process which included some interesting and funny adventures. She finally decided that being a cowgirl was hard work. She decided to become a computer programmer or brain surgeon instead! (The first grade didn't quite appreciate the ending to the story, but it elicited some laughs from the teachers!) The librarian used a large poster of the Big6 to show the students how the girl used the Big6 process to solve her problem. The teacher and librarian introduced the assignment to the students: learn about the life of a cowboy to determine what makes it so difficult. Throughout the assignment, they guided the students step-by-step through the Big6 process.

4. Use extemporaneous dialog with puppets.

Upon arriving in the library, second grade students were met by a glum and grouchy Maybelle the cow puppet. She couldn't understand what the big deal was about that silly nursery rhyme that mothers taught their little children. The librarian had the second graders recite "Hey diddle, diddle" with Maybelle interrupting at the part about the cow jumping over the moon. "Stop! I can't stand it! Why would a self-respecting cow want to go to the moon so far away when there is nice grass to munch on and great books to read right here at Forest Creek Elementary? I just cannot stand the thought of it! The very nerve!" The librarian asked Maybelle how she could make such a determination if she didn't know anything about the moon. She suggested that Maybelle find out about the moon before she makes such a harsh decision "How can I find out about the moon?" asked Maybelle. "Well, I have just the thing.

The second graders are about to use this to study planets in the solar system" said the librarian.

Using storytelling with the Big6 motivates young learners to stay focused on the project from Big6 #1, Task Definition, to the very last word on their Big6 #6, Evaluation. Let your imagination go and you'll have fun finding, creating stories, and designing instructions that will help children love the information problem-solving process!

A Home For Toad: The Actual Story

v1 n6 p7

By Barbara Jansen

Toad was hopping along the hot desert sand looking for a cool place to get out of the heat. She was looking for a home to stay in when the sun was too hot for her bumpy skin. She needed a home that was not too hot, not too hard, and not too prickly. She thought about where she would find out about homes that were not too hot, not too hard, and not too prickly. She knew she could look for one for herself or ask other animals. She decided to ask other animals. So she set off in search of other desert animals to help her find a home that was not too hot, not too hard, and not too prickly. Presently, she found Javelina scampering in and out of mesquite trees, digging for roots and singing a catchy little tune:

Using storytelling with the Big6 motivates young learners to stay focused on the project from Big6 #1, Task Definition, to the very last word on their Big6 #6, Evaluation.

"I'm happy, happy, happy as I can be because my home of mesquite is just right for me. I'm happy, happy, happy as I can be."

Toad liked that tune and wanted to learn it. She asked Javelina about her home and Javelina told her that it suited him perfectly—it was in a sandy hot place to dig for roots, it had some shade to rest in, but it was nice and hot most of the time. She told Javelina that she was looking for a home that was not too hot, not too hard, and not too prickly. Javelina's home was too hot. Javelina told her to find a home that was cooler and that had more water. Toad then asked Javelina to teach her the song. After a number of practice tries, Toad thought she had the song in her head.

As soon as she hopped out of sight of Javelina, Toad tried to sing the song "I'm happy, happy, happy..." but found that she had forgotten the words. She tried and tried to remember the words to that nice song that Javelina taught her when she saw Lizard and heard him singing the same song, but a little differently:

"I'm happy, happy, happy as I can be
because my home of rock is just right for me.
I'm happy, happy, happy as I can be."

Toad liked that tune and wanted to learn it. She asked Lizard about his home and Lizard told her that it suited him perfectly: it was in a hard place to take a nice nap in the sun, it had some shade for him to get out of the sun when it got too hot, and it was nice and flat. Toad told Lizard that she was looking for a home that was not too hot, not too hard, and not too prickly. And Lizard's home was too hard. Lizard told her to find a home that was softer. Toad then asked Lizard to teach her the song. After a number of practice tries, Toad thought she had the song in her head. As soon as she hopped out of sight of Lizard, she tried to sing the song "I'm happy, happy, happy..." but had forgotten the words. She tried and tried to remember the words to that nice song that Lizard taught her when she saw Pack Rat and heard him singing the same song, but a little differently:

"I'm happy, happy, happy as I can be
because my home of cactus is just right for me.
I'm happy, happy, happy as I can be."

Toad liked that tune and wanted to learn it. She asked Pack Rat about her home and Pack Rat told her that it suited her perfectly: it was in a nice place to store things, it had some holes to sleep in, and it stored water to drink. Toad told Pack Rat that she was looking for a home that was not too hot, not too hard, and not too prickly. Pack Rat's home was too prickly. Pack Rat told her to find a home that was smoother. Toad then asked Pack Rat to teach her the song. After a number of practice tries, Toad thought she had the song in her head. As soon as she hopped out of sight of Pack Rat, Toad tried to sing the song "I'm happy, happy, happy..." but had forgotten the words.

This was just too much for Toad. The sun was beating down on her bumpy back, she needed water to drink, and she needed a nice place to rest. To make matters worse, she could not remember the words to that nice song that the other animals kept singing.

"Javelina told me to find a place that was cool and had more water, Lizard told me to find a place that was softer, and Pack Rat told me to find a place that was smoother."

Toad thought about the nice sand under a yucca plant. She dug and dug in the sand until she had buried herself quite deep. The earth was cool under the yucca plant. There was water to drink in the moisture of the roots. And, there were nice fat worms and grubs to eat as she dug deeper in the sand.

"This is nice. It is not too hot, not too hard, and not too prickly. I think I have found my home underneath the desert floor, thanks to my friends' advice."

"I'm happy, happy, happy as I can be
because my home of sand is just right for me.
I'm happy, happy, happy as I can be."

Story and song based on the book Lizard's Song by George Shannon (Greenwillow Books, 1981).

The Bright Bird - A Problem-Solving Allegory

v1 n6 p4-5

By Brian Armour

Brian Armour, Head of Information Services at Redlands College Library, Wellington Point, Queensland, Australia has created an original story illustrating the Big6. He also made a mnemonic from the letters that spell Big6. Both are available on the Redlands College Library website at:
http://www.redlands.qld.edu.au/library/bigsix.html

An adaptation of a PowerPoint version of the allegory is available on the Web site at:
http://www.uq.net.au/~zzredlib/bribird.html

Here's the Story

Living in the deep forest of the Atherton Fableland is a very colorful bird called 'The Bright Bird.' This bird is much admired for its beautiful colors, which

THE BIG6 INFORMATION PROBLEM-SOLVING STRATEGY
STEP 1. **B**e sure you understand the problem, question, and assignment topic. (Task Definition)
STEP 2. **I**dentify the resources that will help you solve this problem, answer this question, and research this assignment topic. (Information Seeking Strategies)
STEP 3. **G**ather relevant information. (Location & Access)
STEP 4. **S**elect an approach, theme, and strategy. (Use of Information)
STEP 5. **I**ntegrate the information you have collected with your own ideas to demonstrate your solution, present your answer to the question, and write the assignment. (Synthesis)
STEP 6. e**X**amine the results and refine the presentation. (Evaluation)

Modified by Brian Armour for use at Redlands College, with permission.

originally earned it its name: 'Bright Bird.' Whenever visitors come to the forest, they try eagerly to catch a glimpse of this wonderful bird. It is an experience to talk about with their family and friends and a tale to pass on to the younger generation.

Our story reaches back into the dim past when the first pair of Bright Birds came to live in the forest. One day, close to dusk, the female was hunting insects and was following a very juicy-looking insect at high speed among the trees. In the semi-dark, she slammed into a tree and suffered brain damage. It seems that the part of the brain which held the nest-making instinct was damaged beyond repair.

Now she had to start from scratch to learn how to make a nest for the approaching spring season. Fortunately, the concussion had rearranged the cells in another part of her brain so that she gained the power to think deeply and to solve problems.

Somehow she heard news of a problem-solving method that they use at Redlands College, based on the Big6 method thought up by Mike and Bob. She decided to give it a try.

The first step was to 'be sure you understand the problem.' She thought about it. Her aim was to raise a healthy family that season but she did not know instinctively how to do it. She understood that the nest would need to be:

- Big enough to hold her eggs and the growing chicks
- Well protected and strong enough to withstand storms and high winds
- High enough to be out of reach of predators
- Snug and warm enough for the comfort of her family.

The second step was to 'identify the sources from which she could get information.' Why not check out what other birds do? After all, these birds had survived for many generations so they must have been doing something right! That seemed like a good idea so she went on to the third step.

The third step was to 'gather the information from these sources.' She went out into the forest to see how other birds made nests.

She observed the crow that made nests high in trees using strong sticks; but she did not admire the untidy jumble that crows made with the sticks and felt sure the nests would not weather the vicious storms that sometimes shook the forest.

She inspected the mud nests that the swallows made in the sheltered crevices of rocky cliffs beside the forest—nests that were so strong that they lasted

Now, ideas are great but they do not get the job done by themselves.

for many years, needing only a new lining and some small repairs each year.

Then there were the nests of the weaver birds into which soft grass and animal hair were entwined to hold the nest together and anchor it to the branch.

In all, she gathered information about ten species of birds, then felt she had enough information to help her make up her own mind.

It was time to go on to the fourth step: 'select the best solution, using the information that is most relevant to the problem.' This is what she said to herself: "I'll borrow some ideas from the crow, the swallow, and the weaver bird, but my nest will be just what I want, to suit the needs of raising my family—large, sturdy, safe, and comfortable."

Now, ideas are great but they do not get the job done by themselves. It was time to take the fifth step: 'Integrate the information you have selected with your own ideas, to demonstrate your solution to the problem.'

She laid a platform of sturdy, crisscrossed sticks across the fork of a tree, high up but sheltered from the rain by the canopy above. She brought sticky mud to cement these sticks together and anchored them to the branches of the tree. She also shaped the mud into a deep hollow in which she built the rest of the nest. She wove grass and animal hair into a circular pattern and placed this inside the hollow, fastening it to the twig foundation using many strands of hair and grass. The deep sides and bottom of the nest were lined with this woven hair-grass combination.

To show other birds that she had borrowed some nest-making ideas, our feathered problem-solver attached a crow's feather to a twig, stuck a swallow's feather in the mud, and sewed a weaver's feather into the lining of the nest.

Having finished the job, she couldn't wait to try it out. She was into the sixth step without really giving it a second thought (the mud had scarcely dried). She snuggled down into the nest to "eXamine the finished product." After an adjustment to a twig here and there and adding further mud where it was a bit thin, she told her mate that all was ready for the new family to be laid and raised.

Several months later, a healthy brood of youngsters added their splash of color to the forest. In the years that followed, these young ones became grown-ups and learned from their mother the new nest-making ways that were so successful.

Nowadays, visitors to the forest are thankful that the Bright Bird species has been so good at bringing up families. There are more of them to give the visitors the great pleasure of glimpsing them as the birds play and hunt in the forest thickets.

And, when these visitors return home and tell the tale about the Bright Bird, they are always careful to tell both reasons why this species is called "The Bright Bird."

Can you tell what those two reasons are?

Be a Big6 Detective: Introducing the Big6 Problem-Solving Process Using Nate the Great

v1 n6 p10-11

By Lynn Spencer

One fun way to help elementary school students learn the Big6 Problem-Solving Process is to use the *Nate the Great* book series by Marjorie Weinman Sharmat. As the plot develops, teachers can help students draw parallels between the actions of the young detective and the six steps of the process.

Before beginning your shared reading time, spend a few minutes discussing a chart of the Big6. The following simplifies the Big6 for the lower grade levels by using key words.

1. WHAT? What do I want to know?
   (Graphic of a large question mark)

2. HOW? How can I find some ideas?
   (Graphic of a child with a thought bubble over his head)

3. WHERE? Where would I go to look for these ideas?
   (Graphic of a large arrow)

4. LOOK! Read, listen, or look. There's people, TV, or books.
   (Graphics of a teacher, TV, books, and computer)

5. SHOW! Make something to show what I learned.
   (Graphics of a videocamera, an easel, and a report paper)

6. WELL? Did I get what I needed? Did I do my job well?
   (Graphic of a child with arms raised in triumph wearing a prize ribbon)

Keep the children on task and involved by making sets of index cards. Write each key word on a separate card. Laminate the cards to extend their usefulness. As the class progresses through the story, ask students to hold up a card if they think the character Nate is using one of the steps. This takes a bit of coaching, but the important point is to reinforce keywords and keep the students actively involved.

There are many different titles in the Nate the Great series, and the plots are predictable. All the adventures fit in well with the steps of the Big6 problem-solving process.

Let's use the original story, Nate the Great, to explain how to apply the Big6. In this story, a young detective must solve a friend's problem: she wants to find a missing painting of her dog.

Point out to the children that we now have our question, or task:

Big6 #1: What do I want to know? Ask everyone to hold up the "WHAT?" card.

Nate then decides he must get information by listening to descriptions from possible witnesses and from studying clues. This is an example of Big6 #2: "HOW?" How can I find some ideas?

Now, ask students to hold up their "WHERE" cards (Big6 #3) when they hear a description about a place where Nate has gone for his clues. Call on students to tell the specific locations. For example, Nate goes to Annie's house and interviews her to find out who has seen the painting, which leads him to interview Annie's friend Rosamund. He also searches Annie's room and backyard, and studies her little brother's painting habits for visual clues.

When Nate puts together what he knows about the colors Annie used, what he has learned about Annie's brother's love of the color red, and what he knows about mixing colors, he discovers the answer to the mystery. This is sometimes a difficult step for students to recognize. Nate is actually doing more thinking than he is looking. There is a useful illustration of Nate putting together his information as he studies the paintings on the little brother's bedroom walls. Ask students to study this illustration and then hold up the card that describes what step is happening "LOOK" (Big6 #4).

Students should hold up the "SHOW" card (Big6 #5) when Nate shows Annie how the wet paint allowed her brother to change her painting by covering it with another color (in the book, there is a "before" and "after" picture for clarification).

In the end, our young detective knows he has done well (WELL?: Big6 #6) because Annie is satisfied and has been given the information that will help her avoid "losing" a picture in the future.

This simple format could also be used in the classroom to give students a framework for the writing process. Using the key words from the Big6, students can think of a question or problem from their daily lives, and try to tell a story that shows how they would find the answer in the tradition of our favorite boy detective, Nate the Great.

It's Primary: Big6 Skills + One Book + Ingenuity = Project Success!

v2 n1 p6-7

By Barbara Jansen

How did life during Christopher Columbus's day compare to ours today? That is what students in **Diane Tredennick's** second grade class at **Forest Creek Elementary, Round Rock, Texas,** wished to find out.

Diane met with the library media specialist (LMS) to plan the project prior to giving the assignment. They decided that they would integrate the Big6 skills and technology into a project that would require students to:

- Analyze the assignment
- Generate questions to answer
- Research to find the answers to the questions
- Produce Venn diagrams comparing and contrasting life today and life in Columbus's day, and
- Present their results orally to the class.

During the planning phase, the teacher and the LMS found that there was only one book in the library that would answer the questions that the students would develop. Undaunted, Diane and the LMS determined that they would employ the "note-taking triad" and word processing to implement Big6 #4, Use of Information. The triad consists of the teacher, the LMS, and the students. Through this process, the teacher and the LMS take turns reading and recording notes as the students identify answers from the text.

The students were divided into five groups: food, occupations, education, recreation, and transportation. To focus on Task Definition, the groups of students used personal observations and surveys to brainstorm and write out questions pertaining to their topic. The LMS taught students how to ask questions that supplied adequate information for use in the final product. For example, in addition to asking, "Did they have hamburgers? Did they have cola?" She discussed adding questions such as "What kind of food did they have?"

Following this, the LMS demonstrated the use of the online catalog (Big6 #3 - Location & Access)

Using the note-taking triad process, the teacher and the Library Media Specialist take turns reading and recording notes as the students identify answers from the text

to find an appropriate book, If You Were There in 1492 by Barbara Brenner (Bradbury Press, 1991).

After the book was retrieved from the shelf, students listened to the LMS read the table of contents out loud to determine if the book held answers to their questions. The students affirmed that the book was appropriate to their task.

Note-taking took place on the floor of the library as students sat in front of a computer hooked to a large TV display. The teacher began by asking one group for its list of questions, which she typed using a large, bold font so that all students could see the questions on the display. The LMS asked that group to identify the chapter in which the answers to its questions would most likely be found. Prior to reading the chapter out loud, the LMS instructed all students to listen for answers to the questions listed on the display and to raise their hands when an answer was detected. This helps students develop critical listening skills and motivates all students to pay attention.

As she read, the LMS stopped each time hands were raised and asked which question was answered. If students missed a passage that answered a question, the LMS or teacher stopped and read it again, instructing the students to listen carefully to match a question to the passage.

The teacher typed in the appropriate information for each question as she and the LMS discussed effective note-taking (Big6 #4.1, Extract Relevant Information). When students came upon unfamiliar terms or objects in the book, the LMS used a CD-ROM encyclopedia to define and display them. Students could see a lute and even hear its music! The process was repeated for each group's questions, with all students listening to answers for all questions.

When students noticed that there was one topic (occupations) that had no chapter in the book, the teacher used the opportunity to present a mini-lesson on inference. For example, from the passage "If you were unlucky enough to get sick..., you would have taken yourself to an apothecary, which was like a drugstore" (p. 34), students could infer that a druggist or sales clerk would be an occupation.

Following the note-taking session, the teacher saved the notes to a shared folder on the file server so that the students had access to their notes both in the classroom and in the computer labs to create the final product, a Venn diagram. Each group created a Venn diagram comparing and contrasting life then and now by using the drawing and text tools in the word processing software (Big6 #5, Synthesis). The students presented their diagrams orally to their classmates and discussed the benefits and drawbacks to living in both times. In summation, students each completed an informal written evaluation (Big6 #6, Evaluation).

This lesson, which might never have happened if the LMS and teacher had been deterred by the lack of materials, provided students with diverse information skills and demonstrated the ingenuity of the teacher and the LMS.

Getting Started with Information Problem-Solving Isn't a Problem When One Begins with a Book

v1 n6 p14-15

By Sally Ray

George Washington Allen, a character in Jean Fritz's book, George Washington's Breakfast *(Coward McCann, 1984), had an information problem. George wanted to know what the famous General and President, George Washington ate for breakfast. Sharing the story about how George Washington Allen solved his problem provides a perfect opportunity to introduce primary students to the Big6. Here's a breakdown of the story from a Big6 perspective.*

Breakfast and the Big6

Big6 #1: Task Definition: What am I supposed to do?

If George Washington Allen could find out what George Washington ate for breakfast, his grandmother promised to cook him the breakfast.

Big6 #2: Information Solving Strategies: How will I begin to find the facts?

George went to the library and asked Miss Willing, the librarian, for help. Miss Willing directed George to the encyclopedia. The answer to his question was not in the encyclopedia. Next Miss Willing showed George the library's card catalog.

Big6 #3 Location & Access: Where will I find the facts?

George located the call numbers for several biographies in the catalog. He began to borrow every biography on George Washington from the library.

Big6 #4 Use of Information: Look and read, look and write.

George took the books home and, with his parents' help, read each one. His grandmother informed

George that she would cook the breakfast, but she would not look in the books. George, his parents, and Miss Willing read all the biographies in the library. They found what people in Colonial Virginia typically ate for breakfast, but they did not find out what George Washington ate for breakfast so they started over with a different source. So, time to loop back—back to:

Big6 #2 Information Seeking Strategies: What are some other sources?

George and his parents decide to visit Mount Vernon, George Washington's home. They stopped en route in Washington, D. C. at a Smithsonian museum. George Allen counted the buttons on Washington's uniform and studied a display at the museum.

Big6 # 3 Location & Access: Where will I find the facts?

He visited the kitchen at Mount Vernon where he could imagine servants preparing breakfast in his imagination. George still did not find out what George Washington ate for breakfast. When the family returned home, grandmother and Miss Willing were waiting for them. Discouraged by his family's desire that he give up the search, George Allen climbed the steps to the attic of his house. In the attic, George accidentally found an old book of American history.

Big6 #4 Use of Information: Look and read, look and write.

This book described Washington's breakfast as three small Indian hoecakes and a cup of weak tea.

Big6 #5 Step 5 Synthesis: Show facts learned to others.

An excited George Allen rushed to tell his grandmother that he had found his answer. Grandmother hesitated. She was glad that George had found the answer, but she had an information problem. Grandmother did not know what Indian hoecakes were. So.... George looked for hoecakes in the dictionary. The description of Indian hoecakes helped Grandmother and George create a recipe. Grandmother cooked the hoecakes.

Big6 #6 Evaluation: Well, did I do a good job?

George ate the hoecakes, but he was still hungry. Surely, he wondered, George Washington would have been hungry too. What would George Washington have eaten for lunch?

Teaching the Lesson

Reading and discussing this fiction book took two thirty-minute sessions or three fifteen-minute sessions. When introducing the Big6, we used modified terms with the first grade classes.

The six modified terms are:

1. "Task" "What"
2. "Strategy" "How"
3. "Locate" "Where"
4. "Use" "Look"
5. "Synthesis" "Show"
6. "Evaluation" "Well?"

These modified terms, taken from a message LM_NET listserv, were written in bold print on six large pieces of posterboard and shown to the class as each step was reviewed.

In addition to introducing the steps to information problem solving, this story about a real person told in an imaginary setting with imaginary characters was used to illustrate the difference in fiction and non-fiction books. By reading the book in February, the story tied in with the curriculum emphasis on President's Day and Washington's birthday.

Following the reading of George Washington's Breakfast, first graders in our school were assigned an information problem about an animal as a part of their class curriculum. While most of the Location & Access and Use of Information were done in class on a computer animal database, children also used First Connections Encyclopedia from Golden Book. This CD-ROM source was introduced to the students during another library visit.

There is a saying that "A picture is worth a thousand words." Using the right story to introduce the Big6 to primary students can be the picture that teaches students more effectively than thousands of words on lists, posters, and charts of explanation.

Sally Ray is a Library Media Specialist, Wells Elementary School, Plano, Texas.

Extra, Extra, Tell All About It!

v1 n6 p16

By Kaye Lindauer

Telling anecdotes from the life of newswoman Nellie Bly (1867-1922) provided the stimulus for exciting research and storytelling for a class of fifth-grade students at **Eagle Hill Middle School, Manlius, New York**. Nellie traveled around the world in an effort to beat the record set by the fictitious Phinneas Fog in Jules Verne's *Around the World in Eighty Days*. Starting from New York City, she went to Southampton, England, Egypt, Singapore, China, San Francisco, and home to New York in 72 days! The sights, smells, customs, and stories from all the places Nellie visited offered rich material for creating biographical fiction about Nellie and her adventures.

Following a storytelling presentation by the library media specialist, students spent two weeks investigating the life and times of Nellie Bly. This research led students to such topics as Stephen Foster, Jules Verne, and Joseph Pulitzer.

The culmination of the research was a storytelling celebration for parents and friends. The students each wrote an essay on one part of Nellie Bly's life, weaving information into their biographical sketches about many aspects of corresponding history and exotic places. The writings were arranged in chronological order and each student told their Nellie story. Students did not memorize their written piece; they shared what they learned by using storytelling techniques (Big6 #5).

To prepare the students, the library media specialist presented two workshops on storytelling. In addition to learning presentation skills, the students learned how to put together and re-tell a good story. The library media specialist and teacher worked with each student to edit their stories. Usually, this meant cutting out some material to make the stories shorter. Students compared editing for storytelling with their previous experiences with editing essays. They were surprised to find that the same techniques didn't always apply. For example, you might repeat the same phrase in a story for emphasis, but you would edit this out in an essay. Once the stories were set, the students practiced their presentation skills by telling their stories to other fifth-grade classes.

Parents and friends were invited to a grand storytelling celebration. Each student in the class told their story from "The Life and Times of Nellie Bly." Following this, students presented "A Live Presentation of a Historical Timeline" as they each shared a historical fact that spanned the years of Nellie's life. Copies of the song, "Nellie Bly," which students learned in music class, were distributed to the audience. Everyone sang as the music teacher directed. Student-created bibliographies of historical fiction and biographies for further reading about the time period corresponding to the life of Nellie Bly were distributed. And, of course, parents and students celebrated their success with cookies.

CHAPTER 5

The BIG 6

Middle Kids

Not Just For the Younger Set: Booktalking Revisited

v1 n6 p8-9

By Mike Eisenberg

In the Beginning

Back in 1979, before there was a "formal" Big6, I wrote my very first article for publication—in *Media & Methods* magazine. The title was "Booktalks: Creating Contagious Enthusiasm," and it focused on getting high school students excited about reading and books. It's good to look back on that article and see the strong connection to my more publicized passion—the Big6 Skills.

The booktalking article described a program that we developed through the library media program that involved classes throughout the school. The library media staff would contact teachers to see what assignments or classwork required students to do some form of outside reading. Typically, this involved some form of required reading in English classes (e.g., 19th century novels, contemporary fiction, essays, speeches, etc.), but it also involved art and humanities classes studying famous artists, a social studies class studying concepts of world history through novels, and a science class involved with weather.

We had one other rule in the booktalk—as soon as someone indicated they wanted the book, we stopped talking, passed it to that student, who could sign it out right on the spot...

Approach to Booktalking

Our approach to booktalking was quick and to-the-point. We would go into the classroom with a bag of books and talk to the students about their assignment and then briefly discuss each book. The goal was to tie the booktalk to a real need, the assignment, and assure the students that the books would fulfill their needs. When discussing a book, we would try to comment on something we knew about the book that might grab the students' attention—the plot, theme, characters, a story about the author—some "hook" to get them to think about reading that book.

We were always up-front and honest with the students. If we hadn't read the book, we said so, but we might discuss another book by the same author or note a review of the book that gave it a good rating. We had one other rule in the booktalk—as soon as someone indicated they wanted the book, we stopped talking, passed it to that student, who could sign it out right on the spot, and went on to discuss another book. This kept the entire event moving and kept the students interested because one student might ask for a book right before another student who wanted it. We also followed up on the booktalk with a display in the library media center targeted to that particular teacher's class and assignment.

These booktalks proved to be highly successful. In my last year on the job, we did 180 booktalks—an

average of one a day! The students seemed appreciative because we made it easier for them to get books for assignments. They also discovered books that they might want to read on their own. Teachers appreciated our active involvement in the classroom and the help in getting appropriate books in their students' hands. We were pleased because students were reading more library books!

Discussing the Program

When discussing the booktalking program, we explained it as part of the library media program's services component. Booktalking was part of our resource provision and reading guidance functions, not part of information skills effort. I now know that it was a mistake. Booktalking can be an integral part of Big6 Skills instruction.

Think about it. Choosing appropriate books for an assignment is an information problem. And, the key to our booktalking was tying it to a real assignment. That's Task Definition! Students, particularly those in high school and college, really have a limited amount of free time. Before linking the booktalks to assignments, trying to get the students excited about books was an uphill battle. But, by tying the effort to their specific tasks, we were able to meet their needs as well as get them to think about interesting books beyond the assignment.

Selecting Appropriate Books

Selecting appropriate books is an Information Seeking Strategies activity. I did some of this by bringing a set of books to the classroom, but the students still had to evaluate the books in terms of their own needs and interest. True, I did short-circuit Big6 #3, Location & Access, but it's not necessary to teach each Big6 skill with every information problem.

As for other stages, the students engaged in Big6 #4, Use of Information, by listening to the booktalk. Most would listen, but some would write down the name of an author or title. Synthesis, from our perspective, was the booktalk itself. From the students' perspective, it was selecting the book. Lastly, for Evaluation, we always asked for feedback—on the books and on the booktalk. Regarding the books, we asked students to let us know if we ever recommended a book that they really didn't like or one they had trouble linking to the assignment. We would discuss this with them, help make the link, and sometimes make a note to not use a particular book again for that assignment.

Booktalks help bridge the artificial gap between books and technology.

Great Success!

As for the booktalking itself, most students really liked them. After a few years, some students mentioned that they preferred that we simply set up a display of books linked to an assignment in the library media center. After evaluating their comments, we cut back a bit on the number of booktalks and expanded the displays. This saved time and effort, but still met students' needs.

Overall, our booktalking was a great success. We were actively engaged in the curriculum and helped students focus on Task Definition and resources to meet their tasks. Today, I would emphasize the connection between booktalking and Big6 information skills instruction even more. Too often we hear the comment that we must choose between books or technology. We disagree. It's all together, and booktalking, Big6-style, demonstrates that!

CHAPTER 6

Big Kids

The Big6: Not Just for Kids!

v1 n3 p1, 8-10

Introduction to the Big6: Information Problem-Solving for Upper High School, College-Age, and Adult Students

By Mike Eisenberg

Here's a first for the Big6 Newsletter—an article to use directly with students. In this case, upper high school and college-age students! Feel free to reproduce the article as is, or adapt it to your own situation.

The article was specifically developed to introduce the Big6 to college freshmen in my "Introduction to Information Management & Technology" course at Syracuse University. My goals were to present an overview of the Big6 process, give examples of each stage, and get students to think about the Big6 in relation to their own situations.

At first, students were skeptical. "Isn't this just common sense? Don't I do this already?" But after I explained the process in relation to their needs and interests (nonacademic as well as for papers and projects), they got it! When I see students in later years, they frequently mention how they still use the overall Big6 process, as well as apply specific Big6 skills to successfully complete various work tasks and

activities. A number of former students refer to the Big6 as their "information advantage."

So, read on—from the perspective of a college student or junior/senior in high school—and think about how you could use this article to teach the Big6 in your setting.

It's the information age, and success in today's information-rich world requires a new form of literacy, "information literacy." Calvin is right. Success and opportunity, today and tomorrow, call for a new set of skills:

- Flexible skills that enable a person to recognize the nature and scope of information needs and then locate, use, organize, present, and evaluate information to meet those needs.
- Skills, as Drucker recognizes, that go beyond simply being able to use computers or any particular software package.
- Skills that encompass the entire information problem-solving process.
- Skills known by many as "the Big6."

The Big6 Skills comprise a unified set of information and technology skills—including the ability to define an information need; to identify sources; and to locate, use, synthesize, and evaluate information. With the Big6, you learn how to recognize your information needs and how to progress through a series of stages to solve information problems effectively and efficiently.

The following pages contain a description of the Big6 approach and exercises to be completed during class sessions. After these sessions, you should be able to:

- List and describe the stages involved in the Big6 information problem-solving model.
- Give examples of information problems.
- Analyze a situation and describe how the Big6 model applies to the situation.
- Evaluate your own information problem-solving abilities.

Information Problem-Solving: The Big6 Approach

The Big6 is a systematic process that can be used any time you are faced with an information problem or with making a decision that is based on information. As a student you encounter many information problems related to course assignments. However, the Big6 is just as applicable to your personal life.

Whether you are tackling personal or academic information problems, information problem-solving is your game plan. The Big6 model encompasses six skill stages, each containing two components (see page viii).

From experience and research, we found that successful information problem-solving does require completing each stage at some point in time: defining the task; selecting, locating, and using appropriate information sources; pulling the information together; and deciding that the task is in fact completed. It's not necessary to complete the stages in order, however all the stages must be completed for overall success.

Figure 1 illustrates that the Big6 is not necessarily a linear, step-by-step process. For example, imagine that you defined your task and decided on your information seeking strategies, you identified sources, however, you find them unavailable. In that case, you would loop back to information seeking strategies to reformulate your plans. Or, suppose when writing a paper (Synthesis), you aren't sure if you have done everything the professor asked. Here, you would return to Task Definition to review the problem and requirements.

The point is to be flexible, to move back and forth in the process, and to be able to do what is essential in each stage. To facilitate this, let's take a closer look at each Big6 stage and what's involved.

Figure 1 *The Big6: A Nonlinear Perspective*

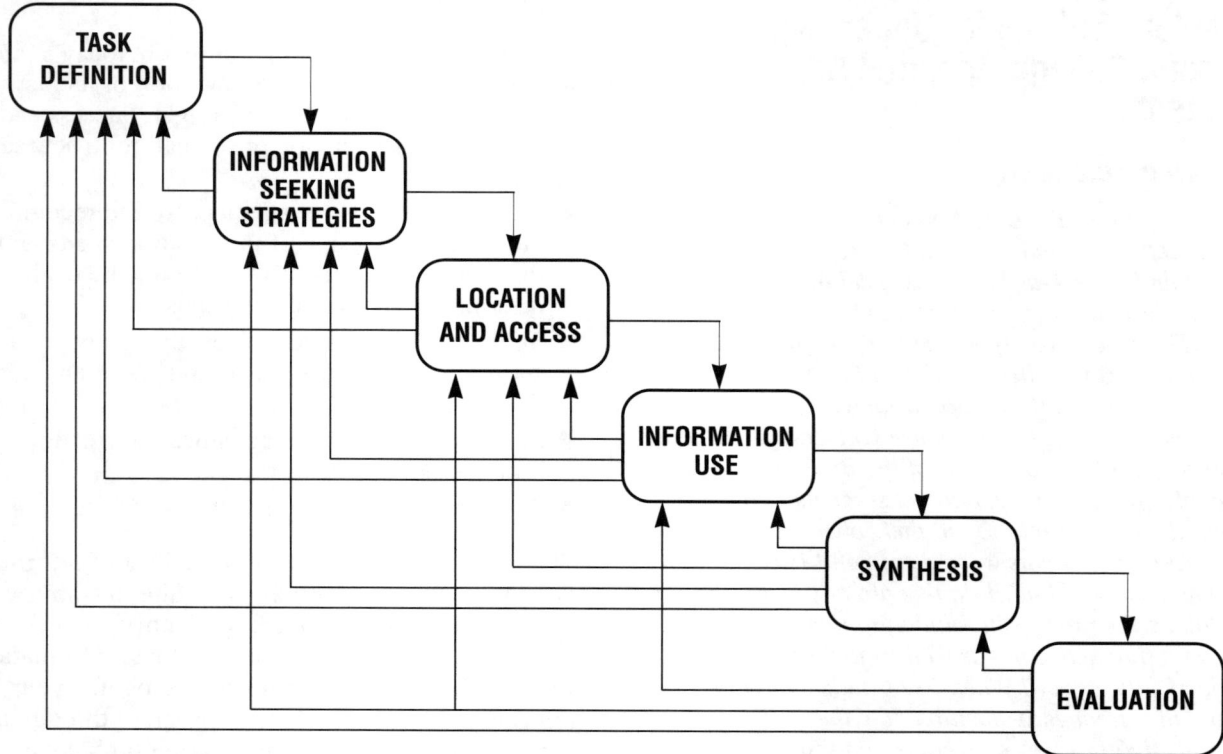

*Design adapted from Koberg, Don and Bagnall, Jim. *The Universal Traveler, A Soft-Sustems Guide to Creativity, Problem-Solving and the Process of Reaching Goals.* William Kaufmann, Inc. 1980.

Task Definition

Task Definition is the stage at which you determine what needs to be done and what information is needed to get the job done. Often, the major problem is not knowing or understanding what's expected of you. There are many reasons for this (instructions aren't clear, the task is confusing, you weren't paying attention). Regardless of the reason, if you do not understand what constitutes success (upon what basis your work will be evaluated), you are at a tremendous disadvantage.

There's a second part to Task Definition: determining the information requirements, the types and amount of information needed. Considering information requirements does not refer to the resources (print, electronic, human) that may be appropriate. They come later. Here, you need to think about what types of information are needed to get the job done (facts, opinions, graphics, numerical information) and about how much information you will need.

Information Seeking Strategies

Once you understand the task and have some idea about the types of information needed, you should turn your attention to possible information sources. This is the brainstorming stage—figuring out all possible information sources, and then selecting the sources that are most relevant based on such criteria as accuracy, quality, completeness, availability, currency, ease-of-use, and cost. Your goal at first is to think as broadly as possible and then to choose appropriate sources for the particular task at hand based upon these criteria. This is a creative stage— open your mind to all kinds of possibilities.

For example, when starting a paper, you usually rely on the traditional sources–books, reference materials, and magazines. But there are other sources to consider as well—databases, electronic references, World Wide Web sites. And don't forget other people. People are often the best sources for relevant information. Being able to consider the full range of sources and then select those sources that really meet your needs contributes to both effectiveness (getting a good grade) and efficiency (saving time and effort).

Before being introduced to the Big6, many people skip the Information Seeking Strategies stage. Don't! Taking a few minutes to think about all possible sources and then deciding on the best ones for the situation can save considerable time and make a big difference in your final product.

Before being introduced to the Big6, many people skip the Information Seeking Strategies stage. Don't!

Location and Access

This should be the easiest stage, but often isn't. It's also not a very exciting or particularly interesting stage. But, it does need to be completed if you are to succeed.

The goal in this stage is to locate the sources selected under the Information Seeking Strategies stage, and then actually get to the information in those sources. One important device that can save lots of time in Location and Access of resources is an index. Indexes of various kinds (yellow pages, directories in shopping malls, back-of-the-book indexes, online periodical databases) make it easier to find the information you want. Indexes may not be exciting, but they really do save time and effort.

One of the big challenges today is finding information on the Internet. One approach is to e-mail to a listserv or newsgroup in order to gain information from other people. Another is to use one or more of the search engines to the World Wide Web (Yahoo!, AltaVista, Excite, Lycos). All of the search tools have limitations due to the dynamic nature and exponential growth of the Web. Experts in WWW searching are aware of these limitations and employ a range of techniques and tools to locate and access Web information.

Use of Information

Locating and accessing information is easy compared to actually making use of the information found in the sources. This requires reading, viewing, or listening; deciding what's important for the particular task at hand; and finally extracting the needed information. This isn't always easy to do, and can certainly take a considerable amount of time.

There are techniques you can learn to help you to use sources effectively and efficiently. Consider various ways to skim or scan a print or electronic reading, to pick out the important points, and to save these key points for later use. There are a range of note-taking methods from traditional notecards to highlighting on photocopies to typing directly into a word processor.

Many students are learning to do all their work on a computer—without printing out from electronic resources. Today's technology facilitates this; however, using CD-ROM, Web, or other computer resources requires you to cut and paste, download, ftp, or use some other data capturing method. It is also crucial to keep track of where the information came from. Proper citing is an important part of stage 4—Use of Information.

Synthesis

Synthesis involves organizing and presenting the information—putting it all together to finish the job. Sometimes Synthesis can be as simple as relaying a specific fact (as in answering a short-answer question) or making a decision (deciding on a topic for a paper, a product to buy, an activity to join). At other times, Synthesis can be very complex and can involve the use of several sources, a variety of media or presentation formats, and the effective communication of abstract ideas.

Computer applications can help you to organize and present information. Word processing, graphics programs, desktop publishing, database management programs, electronic spreadsheets, and presentation packages can all help put information together and present it effectively.

Evaluation

In the Evaluation stage, you are asked to reflect on the result and process of your work. Evaluation determines the effectiveness and efficiency of the information problem-solving process. Effectiveness is another way of saying, how good is the product? What grade are you likely to get? Efficiency refers to time and effort.

If you were to do the work again, how could you do as well, but save some time and effort?

Evaluation is not just an after-the-fact activity. Assessing a paper before turning it in will allow you to make adjustments that can greatly enhance your grade. Similarly, if you seem to be stuck while working on an assignment or trying to solve a problem, consider where in the Big6 process you might be having difficulties and how you might change things or seek assistance.

At the end of the process, you need to think about your result and decide if you are pleased. For example, it's not always necessary to get a top grade—sometimes OK is enough. At other times, you will want to strive for excellence. Understanding and recognizing the difference is crucial. You also need to think about the process. Where did you get stuck? Where did you waste time? This kind of self-reflective action can help you improve your approach in the future.

As noted, successful information problem-solving requires the completion of all six steps regardless of whether they are completed in order. Research shows that some students omit steps in the process. For example, when confronted by an information problem, many students do not adequately define the task before attempting to find required

---

EXERCISE 1

Directions: Below is a list of information problems. Think of three other examples of information problems and write them in the spaces provided.

Information Problems:

- Completing a project for a course.
- Finding a ride home for semester break.
- Deciding which movie to see on the weekend.
- Studying for an exam.
- Applying for financial aid.

_____

_____

EXERCISE 2

A Personal Information Problem

Directions: In the space below, describe each step of the process you used to make a recent purchase (buying textbooks for your courses, a gift for someone, a new car, etc.).

_____

_____

_____

_____

EXERCISE 3

Directions: In the chart below, list some of the assignments for this course and for your other courses. Which Big6 skill areas will be particularly important for each assignment? Indicate with a check mark (✓) and note "why" in the comments section.

ASSIGNMENT	TASK DEFINITION	INFORMATION SEEKING STRATEGIES	LOCATION & ACCESS	USE OF INFORMATION	SYNTHESIS	EVALUATION	COMMENTS

information. Similarly, few students take the time to reflect on the successes and failures of their information problem-solving process, thus short-circuiting their opportunities to learn.

The Big6 information problem-solving process represents a powerful tool for identifying your strengths and weaknesses. You can use the process to help you: (1) recognize when you are having difficulty, and (2) formulate questions to mediate difficulties. This can help you in every aspect of your lives since the Big6 approach is widely applicable across situations–not just in academic settings. Every day–at work, school, and in your personal lives–you are faced with information problems and decisions requiring information. Improving your information problem-solving abilities can help you to be more effective and efficient in all these settings.

Looking at Life through Big6-Colored Glasses

v2 n6 p1, 14-15

By Kathy Spitzer and Mike Eisenberg

How did you first learn about the Big6? We would be willing to bet that it was in an academic, professional conference, or workshop setting. As such, you're probably used to thinking about the Big6 in an educational or curriculum context. It's likely that you've become skilled at coming up with Big6 lessons that relate to social studies, math, or English. And that's how most of our students learn about the Big6. But what about life outside of school? How does the Big6 apply?

In Big6 workshops we often introduce the Big6 by using examples beyond the curriculum, such as buying a birthday present, selecting a new car, deciding what movie to go to on Saturday night. Using these familiar examples helps make the Big6 understandable and demonstrates that the Big6 is applicable to any information problem. And as we like to point out, everything is an information problem!

The question is, how can we make students aware of the applicability of the Big6 to their lives? How can we show them that the Big6 is a process that can help them with virtually any information problem?

The Big6 in Our Lives

First of all, in order to help students we need to be confident in our own Big6 abilities and understanding of the Big6. Ask yourself the question:

"How does the Big6 apply to my own life?"

As experienced information problem solvers, we engage in the Big6 stages without much effort or thought. We already "live" the Big6 and think in Big6 terms because we have had opportunities to work through the process many times. It's likely that the process has become automatic for us; perhaps so automatic that we fail to see the discrete parts of the Big6. However, in order to best help students of all ages, it's useful to do some self-reflection and look at some examples of everyday problems in terms of the Big6.

Problem 1

Your 18 year old daughter has just graduated from high school and has made plans to attend a two-year college in another city located a couple of hours from home. You have agreed to help her fund her education. All of a sudden she announces, "I don't think I want to go to college any more. X and I are thinking about moving in together." (X, of course, is her boyfriend that you can't stand!)

One approach would be to forbid her to move in with X. Another might be to rant and rave. Or, if you (and she) can calm down a bit, you could show her how to use the Big6 to analyze the situation. The conversation might sound something like this:

- **DAUGHTER:** "I don't think I want to go to college any more. I'm thinking about moving in with X."

- **MOTHER:** (controlling her shock and dismay) "Well, that's a pretty big decision. Once you move out, Dad and I won't be responsible for your bills any more and it seems that you would be facing some pretty big expenses."

- **DAUGHTER:** "Yeah."

- **MOTHER:** "Before you make such a big decision, how about if you gather some information about it. You know we believe in making informed decisions—decisions based on information."

- **DAUGHTER:** (groan) "Like what?"

- **MOTHER:** (Task Definition): "Like how much do apartments cost? Where could you live? What other things will you need in the apartment? Furniture? Dishes? Glasses? Silverware? Pots and pans? Cups? Measuring cups?"

- **DAUGHTER:** "He already has a lot of that stuff."

- **MOTHER:** "Okay. I'm just suggesting that you make a list and find out what you would need and how much it would cost. Once you move out you'll need to have your own health insurance. And I guess you'll probably need a car, and that will mean car insurance."

- **DAUGHTER:** "I think I can get health insurance at work."

- **MOTHER:** "Good, but you'd better know if you're covered or not."

- **DAUGHTER:** "Yeah. I guess I'll have to check."

- **MOTHER:**(Information Seeking Strategies): "If you want, I'll be glad to help you brainstorm places where you can find out how much it will cost you to be on your own. You can check Sunday's paper to see how much an apartment costs, but you'd probably want to go look at some of them to see what they are like. It can be expensive to find one that you'd actually want to live in."

We can't guarantee that the problem will resolve to your complete satisfaction, but at least by focusing on the information aspects of the decision, you are still talking and also interjecting a bit of reality into the situation.

Problem 2

You take your lawn mower in for its yearly service and you are told that it will cost $80 to service it because it needs one new wheel and a new throttle—in addition to the regular maintenance. Should you have the lawn mower repaired or should you buy a new one?

Let's take a look at this wearing our Big6 glasses:

■ TASK DEFINITION

What is the cost of a new mower? What would the advantage be of buying a new mower?

■ INFORMATION SEEKING STRATEGIES

Talk with a lawn mower salesperson to find out how much new lawn mowers cost, and determine what advances in lawn mowing technology have taken place since you've owned your mower.

Check *Consumer Reports* to see if they have published an article on lawn mowers lately.

Check the newspapers to see if there are any sales on lawn mowers right now.

Check the Web to read about lawn mowers on various company Web sites.

■ LOCATION & ACCESS

Find and talk with the salesperson.

Visit the *Consumer Reports* Web site and determine that there was an article published about lawn mowers last spring. Call the local library and see if they have a copy that you can access right away.

Pull the Sunday paper out of the recycle bin and look through the ads for sales on lawn mowers.

Use the Web to locate the address of a couple of the companies that manufacture the model of lawn mower you are considering.

■ USE OF INFORMATION

Listen to the salesperson and push each of the two lawn mowers in consideration to assess their maneuverability.

Read the *Consumer Reports* article.

Scan the newspaper ads for lawn mowers on sale.

Read the information about the mowers located on the manufacturer's Web sites.

■ SYNTHESIS

Consider the information that has been gathered from all sources and decide whether to buy a new lawn mower.

If you decide to buy a new one, decide which make and model to buy and where to buy it.

■ EVALUATION

Try out the lawn mower or try your old one. How does it cut the grass? Are you satisfied with the performance and maneuverability?

Do you wish you had done anything differently in arriving at your decision?

The chart to the previous page is a blank Big6 worksheet for you to fill in with a couple problems of your own. Try it out! After you've had a chance to practice a couple of real life examples, you'll feel more comfortable working with students on some of their personal information problems.

P.S.—In relation to problems 1 and 2 above, the answers were: she didn't (move in with X!) and it does (the new mower cuts the grass beautifully).

Spreading the Word: Teaching about the Big6 and Technology

v2 n6 p3-5

By Verna LaBounty

We all agree—information and technology skills are important for our students' success. More and more educators and parents are eager to learn about these information and technology skills and how they can be applied in various educational and even home settings. Classroom teachers and library media specialists who are technology literate and who are already successfully using the Big6 information problem-solving process are often asked to share their knowledge with other professionals. It's relatively easy to explain the Big6 informally—one-to-one or to a small group. But, what about presenting a more extensive or formal workshop on the Big6? That's what this article is all about—how to present a workshop that focuses on technology skills and the Big6.

The challenge

A nearby school district contacted our district's technology committee chairperson and issued a request for a workshop that would focus on integrating technology. The challenge was to create a practical, "hands-on," workshop that would not only provide the participants with technical skills but would allow the participants to develop plans to integrate information and technology skills with any grade level and any curriculum topic. As a library media specialist with experience working with teachers to develop Big6 units incorporating technology in a variety of curricular areas, I accepted the challenge despite the risks of using an unfamiliar computer lab, not knowing the level of the technical skills of the participants, and, last but not least, driving in North Dakota winter weather!

As part of Task Definition (Big6 #1)—planning the workshop—it became apparent that I needed more information. I contacted the requesting district about equipment, lab set up, and expectations and asked the technology coordinator in our district whether thirty simultaneous users could access our Web server throughout a ninety-minute period (Information Seeking Strategies, Big6 #2, and Location & Access, Big6 #3). With answers in hand (Use of Information, Big6 #4), the plan began to take form (Big6 #5, Synthesis).

Figure 1 shows the steps used to plan the workshop—in Big6 form, of course! Sections of the workshop would include:

- Teaching basic technology skills

- Presenting the concepts of information literacy and technology literacy

- Introducing the Big6 information problem-solving process

- Providing participants with time to create a sample unit plan, and

- Evaluating the workshop.

Teaching basic technology skills

Spread the word...

Since participants in the workshop had only very basic information technology skills, the workshop began with learning how to open a Web browser and a word processing application. Participants were shown how they could move between the web browser and the word processor and use the latter to take notes during the session. For many participants this was a new experience; they didn't know that they could have two applications open at the same time.

Now that participants had learned how to move between applications, they were ready to begin the

---

Figure 1 — Steps Used to Plan a Workshop

- **TASK DEFINITION**

  Providing a workshop for teachers on integrating technology and information skills in the curriculum.

- **INFORMATION SEEKING STRATEGIES**

  Determining who to ask about the technological aspects and the expectations of the teachers.

- **LOCATING & ACCESSING INFORMATION**

  Asking representatives of the other school district about equipment, their lab, and the expectations of their participants and asking our school's technology coordinator if our Web server could handle the traffic.

- **USE OF INFORMATION**

  Evaluating the information to create an informative and stimulating workshop that would allow participants to practice information gathering and technology skills.

- **SYNTHESIS**

  Organizing the information and writing a series of Web pages to deliver the content and exercises of the presentation.

- **EVALUATION**

  Evaluating the effectiveness and efficiency by reviewing workshop participants' comments that were forwarded via e-mail.

workshop by using the Web pages that were created for the presentation. Each of the first few pages were easily navigated by the participants by clicking on the "Next" button at the bottom of the screen. The first screen welcomed participants, identified the presenter, and outlined the goals of the workshop which included the following:

1. To introduce an information problem-solving approach to curriculum

2. To model the use of information skills

3. To model the use of technology, and

4. To enjoy meeting and interacting with the participants.

5. Presenting the concepts of information literacy and technology literacy

The next few Web pages explained the terms information literacy and technology literacy and illustrated the interconnection of the workshop strands. Information literacy was explained in terms of the skills involved in the Big6 process. Technology litera-

cy was identified as determining the appropriate medium to locate specific information, using effective search strategies, choosing and using a variety of technology tools, programs, and applications to achieve the best production results, and using technology tools for information and communication in responsible ways.

As the material was presented, participants created their own handouts by copying and pasting any of the material they were viewing to their "note pad," the open word processing document. This helped reinforce what the teachers were learning and allowed them to practice their new skill of moving between one application and another.

Introducing the Big6 information problem-solving process

After this background on information and technology literacy, the next section of the workshop (15-20 minutes) focused on the concept of information problems. A number of everyday situations were presented:

Example *Build a snow person for the contest by...*

TASK DEFINITION	INFORMATION SEEKING STRATEGIES	LOCATION & ACCESS	USE OF INFORMATION	SYNTHESIS	EVALUATION
Building the snow person yourself.	Figure out if you can build a snow person yourself.	Find books on building snow people at the library.	Study books from the library on snow people and choose a picture of the perfect snow person.	Build a snow person using the picture as a model.	The snow was warm and sticky enough and your snow person won first prize.
Buying an inflatable snow person.	Figure out where to buy an inflatable snow person.	Call stores to find an inflatable person.	Look through the list of stores that have inflatable snow person.	Buy the inflatable snow person and install on the front lawn.	Inflatable snow person blew away!!
Hiring a neighbor's kid to build the snow person.	Think about which of your neighbors has kids that might be interested in building a snow person.	Call the neighbor's kid.	Talk with the neighbors kid to see if they are available.	Neighbor's kid builds the snow person.	Neighbor's kid created snow person that looked like a blob!
Putting up a cardboard cut-out of a snow person.	Determine how to create and put up a cardboard cut-out.	See if there's cardboard.	Find out if the cardboard will be large enough.	Cut out snow person from cardboard and install it on the lawn.	Cardboard cut-out was cute but the rules of the contest didn't allow the use of cardboard. You lose.

- Tonight it is your turn to prepare the evening meal for your family.

- You are invited to Hugo's birthday party on Saturday.

- Your parents say you are responsible enough to have a pet.

Participants briefly discussed and analyzed each situation and identified the task and the information that would be needed. Next, the participants used all of the steps in the Big6 model to solve this information problem which was appropriate for wintry North Dakota:

The Jamestown Park Board announces Winter Festival Days, February 25-26, 1998. Festival planners invite you to build a snow person in your yard to create a jolly magical atmosphere of celebration dedicated to the winter season and to welcome visitors to the city. Contest rules are available at all local businesses. Prizes will be awarded!

Using this realistic example, the workshop participants generated ideas for each of the Big6 steps (See Figure 2 on previous page).

To conclude this section of the workshop, participants listed the advantages of using the Big6 information problem-solving model. Some of the advantages that the participants came up with include:

- Ensuring success in dealing with large amounts of information

- Keeping students on track and responsible

- Helping the teacher provide learner-centered, suitable, and clearly defined assignments, and

- Maximizing use of resources within the school and beyond the school walls.

Providing participants with time to create a sample unit plan

During the next section of the workshop, participants browsed through the links of the Big6 home page, **http://www.big6.com**, and through the Big6 examples used at the Kindred School at **http://www.kindred.k12.nd.us/CyLib/B6.html**. They chose a curriculum topic and completed a rough draft of a unit using the Big6 plan. The library media specialist acted as a guide and mentor by moving around the lab to answer questions, providing explanations, giving ideas and hints for activities and skills appropriate for each step, and providing encouragement and support to the participants.

Evaluating the workshop

To wrap up the workshop, participants printed their notes and unit plans and sent the instructor an e-mail evaluation of the workshop. They collected several handouts including the Big6 organizer, a Big6 bookmark, and a sample rubric. In reviewing the evaluations, the workshop was deemed a success. Teachers not only learned about technology and the Big6 information problem solving process but applied their knowledge to create a sample unit plan they could use with their students.

CHAPTER 7

The BIG 6

Special Kids

Including All Students: The Big6 Helps to Level the Playing Field

v1 n4 p1, 6-7, 10

By Bob Berkowitz

This article is the first in a series about applying Big6 principles to the instruction of youngsters with diverse abilities. Today's classrooms bring together students with a wide range of needs. To meet these needs, teachers must juggle the classroom environment, materials and resources, and time. Teachers need to plan appropriate instruction for a wide variety of student abilities, and consider the scope of many learning styles. This is no simple feat. It is not surprising that many teachers are either reluctant to accept the challenge, become frustrated at making the attempt, or exhaust their professional and personal resources by accepting the responsibility.

In this first article, I will identify some of the challenges associated with instructing students of widely varying talents, review Big6 principles, and offer some suggestions for meeting these daily challenges by using the Big6. At the conclusion, I hope you will agree that the Big6 is a valuable tool to help teachers welcome all children as fully participating members of their classrooms.

> *Teachers can build on the Big6. They can work with individual students as they go through the Big6 process to complete tasks and assignments.*

Common Understandings

To begin, we need to define two modes of instruction, "inclusion" and "mainstreaming."

Though many people use these terms interchangeably, there is a difference between the two approaches. The inclusion model brings all students into the same classroom, but has little expectation that differently-abled youngsters will engage in the regular curriculum. Special needs children work on their individualized goals and objectives in the context of the regular class. (Tucker and Goldstein, chapter 13, p. 15, chapter 16, p. 22.)

For example, in an inclusion situation, a child may work on language skills while the rest of the class works on grammar, or the child may be learning to count to five while the others are practicing long division. Overall goals and objectives are usually determined at a team meeting that focuses on strengths and addresses needs. The resulting goals and objectives form the basis for an "individualized education program"—commonly referred to as an IEP. (Tucker and Goldstein, chapter 19.)

A teacher using the mainstreaming model, on the other hand, expects the special needs student to engage the regular curriculum in a modified form. The mainstreamed student works on the same curriculum as the rest of the class with some possible adaptations. For example, the child's homework load may be reduced or the child may be given prepared notes from which to learn vocabulary and concepts before a lesson, or he or she may be responsible for only a percentage of the class material.

There are many benefits to both inclusion and mainstreaming. For example, youngsters learn from each other how to act appropriately, to have compassion and understanding, to appreciate differences. This is known as peer modeling. Peer modeling can facilitate these skills and attributes and many others. All of the children gain experience and practice they might not otherwise have received.

It is a fundamental principle of both the inclusion and mainstreaming models that children with special needs will benefit from participating in regular classes. To varying degrees, differently-abled students are just as capable as their classmates. They can:

- participate in the learning process with their peers,
- build academic and process skills related to problem-solving and decision-making,
- learn to use Big6 to solve age-appropriate academic and personal problems,
- be active participants in the school and community at large.

It is important to reaffirm that good teaching takes individual needs into account. This is nothing new. However, when generating instructional plans for children with special needs, all teachers—classroom, resource, library media, technology—must be more cognizant of learning strategies and outcomes and how they impact the individual youngster. Providing teacher-prepared notes is one example. A learning disabled child is likely to need-prepared notes in order to learn fundamental vocabulary and concepts before the lesson or to attend to the class discussion without having to struggle with note-taking. These notes are helpful to other students as well, for instance, those who have been absent or whose note taking skills are still emerging. Another illustration: Some children require specific positioning in a wheelchair in order to see, attend, and communicate. A teacher who accepts this child's needs is more likely to recognize and honor other students' needs for unconventional learning and working positions such as leaning over a desk, standing, lying on the floor, or roaming about the room.

A Few of the Challenges

One major challenge associated with inclusion or mainstreaming is time—time spent by students and time for teachers to plan. The classroom teacher must structure the instructional day, establish the goals of

Where, amoung the stages of the Big6, are the students likely to have problems.

various groups' lessons, and address the IEP goals and objectives of individual students. This often means additional meetings with other professional staff such as therapists, school social workers or psychologists, and special education teachers.

The classroom teacher must also coordinate with various staff working in this classroom or scheduling students for special services. Therapists, special teachers, and other staff may come to the classroom to work with individual students or small groups who need extra support. Sometimes students' therapy or tutoring sessions may occur at a separate location.

Beyond academic concerns, the classroom teacher is also expected to be able to address social and other needs of students. Some children frequently display inappropriate behavior, which affects their ability to make friends, and their self-esteem, as well as the general class decorum. Teachers are often confronted with a conflict regarding behavioral expectations. On the one hand, students are expected to conform to a set of rules; on the other hand, some students cannot be held responsible for these rules—they have individualized behavioral plans. The goal is to hold each child accountable for his or her ability to conform to social norms while promoting class-wide understanding that "fairness" means that everyone gets what he or she needs, not just what the other person gets.

Clearly, working in inclusive or mainstream classrooms presents unique challenges for all teaching and support staff. Some ways to meet the challenges include better coordination of the work of various professionals as well as providing additional skills and insights through training and staff development. Considering the challenges from a Big6 perspective can also make a difference.

The Big6 approach to information problems is a broadly applicable process that is not restricted to ability or skill level. Persons at varying levels of sophistication can still accomplish each of the six stages of the Big6 to some degree. The Big6 is also applicable to a range of problems and situations. For example, the Big6 can be used by students to complete school assignments and also used by teachers for instructional design and implementation. Therefore, when considering students with special needs and the inclusive or mainstreamed classroom, the Big6 can be used to guide and help individual student efforts and to design learning and instruction to provide for a range of options for all students.

The Big6 Applied: Using the Big6 to Guide Students

All students can and do use the Big6 process. Certainly, they may do so at different levels of expertise, but all still engage in:

- Task Definition—figuring out what they are supposed to do
- Information Seeking Strategies—selecting a source for information
- Location and Access—getting the source(s)
- Use of Information—engaging the information
- Synthesis—completing the task or reaching a decision
- Evaluation—determining that the task is completed.

Teachers can build on this. They can work with individual students as they go through the Big6 process to complete tasks and assignments. With the Big6, teachers can help students break down instructional objectives into smaller, doable tasks. Perhaps Jamie can readily identify the task at hand (e.g. perform long division). Corrine understands what to do, but is confused about the order. Alex cannot even begin; he has trouble determining parts from a whole and independently starting a task. The teacher doesn't have to spend much time with Jamie. She can offer Corrine a model to follow based on the Big6. The teacher now has more time to help Alex begin to identify the nature of the task and the steps involved, and to integrate other skills that Alex may need to improve (e.g. using manipulatives to make sets, completing a puzzle). Alternatively, the teacher may decide to pair Alex with another student to work on one of his other objectives, such as making eye contact. Since not all students are expected to perform the same tasks at the same time nor to the same level of proficiency, the classroom teacher has the ability to identify those students who need more help. She can then arrange for other support systems such as instructional aides to lend a hand. The teacher also has flexibility to design the lesson for the benefit of all.

For example, Task Definition is a major concern for most students. Applying the overall Big6 process to fully understand the task can really help students. Here's an example modified from work contributed by Catherine Anderson, a speech-language pathologist in the Rochester City Schools, Rochester, New York, Schools:

- Students read through the written assignment in its entirety. Depending on the reading level of the students, the students take turns reading or the instructor reads it aloud. (Task Definition and Use of Information)
- Students go back through the assignment line by line. They highlight any unfamiliar words. (Use of Information)
- Students determine the meanings of unknown words using various resources: project vocabulary worksheet, dictionary, teacher or other students. (Information Seeking Strategies, Location and Access, Use of Information)
- Students paraphrase each line of the assignment and share the paraphrasings with the entire class. Make sure that the paraphrased information is clearly understood by everyone. (Synthesis, Evaluation)
- Copy the paraphrased steps of the assignment in checklist form. This now creates a quick evaluation tool. (Task Definition, Evaluation)

The Big6 Applied: Using the Big6 to Design Learning and Instruction

The Big6 is also a useful framework for instructional design. Teachers can consider the content and objectives of a learning situation in terms of the Big6 process and the range of abilities of students in the class. This can involve answering the following questions:

- What are the learning objectives?
- What do you want your diverse group of students to learn?
- What are the capabilities of the students with varying abilities?
- Where, among the Big6 stages, are the students likely to have problems?
- What additional Big6 instruction or assistance help these students?
- What alternatives, in the assignment, expectations, or approach, can be provided to students?

By answering these questions, teachers may decide to adjust the task by varying the requirements for some students or providing special assistance or instruction to others. Here are some examples of providing alternatives from a Big6 perspective:

- The topic is photosynthesis in plants. Some students are required to demonstrate photosynthesis by creating a model of the process, others comprehend by answering "how" questions, and still others express literal level skill by labeling a chart depicting the process.

This is an example of providing options for Big6 stage #5 – Synthesis.

- Students are studying the book, *The Red Badge of Courage* by Stephen Crane. While most of the class reads the book, other students are provided a simplified comic book version, and still others view a video of the story.

This is an example of alternatives for Big6 stage #4—Use of Information.

- Students are learning about whales and dolphins. Each student helps to create a scoring guide which indicates what he or she is expected to do and how much time he or she will be allowed.

This is an example of accommodating differences through Big6 stage #5 – Evaluation.

Conclusion

Educating children with special needs is a responsibility for all teachers. There are considerable challenges inherent in the inclusion and mainstreaming models of instruction, not the least of which is the amount of time a teacher must spend on organization and planning. The Big6 process provides a framework to help teachers develop a range of instructional and learning opportunities to meet the needs of all students. Figure 1 summarizes a Big6 view of special needs situations and identifies possible alternatives.

In the next issue of the Big6 Newsletter, I will expand on these and other options.

Sources

Tucker, B. & Goldstein B. (1991). *Legal rights of persons with disabilities: An analysis of federal law*, Horsham, PA: LRP Publications.

Maryland Coalition for Integrated Education, 7257 Parkway Dr., Hanover, MD, 21076.

The ERIC Clearinghouse on Disabilities and Gifted Education (ERIC EC), The Council for Exceptional Children (CEC) 1-800-328-0272 (V); 703-264-9449 (TTY); http://ericec.org/

The Council for Exceptional Children. 1920 Association Dr., Reston, VA 20191-1589. http://www.cec.sped.org/

National Information Center for Children and Youth with Disabilities (NICHCY) P.O. Box 1492, Washington, D.C. 20013.

Additional Web Sources

Consortium on Inclusive Schooling Practices: http://www.asri.edu/cfsp/brochure/abtcons.htm

Renaissance Group, Inclusive Education Web Site: http://www.uni.edu/coe/inclusion/index.html

Education Resources, Special Education Inclusion: http://www.weac.org/resource/june96/speced.htm

Circle of Inclusion: http://circleofinclusion.org/

Office of Special Education and Rehabilitative Services: http://www.ed.gov/offices/OSERS/

LD Online (Includes Understanding the IEP): http://www.ldonline.org/index.html

Figure 1: *Special Needs from a Big6 Perspective*

CHALLENGES	BIG6	POSSIBLE ACTIONS
■ Diverse student needs ■ Time to plan ■ Time to teach, help students ■ Academic and social learning	Task Definition Information Seeking Strategies Location & Access Use of Information Synthesis Evaluation	1. Walk students through tasks with the Big6. 2. Reconsider tasks, offer options. 3. Provide options within each stage of the process. 4. Intervene—provide special instruction or assistance. 5. Design learning and instruction from a Big6 perspective.

Leveling the Playing Field - Part II: Using the Big6 Model to Plan Instruction for Students with Special Needs

v1 n5 p4-5

By Bob Berkowitz

Through inclusion and mainstreaming, all educators work with students of varying physical and mental abilities. The challenge for the classroom teachers, special education teachers, library media specialists, technology teachers, and others is to mediate the educational process for each individual's maximum benefit.

To do so rests on the following assumption: All children can learn. The difference among children is the rate at which they learn, the quantity of materials they can learn, and their ability to demonstrate a mastery of skills in a variety of settings. Every child needs his or her teacher to consider individual learning needs when designing and implementing instruction. If the teacher does not account for individual learning styles and needs, the students may fail to adequately learn the lesson. It is the responsibility of all educational professionals to plan for each and every student's success. Parents and administrators expect no less. A carefully thought out instructional plan is important to the success of each lesson for each student.

One useful way to focus on individual students' needs is to look at each situation from a Big6 perspective. That is, every lesson is about solving an information problem.

The Big6 and Instruction

The Big6 Skills provide a framework for analyzing instructional variables in terms of a diverse student body. Prior to designing instruction, teachers can use the Big6 model to identify each student's strengths and weaknesses. In this context, the Big6 model can be phrased as a series of questions for analysis:

1. TASK DEFINITION

Can the student define the task? Is it a requirement of the lesson that the student define the task or could the task be pre-defined?

2. INFORMATION SEEKING STRATEGIES

Can the student brainstorm or use other strategies for identifying information sources? Is it required that the student identify sources or can they be given to the student?

3. LOCATION & ACCESS

Can the student find and physically retrieve information? What equipment might the student need in order to accomplish this step as independently as possible?

4. USE OF INFORMATION

Can the student read, hear, view, or touch the information? Is there equipment or assistance that can help?

5. SYNTHESIS

Can the student organize information and present a result? Does every product have to be the same for everyone?

6. EVALUATION

Can the student judge the resulting product against a model? Can the student articulate the process?

By considering the answers to these questions, a teacher can help the student meet the challenges posed by the assignment by:

- Pairing the student with another student,
- Planning to use assistance from a student's aide, assistant, or therapist, or
- Using appropriate adaptations such as computers, other media, or equipment.

A Specific Example

To cite an example of using the Big6 to analyze an instructional situation, we will use a fictional teacher and class. Ms. Hawkins' seventh graders include 25 children of mixed abilities: some have average intelligence, some have above average intelligence. She has one student with attention deficit hyperactivity disorder, three students who have specific learning disabilities, one student who is visually and hearing impaired, and one student who is mobility impaired.

Ms. Hawkins is planning a unit focusing on how math is used in everyday life. As a final project for the unit, students will develop a monthly budget by:

- Looking at the classified advertisements for housing costs,
- Using grocery circulars to determine food costs,
- Reading catalogs and advertisements for clothing costs, and
- Determining an amount for entertainment costs.

Students will then create a pie chart representing the percentage of each cost within the total monthly budget. Students will work in pairs and present their results to the class.

Let's now explore how this task could be analyzed using the Big6 model:

1. TASK DEFINITION

Ms. Hawkins believes that some students will have difficulty since this project involves a number of steps. Students will work in pairs and explain to each other what the task requires. Each student pair will then create a plan for achieving the task. Those students who may have particular difficulty in planning will be helped by the teacher's assistant. Even with this arrangement, Ms. Hawkins knows that one learning disabled student will have difficulty with this step. Ms. Hawkins plans to help the learning disabled student understand all of the tasks involved, prioritize their completion, estimate the time needed to complete each step, and appreciate how each task relates to the completed project.

2. INFORMATION SEEKING STRATEGIES

Ms. Hawkins has pre-defined the information sources that the students will use. Information-seeking strategies are therefore not the focus of this unit.

3. LOCATION & ACCESS

Ms. Hawkins was originally going to ask students to bring newspapers, circulars, and catalogs from home. Since some of the children come from impoverished homes, Ms. Hawkins has decided to collect several of these items ahead of time from other teachers. The visually impaired student will receive help from her partner and her assistant in locating and accessing these items.

4. USE OF INFORMATION

Ms. Hawkins knows that the student with hyperactivity disorder will have difficulty engaging the information in the sources. She will ask an aide to help this student. Ms. Hawkins will also check in frequently with the student.

5. SYNTHESIS

Students with disabilities may experience more difficulty than other students with this step. Ms. Hawkins decides that each student pair will complete the research for the project and create a pie chart. She arranges for the visually and hearing impaired student to use a specially adapted computer.

6. EVALUATION

This step may be difficult for many students. They may be able to discern the difference between their product and the teacher's model and instructions, but assessing the efficiency and effectiveness of the process requires students to understand how to prioritize, make decisions, ask relevant questions and identify relevant answers. Children with disabilities are at a disadvantage at this step of the Big6 process. Ms. Hawkins has identified several students who will need help with this step and has arranged to meet with each individually to assist them with this task.

This example shows how the Big6 provides a framework for teachers to identify and plan for various needs of all. When teachers anticipate requirements throughout the Big6 problem-solving process, they are better able to implement the instructional plan.

CHAPTER 8

The BIG 6

Kids & Sports

Sports and the Big6: The Information Advantage

v1 n2 p8-10

By Mike Eisenberg

Don't turn the page! This is still the Big6 Newsletter, *not* Sports Illustrated. *But, yes, the topic is sports—sports from a Big6 perspective; it's a natural combination. So, read & enjoy. You'll never look at a game or information problem-solving in quite the same way.*

Sports occupy a central place in our society. Fitness clubs, the Olympics, interscholastic sports, Monday Night Football—most people enjoy sports in some form, at some time. Even people who would never think of attending a baseball or football game, might be avid hikers or eagerly watch broadcasts of gymnastics, track and field, or Olympic ice skating.

So, if sports are such a big part of our lives, and we promote the Big6 as applicable to any situation—academic or personal—is there a connection between the Big6 and sports? Absolutely! We've all heard the phrase, "information is power." Well, that's true for sports as well.

Consider what it takes to succeed in sports. Athletic ability? Physical size, speed, and strength? Absolutely. But having a "game plan," a systematic training program, and scouting reports can be just as

important. Whether it's working to get in shape, trying to improve your tennis game, or developing that winning soccer team—information is as much a key to success as physical ability.

This article explores the "information-sports-Big6" connection and how sports provides an ideal setting for learning and teaching about the Big6. It covers the information aspects of various sports and walks through a typical sports situation/problem from a Big6 perspective. The next issue of the Big6 Newsletter will continue the discussion, offering additional examples and ways to use sports to motivate students and teach the Big6.

The Information Aspects of Sports

If asked about the keys to success in sports, most people would probably state athletic ability and physical skills. However, once you begin to think about it, it's easy to see the importance of information and information processes.

Consider a baseball game. Before anyone throws, hits, or catches a ball, there's "information action" going on. Players, coaches, and even umpires are engaged in solving a series of information problems.

For example, the pitcher and catcher are trying to figure out how to get a batter out. The catcher signals the pitcher to throw a certain type of pitch in a certain location—one that he thinks the batter is least likely to hit. How does the catcher know this? From experience and statistical analysis of the batter's past performance in various situations. That's information.

Sports-related Big6 Activities

In addition to walking through the entire process, there are a number of activities that use the sports-Big6 connection and help students to learn about information and the Big6 process:

- Show short video clips of various sports. Ask students to identify what's going on in each from an information perspective. What are the information aspects of these sports? What are some of the key information requirements (Big6 #1.1) to succeed in a sports contest and what are potential information sources (Big6 #2.1) to help?

- Show a video (5-10 minutes) of a sporting event. Play through once. Then go back and review, stopping at every point that there's something going on related to information. Write each information incident on the board. Afterwards, discuss, sort, and summarize in relation to the Big6.

- Break students into small groups and give each group the sports section from a newspaper. Have the groups identify the various information aspects of sports as demonstrated in the newspaper.

- Break the students into groups and have each group interview a coach to determine how they use information, the sources they use, and the information systems (manual and computer-based) that they use.

- Show a video of a sport that students are probably not familiar with (e.g., in the U.S. you might show a cricket game; in other countries U.S. football is usually a good choice). In groups, to the best of their abilities, the students are to: (a) determine the rules of the game and (b) identify information aspects that might gain them a competitive advantage.

- Instead of typical "reports on sports," have students analyze a particular sport from an information, Big6 perspective. They should include personal experience, observation, and use of sources.

Stay tuned for more Sports and the Big6 Activities in the next issue!

Major league baseball players talk about keeping a "book" on other teams. Catchers, pitchers, managers—they all compile and process information about the opposition. In the past, the player or manager might just try to remember this information, or write down a few notes. Today, it's just as likely to be computerized—in databases and spreadsheets that can be selected, sorted, and displayed in dozens of ways—and viewed on laptop computers in the dugout.

On the other side, the batter and his team have a "book" as well, with all kinds of information about the pitcher and the other players in the field. Before each pitch, the manager signals to the third base coach who signals to the batter about the pitcher, the situation, and what the manager would like the batter to do—e.g., swing away, "take" a pitch (not swing), bunt, or any number of other possibilities.

Again, all this takes place before anything physical (like throwing or hitting a ball) happens at all! What seems like a fairly simple sports activity—pitching and batting—turns out to be an intensive information experience, one that directly relates to the Big6 process and Big6 skills.

Baseball is not unique in its reliance on information. Aspects of information that relate to most sports include:

- the rules of the game
- game strategy (offense and defense, teamwork)
- equipment (particularly new developments)
- player selection (recruiting, drafting, positioning)
- preparation (training and practice, long-term player development)
- planning and coaching
- business management (scheduling, finances)
- public relations
- communicating (before and during a game)

Examples of information in other sports situations include:

FOOTBALL: American football is essentially a contest between two information systems. Each team has a system of offensive and defensive plays and formations. The major information problem in football involves trying to figure out what your opponent is going to do, and then doing something yourself that the other team doesn't expect. This happens over and over in a football game. The actual play on the field is surrounded by elaborate information systems to monitor and analyze the other team's performance, assess your own play, communicate information to/from coaches and players, track the time and other game situations. Teams constantly review their information seeking strategies, seeking to speed up location and access, and find new ways to organize and present the information.

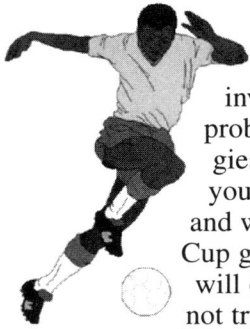

SOCCER: While more fluid and continuous than football, soccer still involves solving a series of information problems. Offensive and defensive strategies dominate soccer at all levels. Even young children learn where to line up and whom to "cover" on defense. In World Cup games, a team with a one goal lead will often decide to play tight defense and not try to score at all. Here the task may be redefined from scoring goals to containing the other team. Information about the situation is quickly gathered and analyzed, and a decision is made about how to proceed. Penalties can also greatly affect a soccer game. Referees must make split-second decisions based on interpretations of rules as much as on the actions of players.

BASKETBALL: Basketball is also a continuous action sport. Players process information about what's going on and make quick decisions about when to pass or shoot, or whom to guard. There's also considerable advance preparation in terms of practicing plays and learning how to play a certain style of defense. The information problem here is to develop a team rather than to perform well in a given game. In division I college basketball, there's also a concerted effort to "level the information playing field." For example, it is not permissible to send scouts to opponents' games. Coaches must rely on videotapes because the schools who can afford to send scouts would have an unfair information advantage over those who don't. Videotapes becomes the major source of information and, the coaching staff spends much of their time sorting and analyzing the information in tapes. The result may be an highly edited subset video on an opponent as well as written and graphic summaries of tendencies, strengths, and weaknesses.

FIGURE SKATING: Figure skating is representative of a number of sports that rely on human judgments of performance. Figure skating, as well as gymnastics, diving, and even skateboarding require a competitor to be fully informed of what's expected and permissible, the criteria for evaluation, and what other competitors are likely to do. The skater's information problems include finding ways to score well with the judges. The judges' information problem is to objectively and fairly score each skater. These sports also require carefully planned training regimens that monitor progress and build to optimal performance at key events.

TRACK AND FIELD: Track and field sports also require systematic and detailed training and prepa-

ration. Information problem-solving is crucial to gaining even the smallest competitive edge. For example, athletes and coaches must keep information about the latest developments in equipment.

GOLF: Information about equipment is also crucial to golf. During a golf match, the player and caddie continually solve information problems—consulting on proper club selection based on weather conditions, position of the ball on the course, the player's abilities, and the overall situation in the match.

The Big6 Information Problem-Solving Process Applied to Sports

Since information is so crucial to sports, it's highly appropriate and easy to apply the Big6 to any sports problem. For example, you can go through the entire Big6 process with the problem being winning (or doing well) in basketball, soccer, swimming, or volleyball. The most direct way to teach the Big6 using sports situations is to "walk students through" preparing for an upcoming sports contest as an information problem.

TASK DEFINITION: Students can easily grasp the overall problem, but have them think about subtasks—preparation, developing a game plan, or communicating information during a game. Consider the types of information required—facts and opinions about the other team; their strengths, weaknesses, and tendencies; our own strengths and weaknesses; offense and defensive strategies, and more. Graphic summaries of much of this information is preferred.

INFORMATION SEEKING STRATEGIES: For each type of information needed, brainstorm all possible sources: scouting reports; videotapes of games; magazine, newspaper or WWW articles; expert opinion; books on strategies; observations of our own practices and games. Determine which sources are the most appropriate for the situation.

LOCATION & ACCESS: What is the easiest and quickest way to get the sources needed: How can you find the information in the sources? For example, in college sports, teams usually exchange videotapes of games. To locate articles, WWW sites, or books, you might use some form of index. Experts can be consulted in-person or via telephone or e-mail.

USE OF INFORMATION: The amount of sports information available can be overwhelming. Discuss how to best process the information. After viewing, interviewing, or reading information, the key is to filter out what's important, summarize, and consolidate. Professional teams use database technology for this purpose. In football, every play from a videotape is indexed and entered into a database for easy retrieval. What do the students recommend for the situation at hand?

SYNTHESIS: In synthesis, you link back to the original problem. Students also need to consider who will use the information—coaches, players, or both? Synthesis may involve outlining the key points for training or practice, compiling a full analysis on an opponent, or developing a game plan for a particular competition. Ultimately, synthesis is actually playing the game.

EVALUATION: Evaluation is more than just determining whether you won or lost. Have students consider how to assess performance in relation to expectations. Those who succeed in sports learn from their mistakes. Therefore, have the students reflect on how to improve on the information aspects—the information processes and systems used as well as the strategies and decisions.

These are just some of the possibilities—mostly dealing with team sports . Recreational sports provide additional opportunities to develop Big6 understandings and skills. The role of technology in sports is also a fertile area for exploration. Future issues of the Big6 Newsletter will expand more on these topics as well as provide additional examples of teaching the Big6 through sports.

More On Sports and the Big6

v1 n3 p6

By Mike Eisenberg

In the last issue, we discussed how sports is an information activity and how using sports as the context for information skills instruction can be highly motivating. Difficulty in motivating students can happen at any level. After numerous lessons in study skills, library skills, or the research paper, a glaze may come over students' eyes when you start talking about information processes and, yes, even when you present the Big6.

I've experienced this first hand with students in elementary schools, grades 10-12, and more recently with my college-level classes. But, I've also found

that if you can link this learning to their personal interests and needs, students do get interested. The challenges are to gain their attention, sustain their attention, and make the instruction relevant to their interests. Linking the Big6 to sports can do this. Here are some additional ideas on how to teach the Big6 in a sports context:

- Have a coach speak to students about scouting a game: what a scout looks for, how to go about scouting, the forms used, how to summarize and present the information. Have the students go to a live game or practice and scout the action. Students should compile a "scouting report" and also report back to the class in terms of their information gathering, use, and Synthesis. Students should compare their efforts to using the Big6 in other settings.

- Get one of the computer-based football games, the kind that has player profiles and involves offensive and defensive play-calling. Have the class analyze the game to determine what are the key information components of the game. Also have the class analyze the game from a Big6 perspective—what Big6 processes are going on and how the students can use the Big6 to be more effective in playing the game. Alternatively, divide the class into teams and have them play against each other. Afterwards, have them describe their game strategies and their Use of Information while playing the game.

- Focus on the Big6 for recreational sports and activities. Discuss the process of using information to learn about the sport, training, preparation, and conditioning.

- Consider information sources available for the sports enthusiast. Compare print sports magazines and books to Web sites, online databases, and other electronic resources. Students should first brainstorm and then apply criteria for comparing sources (Big6 #2—Information Seeking Strategies):

  - complete
  - reliable (authoritative)
  - valid and precise (on target)
  - available
  - current
  - easy-to-use
  - affordable
  - entertaining.

> "It may be hard to believe, but sometimes students aren't interested in hearing about the Big6. Linking the Big6 to sports grabs their attentions

- Consider technology in sports—particularly information technology. Challenge the students to track the use of information technology in a particular sport, noting how the technology is applied and how it may have changed the sport. Then, have students identify the Big6 connection—how is the technology fulfilling one or more of the Big6 stages?
- Videotape arena horse jumping or some other sport that involves human judging. Show the tape to the students without the sound and have the students try to determine the criteria for judging. Don't show the parts where the judges give their scores. Then have the students judge a few of the contestants. Have the students compare among themselves and then compare to the actual judging. Evaluate their success in judging and also which Big6 Skills they relied on most.

In these situations, the challenge is to grab the students' interest, focus on the information aspects of the sports situation, identify relevant Big6 skills, and further develop those skills.

CHAPTER 9

The BIG 6

Kids & the Internet

Technology - More Than an Answer in Search of a Question

v1 n1 p1, 12-13

By Mike Eisenberg

Technology—computers—the Internet. Everywhere you turn, there's talk about the importance of technology and how technology and the Internet are changing our lives. Technology seems to be "hyped" as the answer, regardless of the question. Here's some of the hype:

■ Technology is the key to getting a good job.

■ The Internet is the answer to all our information needs.

■ Technology and the Internet are essential for learning and teaching.

■ Technology will fundamentally change the way we teach and learn.

Of course there's also the "anti-hype." According to Clifford Stoll (Silicon Snake Oil, 1995), for example:

■ The Internet isolates us from one another.

■ Technology cheapens the meaning of actual experience.

■ Technology works against literacy and creativity.

> *But the key isn't in the technology itself, rather it's what the technology allows us to do....*

■ Technology and the Internet will undercut our schools and libraries.

Which set of views is correct? Well, both. . . and neither. Technology is certainly important in our society. For example, we increasingly rely on the Internet to communicate with one another. The Internet is also a source of information. But the key isn't in the technology itself, rather it's what the technology allows us to do. We inter act person-to-person (through e-mail) or think about ideas we've read, viewed or heard on the Web. Technology is a tool—that's the key.

For most of us, there's a certain excitement when we learn to use a new technology. Remember what it felt like to drive a car for the first time? Exhilarating yes, but also a bit over whelming, and for some, even terrifying. What power, what responsibility!

But over time, we learned to harness the power and use it as a part of our everyday lives. So too with computers, the Internet, and other technologies— first interactions can be intimidating and overwhelming, Remember the thrill of writing and printing out your first word processed document or the first time you conducted a successful search on the World Wide Web? Regular users of the Internet know that it is decidedly NOT warm and fuzzy, friendly, easy to use, easy to learn about, easy to teach, fully reliable, search efficient, or a panacea. But we also know that the Internet has the potential to bring people together and provide unique learning and teaching opportunities.

That's the challenge—to use technology and the Internet in meaningful ways to help achieve educational goals. Our "technology and Internet challenge" is to continually focus on what we are trying to accomplish—in terms of learning and teaching—and how we can use technology and the Internet to help us to do so.

Helping students to use computers proficiently is our goal. We're pleased to see that there's support for computer literacy at the highest levels. In his April 19, 1997 radio address, President Clinton stated, "we have to do everything we can to make technology literacy a reality for every child in America." Students clearly need to be "technology literate," but there's more to it than just knowing keyboarding, the parts of a computer, or even writing with a word processor. Learning individual skills may address the "how" of computer use, but rarely the "when" or "why." Students may learn a particular tool but they will still lack an understanding of how those various tools fit together to solve problems and complete tasks.

That's where the Big6™ approach comes in. (For a complete explanation of the Big6 Skills™ please see pages viii.) Individual computer skills take on a new meaning when they are integrated within the Big6™ information problem-solving process. For example, students may have fun using e-mail to contact other students around the world, but e-mail becomes a much more powerful tool for information problem-solving when students realize that e-mail can help them in Task Definition. (Big6™ #1)—stu-

Technology is a tool— that's the key.

dents might use e-mail to clarify an assignment by interacting with teachers and group members. E-mail is also highly useful for consulting with others about the best strategies for seeking information (Big6™ #2), to locate and access the information itself (Big6™ #3), to present the results (Big6™ #5), and to seek reaction to their work (Big6™ #6).

The chart below offers examples of how other Internet and computer technologies can be placed in the Big6™ information problem-solving context. The chart is easily modified as new technological capabilities and resources are made available. The Big6TM provides an adaptable context for learning and teaching any electronic networking or information technology skills. We worked with Doug Johnson from Mankato, Minnesota to develop a computer skills curriculum based on an integrated, Big6™ approach. (See Eisenberg and Johnson, 1996 "Computer Skills for Information Problem-Solving," ERIC/IT, **http://ericir.syr.edu/ithome/digests/ computerskills.html**).

In addition to promoting the teaching of technology skills as part of a process, we champion integrating technical skills instruction with classroom curriculum. Technology and information skills should not be taught in isolation. Separate technology or computer classes do not really help students learn to apply computer skills in meaningful ways. This is an important shift in approach and emphasis and it mirrors a similar shift by library media specialists concerning teaching library and information skills.

Over the past 20 years, library media profes-

Technology Applications in a Big6™ Context

BIG6 SKILLS™	TECHNOLOGY APPLICATIONS
Task Definition	■ e-mail, listservs, live chat (e.g., IRC, MOO), video conferencing (e.g., CUSeeMe), Internet Telephone
Information Seeking Strategies	■ CD-ROMs, WWW navigation, e-mail, listservs, electronic full-text resources
Location & Access	■ WWW browsers (*Netscape, Internet Explorer),* WWW search *tools (Yahoo, Webcrawler, Excite),* online catalogs, electronic indexes
Use of Information	■ download, upload, file transfer (ftp), cut-paste in word processing
Synthesis	■ word processing, multimedia presentation (e.g., *Hyperstudio, PowerPoint),* electronic spreadsheets, database management systems, WWW page creation
Evaluation	■ e-mail, listservs, live chat (e.g., IRC, MOO), video conferencing (e.g., CUSeeMe), Internet Telephone

sionals have worked hard to move from teaching isolated "library skills" to teaching integrated
information skills. While it is certainly possible to
learn skills in isolation, practice and research confirm
that people learn best when the use and purpose are
clear. Students can probably learn to communicate
via e-mail or to access a WWW site, but they will
eagerly engage and internalize these skills if they see
how they directly relate to their school assignments,
personal interests, or work requirements. Electronic
mail, for example, is more than a novelty if students
realize that it can help them to work with students
from another state or country to complete a project
for social studies. Accessing a WWW site has a purpose when it relates directly to answering homework
questions or for a project or report.

In the rush to bring technology into our schools,
the focus has centered primarily on the hardware and
software and the commands and capabilities. School
districts are investing considerable amounts of money,
time, and effort on getting connected to the Internet
and adding computers to labs, classrooms, and
libraries. But, technology is NOT the answer regardless of the question. Technology is AN answer when
infused into the Big6™ information problem-solving
process and applied to meaningful curriculum or personal needs situations.

Through this and future issues of the *Big6™
Newsletter*, we look forward to providing further
explanations and practical examples of how to provide a range of integrated learning experiences to
ensure our students' success.

Netting the Big6: Integrating Instruction, Information Skills, and the Internet

v2 n1 p1, 10-11, 13

By Margaret Buehler & Patrick Jones

*"The Big6 process helped me find information
more efficiently, allowing me to find it quickly and
in more depth, and with a wider range than my
previous research attempts."*

—Caroline Helton,
Eleventh-grade student

Caroline's comments are just one example of the
many positive things students at the Saint Agnes
Academy, a private college prep school in Houston,
Texas, had to say about the use of the Big6 in their
school during the past two school years. For the
1996-1997 school year, the school library program

developed four primary goals:

- To acquaint more students with the Internet for
  research projects
- To increase both the quantity and quality of information skills instruction
- To introduce students and faculty to the Big6, and
- To work more closely with teachers in planning
  and implementing research projects.

All four of these goals were met through one program: the Big6 Project Pages. These Web pages use
the Big6 steps to guide students through a process of
critical thinking, skill building, and problem solving
(see the St. Agnes Academy Web page at www.st-
agnes.org/library).

Originally planned to coincide with only four
major projects a year, the Big6 Project Page idea was
expanded during the 1997-1998 school year with the
creation of more than 20 Web pages. Students have
been very successful at using the Web pages, but the
greatest impact has been the increased cooperation of
the faculty with the library media specialists. In addition to providing more time for instruction in the
library, teachers are starting to use the Big6 to transform research and writing assignments—to make them
clearer, more focused, and more student-centered.

Transforming Assignments

Once teachers "bought in" to the Big6 and viewed
the Internet as a viable and valuable research tool,
they began to transform assignments from traditional
exercises of handing back information to exciting
forays requiring critical thinking. For example, to
study *The Great Gatsby* during 11th grade English,
students used to complete a basic library book
research project offering little opportunity for information skills instruction. However, through the Big6
process, the project evolved over a three-year period
into an information-rich activity with numerous
opportunities for instruction in research and critical
thinking skills. Students used the Big6 Project Pages
to research topics (fads, sports, fashion, and more)
from the 1920s and presented the content to their
classmates through posters, skits, and other formats.
This required the students to be much more selective
in the information they included and allowed them to
be creative in the use of graphics and various presentation styles.

The metamorphosis from a project that just
focused on the content aspects into an information
skills-oriented Big6 project empowered the teachers
to rethink, revise, and rewrite the assignment. It also
became more student-centered since students were
undertaking research for the purpose of teaching other

students. And, it became a critical thinking exercise because students were learning not just how to find information but also how to evaluate and use it. For the majority of students, this type of assignment was new, and the Big6 process provided them with a useful framework for thinking about, then doing research. **Teresita Sarmiento**, a student, stated, "It showed me a step-by-step process that I could use to organize myself and minimize the time it would take me to research." Moreover, this assignment provided eleventh-graders with a strong foundation for solving future information problems such as the two other big research projects they would face later in the term.

The *Gatsby* assignment was not the only one transformed through the implementation of the Big6. Another example was the evolution of a literary analysis paper on "early American romanticism." Five years ago, students would read stories from a textbook (e.g., *The Devil and Tom Walker* by *Washington Irving* and *The Fall of the House of Usher* by Edgar Allen Poe) then discuss in class the authors' use of romanticism and write a paper that merely regurgitated the class discussion. Now students choose their own themes from a story that is not discussed in class or found in their textbook. This requires students to develop their own ideas on a theme and to use the analysis skills they have been taught. Student **Caroline Helton** commented that the assignment "made me analyze the topic more thoroughly." In addition, rather than reading from the text, students are introduced to the valuable resource of electronic text centers (for example, Virginia Tech Electronic Text Center, **gopher://gopher.vt.edu: 10010/10/33**) as they use the Internet to find primary source material.

The end result is that students write better papers about themes that intrigue them rather than those that interest their teacher.

Simply by changing the medium for source material from a textbook to the Internet, the assignment undergoes a transformation for many students. It is no longer just a traditional paper, but rather a "cool" assignment because they need to use "the Net." They learn that the same place they chat, check their e-mail, and search for the latest entry in the "hunk-of-the-month club," also has a more useful, educational purpose. For students who are economically disadvantaged or without home access to the Internet, this type of assignment opens a new world for them. When teachers notice that their students' papers and projects are more interesting and that students are more engaged, a momentum starts building towards using the Big6 in other projects.

Teachers are astarting to use the Big6 to transform research and writing assignments— to make them clearer, more focused, and more student-centered.

Creating Big6 Project Pages

The Web-based project pages use the Big6 as the structure for their efforts. When students come to the library for instruction, they find project pages for their research task. During instruction, the library media specialists and teachers discuss their assignment and walk students through the Big6 process using the project pages to cover the six stages. Each stage asks Big6 questions, such as "what am I supposed to do?" then provides part of the answer via hypertext links. Eleventh grader **Wendy Vickery** found this part of the process helpful, stating, "It made me think about the questions I am supposed to ask myself." Using the Big6 Project Pages helps all students learn the Big6 process in the context of their own assignment.

Each project page begins with the title of the research project and a short introductory statement. This statement contains a hypertext link to a specific page or, as in the *Gatsby* project, to the best category heading in *Yahoo* regarding the research subject. Providing such a link gives students immediate access to a useful information resource and also demonstrates the Internet's value for student research.

Teachers provide the library media specialists with a copy of the assignment for the Task Definition section. The assignment sheet explains the details of the task to be completed. For some teachers, this is just a paragraph or two while others provide a lengthier document. Many teachers ask for the librarians' input on designing the research assignment. The library media specialists then "mark up" the document in HTML and set it up as a separate Web page linked from the Big6 Project Page.

Information Seeking Strategies is the most labor-intensive task in constructing the project pages. In this part of the project page, the library media specialists define types of sources, identify the appropriate search tools, and suggest possible resources. In many ways, this section is nothing more than a hypertext pathfinder. It still lists reference books, but expands to list electronic resources, many of which are only a click away. There is also a short list of search engines. As part of instruction on accessing information (Big6 #3), students learn the basics of searching *Yahoo, Alta Vista,* or *Hotbot.* Following the search engines is a list of six to twelve appropriate Web pages to find information for the task. Some of these are links to specific pages or to sites that are indexes or hotlists for the selected topic, such as Flapper Station (**www.sns.com/ ~rbotti/**) for the *Gatsby* assignment. Other links might include a *Yahoo* category subject heading, a commercial information site with a search engine of its own, like CNN, or online periodicals, such as the *New York Times*. The sites listed are suggestions, and students are not required to use them. The hope is that by providing these links, library media specialists "level the playing field" and give everyone a chance to find some basic information. It is also hoped that students will be encouraged to find more information on their own.

The library media specialists teach Location & Access skills through direct instruction. In addition to teaching students how to use search engines, to develop complex searches, and to understand search results, the library media specialists provide basic instruction on using the *Netscape* browser. It does no good to elaborate on complicated searches if students don't know how to do simple tasks such as downloading, print previewing, or just clicking.

Evaluating Web resources is the main emphasis of the Use of Information section of the project pages. There is a link to a page about Evaluation, and this is reinforced through instruction. Students need to learn this critical thinking skill as well as how to determine a Web page's value to their particular research. Many students view the Internet as a panacea and think that because information is on the Net that it is as good as gold. Separating the real gold from fool's gold is an important skill for students to master. Eleventh-grader **Angela Dunn** noted that the Big6 "made me think about the sources I was using and their reliability. It also helped me to narrow down all of the information until I got to just the necessities."

Synthesis includes a link to a document on citing electronic resources. In addition, students receive a handout during instruction with more detailed information. For most students, the teacher determines how the research will be presented. Students who want to include a great number of graphics in their presentations are instructed in the use of color printers, graphic converters, scanners, and *PowerPoint*. As the final step of the Big6 Project Pages, students are encouraged to Evaluate their process. Students use a form that is submitted to the library media specialist to answer questions about their work on the project as well on the effectiveness of the project page. Their comments are insightful and rewarding, such as those of eleventh-grader **Courtney Samohyl** who noted that the "Big6 process taught me how to research my project quickly and efficiently. I was able to learn about the different search engines and use them without difficulty." Similarly, **Kate Kraycirik** commented that the Big6 "helped me organize myself, my thoughts, and my information." By taking time to

examine the process, students should begin to see areas for improvement in solving information problems.

The faculty have responded terrifically to these Big6 Pages and have become advocates of the process. After the Gatsby project, teacher Margaret Buehler noted that:

"As an English teacher, I tended to be stuck between the covers of books—they were my comfort zone. Since the introduction of Big6 Project Pages, I have been able to incorporate books and Internet into exciting lessons and projects, which have offered my students real data and the opportunity to do their own research. The kids have become much more adept both with technical use of the Net and with sifting through the information to find what is valuable and reliable."

Everybody Wins

These project pages present winning situations for all involved. Teachers win as they use the Big6 process to write better assignments. Through these more clearly written instructions, students understand what to do, how to approach the task, and the criteria for evaluation before beginning the assignment. As a result, students are writing better research projects.

The library media program wins as these Big6 Project Pages have illustrated the importance of information skills instruction and the use of the Internet. In providing this instruction, the library serves students better, works more closely with faculty, and demonstrates the significance of the library media program to the school.

Most important, students win because they get a practical and philosophical framework to complete research. Helping students improve their information skills is the goal of the Big6 Project Pages. We want to see our students working efficiently, effectively, and always improving. We want them to work smarter, not harder, on every project! We want all students to be able to say, as eleventh-grader **Natalia Lentino** did, "I was able to make connections from what I had learned from the Big6 and facilitate the research of the next assignment paper."

For more information about the Big6 Project Pages, please contact Lynne Webb, library media specialist (**lwebb@ st-agnes.org**), or article authors Patrick Jones(**naughyde@aol.com**) or Margaret Buehler (**mbuehler@st-agnes.org**).

Margaret Buehler is the chairperson of the English Department at Saint Agnes Academy. Patrick Jones, formerly a library assistant at St. Agnes Academy, is also the author of Connecting Young Adults and Libraries (Neal-Schuman, 1998).

Use the Big6 to Harness the Internet!

v2 n3 p10-11, 13

By Rob Darrow

The World Wide Web is doubling every 90 days. A new Web site is appearing every four seconds! The amount of information in the world is doubling every two years. (Jukes, 1997).

- How can teachers learn to make sense of the Web? How can teachers help students to find and organize information from the Web?

- How can library media specialists train students and teachers to sift and sort through what is important and what is not on the Web?

The answer to these questions is very simple: Use the Big6!

The Big6 fits perfectly when teaching others how to find and use information from the World Wide Web. For example, here's the process that has worked with more than 25 different classes of seventh and eighth grade students at **Alta Sierra Intermediate School in Clovis, California**. That's well over 600 students a year!

Here's an example of what takes place. Imagine that there are two students working together on each computer.

Big6 Skill #1: Task Definition

The teacher or library media specialist states, "Let's start today as we always do, looking at defining our task which is Stage 1 of the Big6. What information are we looking for? What is our end product supposed to look like?"

One student responds, "We need to find information about our careers." Another says, "We're supposed to use the Web to find out stuff about jobs we want in the future." Still another adds, "We're gonna make a slide show."

Right. The end product for each pair of students is supposed to be a PowerPoint presentation about a particular career to be presented to their peers next week. Students are to find information about their chosen career that discussed education and training needed, personality traits needed for particular jobs, salary range and opportunities for job advancement.

It is important that students learn how to use the Web in the context of a specific class assignment rather than as a stand alone venture. Once the assignment is given, the key questions to train students to ask regarding Task Definition are: What am I looking for, and what are my keywords?

This group of students goes on to define their keyword search terms as: careers, jobs, the specific job title, or some combination of all of these words.

Big6 Skill #2: Information Seeking Strategies

Part of Information Seeking Strategies (Stage 2) is to select the best sources. When applying this to the Web, students need to learn which search mechanisms will help them find what they want. The library media specialist spends time with neophyte Web searchers on how different search mechanisms work, how these mechanisms display information, and how various mechanisms may help locate certain information. Donna Baumbach of the University of Central Florida Instructional Technology Resource Center has provided an excellent guide for this purpose.

Students in this class type in keywords or phrases such as "lawyer careers" or "mechanical engineer" in several search mechanisms. Students then discuss how different searches displayed information in different ways. Specific search mechanisms used included:

- *AltaVista (**altavista.digital.com**)*
- *Yahoo (**www.yahoo.com**)*
- *Dogpile (**www.dogpile.com**)*
- *NorthernLight (**www.northernlight.com**).*

The students then determine which search mechanism they would use for their own individual searches and then began the process of finding information about their careers. This part is usually accomplished in an hour with two students per computer.

Big6 Skill #3: Location & Access

Actually searching for information on the Web is Stage 3, Location & Access. Once students have the "search results" showing from whichever search mechanism they have deemed best, they learn to assess their search results, select promising links, click on them, and bookmark their sites for later use. Students learn the following process:

- Read and scan the "front page" of several Web sites from the search results. When scanning the Web site, students ask one major question: "Will this give me any information I need for my topic?"

- If the answer is NO, then click on the "Back" button and look at the next Web site.

- If the answer is YES, bookmark or mark the site as a favorite, and then go "Back" to the search results page to look for other useful Web sites.
- Repeat this process until an adequate number of Web sites are found.

Depending on the information needed, the amount of time available, and the age of the students, a goal number of chosen Web sites should be set. In most cases, it is adequate if students select between 3-5 Web sites.

While looking for career Web sites, this group of seventh graders discovered that using the word "careers" following their chosen job worked best. For example, using the phrase "teacher careers" worked better than simply typing in "teacher." During this stage, students also learned that putting search terms in parentheses narrowed their search and resulted in more successful hits.

Big6 Skill #4: Use of Information

Stage 4 of the Big6, Use of Information requires students to revisit their bookmarked sites and ask more important questions:

- Is this information from a reliable source?
- What information is worth applying to my task? (in this case a *PowerPoint* presentation on a career).

Just as with print sources, students need to learn how to evaluate and select the information needed to complete an assignment. This entire process can be done on the computer by highlighting and copying from a Web site then pasting into a word processing or *PowerPoint* document to store key information for use at a later date.

Students learn to follow this process:

- Open a bookmarked Web site.
- Read to find important information.
- Highlight and copy information from a Web site to a word processing or *PowerPoint* document.
- Copy the Web location and title of the Web site to word processing document for a bibliography.

Big6 Skill #5: Synthesis

To complete the Synthesis Stage, #5 of the Big6, students access the information that they previously saved to disk. This saved information can then be organized and used for countless numbers of synthesis projects such as:

- Newsletter articles
- *HyperStudio* or *PowerPoint* projects

- Creation of a Web page
- Notes for an oral presentation.

For the career PowerPoint presentation, students put certain facts on certain slides. Each fact could be no longer than seven words and there could not be more than 25 words per slide.

Big6 Skill #6: Evaluation

As students finish their search for information on the Web, they are asked to reflect on the following questions designed to help refine and improve their search strategies for their next project (part of Evaluation, Big6 Skill #6):

- Which search engine worked best for me? Why? (Efficiency/process)
- Did this search strategy work for me? Why or why not? (Efficiency/process)
- Did I get the information I wanted? Why or Why not? (Effectiveness/result)

Students respond to these questions in a variety of ways. One student says, "I learned how *AltaVista* works better than *Yahoo*." Another responds, "It's easier finding and using information off the Web." Finally, one more added, "I learned how to find the information I need on the Web and then put it into something I can use for my class projects."

This final stage can be done orally at the end of the class or as a short written assignment to assess what students learned. This stage is also critical in helping students think about the information they have found and determine what they have learned, so that they begin to internalize the Big6 process.

In Summary

There's lots of talk in education circles and in the popular press about whether or not the World Wide Web is really helpful to students and teachers. Too often, Web use is a haphazard and disconnected event—with questionable results from a learning or teaching perspective. But not with the Big6! The Big6 provides the necessary direction and context to finding information on the Web.

By repeatedly using the Big6 process, students become more refined users of the Web, and ultimately more effective users of information. And, there's little question that these information literacy skills are becoming more and more important in society. Just ask anyone in business looking for new employees.

Sources

Eisenberg, M. B. & Berkowitz, R. E. (1988). *Curriculum initiative: An agenda and strategy for library media programs.* Noorwood, NJ: Ablex Publishing.

Eisenberg, M. B. & Berkowitz, R. E. (1990). *Information problem-solving: The Big Six Skills approach to library and information skills instruction.* Noorwood, NJ: Ablex Publishing.

Eisenberg, M. B. & Johnson, D. (1996). *Computer skills for information problem-solving: Learning and teaching technology in context.* ERIC Digest. (Report no. EDO-IR-96-04). Syracuse, NY: ERIC Clearinghouse on Information and Technology. (ED 392 463).

Jukes, I. (1997, November 19). *Opening Address to California School Library Association Conference.* Pasadena, CA. Thornburg Center for Professional Development. Available: www.tcpd.org/

About the Author

Rob Darrow, Library Media Specialist at Alta Sierra Intermediate School Clovis, California, is an enthusiastic user of the Big6. Rob has built his entire information skills instructional program around the Big6. He works with teachers across the curriculum and grade levels, and his students respond with great excitement. Rob once commented that a student came up to him in the library media center and said, "Mr. Darrow, you have the greatest job. I hope when I grow up I can do just what you do." High praise indeed.

JASON and Big6 On the Web: A Media Specialist and a Computer Application Instructor Join Forces to Teach a Web-Based Research Class

v2 n5 p1, 12-14

By Karen Becknell & Marjorie Alexander

The Big6 is everywhere—or at the very least applicable everywhere. Here, we see how the Big6 is used in conjunction with one of the most successful and high quality Web-based curriculum projects: The JASON Project. This is a perfect example of teaching information and technology skills in context. Nice work Karen, Marjorie, and the students at John Page Middle School.

The JASON Project (**http://www.jasonproject. org**), developed by Dr. Robert Ballard, the famous undersea explorer, is now in its tenth year. Each year, JASON visits one or more new locations to study the questions, "What are the Earth's dynamic systems?"; "How do these systems affect life on Earth?"; and "What technologies are used to study these systems?" The project provides students access to real scientists through telecommunication and includes live broadcasts and chat sessions. In 1998, JASON IX focused on the Earth's oceans.

The **Lamphere Schools** in **Madison Heights, MI,** have been involved with the JASON Project for the past five years. For the past two years, Lamphere High School has been a JASON PINS (Primary Interactive Network Site) site. This is one of 34 sites, nationwide, to which a satellite transmission from a JASON Expedition site is directly broadcast. Each spring, thousands of students, including those in the Lamphere schools, attend these live tele-broadcasts from the JASON exploration sites around the world. The library media specialist (LMS) and computer teacher realized that the JASON Project would make the perfect research vehicle for a class at **John Page Middle School.** The class consisted of 20 sixth grade students with varying degrees of computer knowledge and no exposure to the Big6!

The Big6, JASON, Teamwork and Technology!

The JASON curriculum was the educational focus of a project that required students to use technology to complete research using electronic and online sources and to use software to produce a Web page to report their research findings. The project was a team effort which reflects the approach that might be taken on the job. The emphasis on teamwork fit nicely with the Lamphere Schools' School-to-Work goal of providing real-life experiences that transfer to the workplace. Five major objectives for the project were identified. These were:

Using the Big6 Skills to conduct research

- Understanding the process behind each of the Big6 steps
- Recognizing that the Big6 process was a life-long skill
- Gaining real-life experiences that transfer to the workplace
- Working as part of a team to accomplish a goal.

The JASON Project provides focus questions as part of the scientific process. The library media specialist LMS and technology teacher adapted these questions so that each group would have two questions to guide their research: (See our link for JASON Focus Questions.)

OCEAN STRUCTURE:

- What properties determine the ocean's structure?
- How do these properties influence where different kinds of marine organisms live?

CORAL REEF:

- What organisms make up the coral reef community, and how do they survive?
- Where are coral reefs found, and what tools are used to monitor their health?

SURFACE AND MID-WATER:

- What organisms make up the mid-water community, and how do they survive?

- How do zooplankton contribute to the global carbon cycle?

KELP FOREST:

- What organisms make up the kelp forest community, and how do they survive?
- What tools are researchers using to study kelp forests?

DEEP-WATER:

- What organisms make up the deep-water community, and how do they survive?
- What tools do scientists use to gather samples from the deep sea?

Students were assigned to groups of four based on an interest survey that the LMS and technology teacher developed after the initial introduction to the JASON Project. To emphasize the teamwork approach, the students gave weekly update reports to

Figure 1: *Web Page Planning Guide*

Created by:_____	
File Name:_____.html	Page #:_____Of_____
Title:_____	**Pages that point to this page:**
Heading Information:	_____
_____	_____
_____	_____
_____	
	Color or type of background:
	_____
Body:	**Color of text:**
_____	_____
_____	
_____	**Pages this page will link to:**
	Site:_____
	Address:_____
Footer Information:	Site:_____
_____	Address:_____
_____	Site:_____
_____	Address:_____

Sources: G. Gandolfi and S. Sutherland: Northville Schools, Northville, MI, 1977.

the class on the information they had discovered in their research activities. Students were encouraged to look for "links" from other groups' findings to their own research questions.

The Strategy

The first week of the project, the LMS and technology teacher introduced the JASON Project, reviewed teamwork skills, and began instruction on note-taking. The LMS used the "Trash-N-Treasure" process (see **http://www.Big6.com** for details, and click on In Action and Lessons), as she does with all research instruction. Students practiced note-taking skills using articles from the JASON curriculum. The next two weeks were devoted to instruction using the Big6 model. As the class progressed through the steps, they continued to practice note-taking skills as homework. Students initially practiced note-taking from print sources. As research continued, instruction was customized for Internet searching, and retrieval. Students also learned techniques for taking notes from video and television broadcasts. During the fifth week, the LMS and technology teacher introduced the elements of designing a good Web page. Under the technology teacher's guidance, students discussed the purpose of their page, what information should be presented, and the importance of accuracy and of ease of use.

Prior to designing their Web pages, each group was required to fill in a worksheet (Figure 1 on page 85) with information on content and resources (including graphics). The technology teacher and LMS introduced students to Microsoft FrontPage which they would use to create their Web pages. As groups became ready to create their pages, members were assigned to workstations. Two group members at a time were allowed to work on the page while the remaining members continued researching. Group members met on a regular basis to monitor their progress and update each other on their accomplishments and needs for more information, etc.

By the eighth week, research was more focused, and the Web pages were well under way. Students began to realize that the Big6 steps were not a linear progression. Several recognized that note-taking (Step 4) was introduced first, and that as they worked, they moved from Steps 3, 4, and 5, and back again, always referring to the focus questions (Step 1). Each research session always began with a review of the group's focus questions and current information needs. As students created their Web pages, they began evaluating them (Step 6) using the guidelines they were given (Figures 2 and 3). As the whole project came to a close, students were asked to describe

---

Figure 2: Web Page Design Guidelines

Is the page easy to use?
- Are there headings and sub-headings on the page to help you?
- Is it easy to move from page to page within the site?

How does the page look?
- Do the pictures on the page add to the information?
- Do the colors allow the page to be read easily?
- Is the page design easy to follow, or is it too cluttered?

Is the information correct?
- Can you verify the information found on the Web site in a recognized, authoritative print source?
- Is the information provided in an easily understood format?
- Does this page have current, up-to-date information?

Is information about the author included?
- Did the author sign his/her real name?
- Did the author give an e-mail address?
- Is there a page with the information about the author?
- Is the date of the last update of the page included?

What else does this site include?
- Does this site lead to some other good links on the same topic:
- Does this site provide information that you could not find anywhere else?
- Does this site provide better information or in a better format than a print source in your school library media center?

Elements of a good Web site:
- It is easy to use and navigate.
- It provides enough information about the author that you can assesss whether the author is knowledgeable about the topic.
- The information can be verified elsewhere.
- The site includes links to other useful sites.

Excerpted from *Evaluating Internet Web Sites: An Educator's Guide* by Kathleen Schrock, ©1997 by the MASTER Teacher, Inc. Used with permission of the publisher.

how each of the steps was used to guide the research (see our link "How the Big6 Guided our Research").

During the ninth week, the Lamphere Schools held "JASON Family Day." This event provides opportunities for students to share their learning with the community. Although the pages were not yet finished, several students came to the event (held on a Saturday) to work on their pages and to explain the process to visitors (see our link "JASON Family Day").

The Web pages are now posted (**http://www.lamphere.k12.mi.us** under JASON Project; JASON IX and the Big6) along with a letter that one of the groups wrote explaining the project to a visiting dignitary (see "How We Build a Coral Reef Web Page" on page 88).

Even though the BIG6 is not mentioned specifically, as you read this student's explanation, you will recognize that all of the steps are there.

Evaluation

At the last class meeting, the LMS and technology teacher reviewed the goals and asked students which skills they thought they would use again, and why. A majority said they would use the researching and note-taking skills again. A surprising number said they found the teamwork skills valuable. The LMS and technology teacher found this comment surprising because the students really hated using teamwork skills, especially to resolve conflict. As expected, a large number indicated they would use the Internet searching skills, and everyone plans to use the Web authoring skills to build their own Web pages!

The technology teacher and LMS reviewed the project as well and asked themselves what they

Figure 3: *Web Page Rubric*

	LEVEL 1	LEVEL 2	LEVEL 3	LEVEL 4	LEVEL 5
Thinking process	Disconnected and unrelated thoughts; vague ideas.	Concrete description and evaluation; no analysis of causes; no meaning.	Description, analysis, meaning, evaluation; identifies problems and solutions.	Integrates multiple sources of information to access issue.	Identifies and examines root causes as well as immediate issues; persuasive and connected.
Writing Process	Difficult to understand, tangents, spelling and other errors.	Many errors but consistent line of thought.	Easy to understand; perfect spelling; one or two grammar, syntax, or semantic problems.	Same as Level 3, but no errors.	Clear, concise, well-written online content.
Web Page Creation Skill	Text is not broken into paragraphs.	Text is broken into paragraphs; headings are used.	Headings, titles used in addition to text style, centering and horizontal rules.	Same as Level 3 plus images and hyperlinks to related material.	Same as Level 4 plus uses images as hyperlinks, colored text/ background images.
Web Page Layout	Layout has no structure or organization.	Text is broken into paragraphs; and or sections.	Headings label sections and create hierarchy;some consistency.	Hierarchy closely follows meaning; headings and style are consistent within pages; text, images, and links flow together.	Consistent format; extended information from page to page; attention to different browsers and their quirks.
Navigation	One Page.	One page with title bar added; heading and student first names are given.	Two pages or one page with links to other resources.	Three pages with clear order labeling, and navigation between pages; all links work.	Title page with other pages branching off; and at least five pages total; navigation clear and logical; all links work.
Graphics	Lacks graphics.	Graphics not appropriate.	At least one page per page. Appropriate placement.	Graphics enhance page.	Appropriate graphic used as links.

How We Built a Coral Reef Web Page

Our first step in this project was to find out what we were going to be researching. Which would be, the organisms that live in a coral reef, and how do they survive? Our second research question was: What tools do researchers use to study coral reefs? We used some of the same focus questions the JASON scientists used. We also wanted to show where coral reefs are located.

Once we decided on our questions, we started our research. We used a variety of research tools. We used articles our teachers gave us, books, electronic encyclopedias, magazines, the Internet and public television programs and videos.

When we had all our info we made a rough draft of our web pages. We revised and drew, and put all the info in again. Then when we were ready, we started to create our web pages, storing all the info onto disks. We entered our text and found our graphics for our pages. We loaded our graphics on a disk and brought them up and placed them where they were supposed to be. The last thing we had to do was to add our links to the different pages.

— Megan, John Page Middle School, Sixth Grade

would do differently. They decided that since students were overwhelmed with the amount of information needed to produce one Web page, they would ask students to research one question, build the resulting Web page, then research the second question. They reasoned that this format would help sustain interest in the project and would provide students with more time at the computers. Having students synthesize the results sooner would afford them the opportunity to analyze their results and to determine any additional information they would need (Step 6).

Conclusion

Several colleagues described this project as very rigorous. It was, but students experienced success due to clearly outlined expectations and the power of The Big6!

NOTE: To access the pages to which you are referred, go to: **http://www.lamphere.k12.mi.us**. Click, JASON IX & the Big6; then click on the links in parentheses.

How I Cloned Myself with Big6 on the World Wide Web

v2 n6 p6-7

By Melissa R. Gibson

Once upon a time, there was a music teacher who was so completely burned out that she went back to school to become a librarian. Little did she realize that a librarian's job was just as busy and hectic! Despite the challenges, she felt that she could make a difference in the lives of her students, especially by using the Big6.

With so many students and so little time, she found that there was never enough of her to go around. Even though she promoted an open-door policy in her library, she was not able to help children who came willingly for information if she was working with a scheduled class. There wasn't enough time in the 30 minutes every five days she had with the children to adequately teach them the steps for the Big6. So, this teacher-librarian decided to use the school's new Internet connections to her advantage. She created a bevy of Web pages that would help guide her older children through the steps of the Big 6 so that if the children came in and she was busy, they could use these pages to help themselves to information.

Cloning Myself

This teacher-librarian is me—Melissa Gibson! And, in order to better help my students, I needed to find a way to "clone myself." Well, I did it—I cloned myself by creating a set of web pages in a Web site that I call the "Research Buddy" (**http://www.squires. fayette.k12.ky.us/library/research/research.htm**). The Research Buddy site is set up according to the stages of Big 6, beginning with Task Definition and ending with Evaluation. However, the beauty presenting this in a Web, hypertext format is that no reader is limited to reading one page after another to access information. When students are reading about Big6 #4, "Use of Information," they can immediately get information about citing sources or evaluating sources. The Big6 process is not linear—and neither is using hypertext. They're a perfect combination.

What made me think of the computer? Why not just write a pathfinder or booklet? The students. I noticed when children came into the library looking for information that they made a beeline for the computers. Why? When I asked them, I was told how much easier computers were, and faster, and how much better the information was from computers. They could get pictures from the computer! Right then, I knew they desperately needed evaluation skills! But I also decided to build on their love and interest for computers. If they would go to a computer for information, maybe they would go to a computer for help with looking for information.

Elements of Design

The design of the Research Buddy is based on the learning theory of constructivism, because teaching information literacy skills requires the strategies that constructivism provides. Judy Pitts (1992) outlined the strategies of constructivism noting that students must:

- Examine their own ideas
- Interact with others
- Think critically, and
- Pause for reflection.

Within the Research Buddy, students have the opportunity to record their thoughts by creating a journal as they answer the questions that are provided after each stage of the Big6 is completed. These questions are designed to help students reflect on their performance and to think about how they might change what they did. This stimulates the self-reflection, the metacognitive thinking that is required for lifelong learning. With the Research Buddy acting as a mentor, students can be guided through a research process, thinking critically about each step they complete.

The first design for the Research Buddy featured fairly long pages that required the students to scroll down the screen to read. As I noticed that students weren't scrolling, I started editing the long pages into smaller ones. Now, a previously long page appears as 4 or 5 different screens, with "Next" and "Back" buttons at the bottom. Most of the pages are small enough to be seen in one window without scrolling. On these type of pages, there is no navigation bar at the bottom, a design element that should "force" reading to the end of the pages of information. I find that this design can be aggravating and limiting, but I am waiting to see if it keeps the students on track.

Determining if Research Buddy Works

In the Spring of 1998, an exploratory study involving fifth graders demonstrated that they had some trouble

If they would go to a computer for information, maybe they would go to a computer for help with looking for information.

with the Research Buddy. They tended to get "lost in hyperspace," and became distracted by going into different, more entertaining sites. In observing the students, I determined that even though most pages have a navigation bar at the bottom where students can access the Program Map (like a table of contents), the Big6 page, a help page, a glossary, and an index, students didn't have enough experience with the Web to navigate the Research Buddy.

In an updated study, students were given two months of instruction on using the Web prior to using Research Buddy.

Presently, I am preparing a dissertation study focusing on fifth-graders' perceptions of using the Research Buddy as a mentor for information problem solving. I'm not sure just what I'm going to find out from this study, but I hope it will be useful to teacher-librarians who have the same problems as I do in their libraries!

My research focus questions include: Does "on-line mentoring" occur with the Research Buddy? If so, in what ways? How do students use the Research Buddy? For what purposes? For information seeking skills? For organization of information? For presentation of information?

What features do they think are most and least helpful? For which tasks? Will the students think that they have learned new research skills because they used the Research Buddy? What new skills might those be? Are there patterns in the students' perceptions and use of the Research Buddy? By studying students' perceptions of the Research Buddy, will a model of information-seeking in an electronic environment evolve? Do students' perceptions differ from their actual use? If so, how?

An Invitation

Colleagues on the Big6, LM_NET, and KYLMS (Kentucky Library Media Specialists) listservs have been a great help to me in "cleaning up" such things as grammar, spelling and the appearance of the pages. I invite my Big6 colleagues to use the Research Buddy and see what you think. Make a link to it from your page, and let your students go. Watch how they use it, and let me know their responses to it.

References

Pitts, J. (1992). Constructivism: Learning rethought. In Smith, J. B. & Coleman, J. G. (eds.) School *Library Media Annual, Vol. 10.* Englewood, CO: Libraries Unlimited.

The BIG6

Teaching Technology & Information Skills

PART IV

TIPS:
(Teaching Information Problem Solving)

CHAPTER 10

The BIG 6

Getting Their Attention

Teaching the Process with Calvin & Hobbes

v1 n3 p16

By Mike Eisenberg

Want to avoid that "same old, same old" feeling when going through the Big6 process with students? How about working through a problem with that expert information problem-solver, Calvin?

Calvin is a master at avoiding work. He really does understand what it takes to do well—he's a natural Big6er—but he'd prefer to get others to do it. In *The Indispensable Calvin and Hobbes* (Universal Press Syndicate, 1992, p. 152-154), Calvin has the problem of writing a report for school on the topic of bats. He says, "Heck, I don't know anything about bats! How am I supposed to write a report on a subject I know nothing about? It's impossible!" Hobbes asks, "I suppose research is out of the question?" And Calvin answers, "Oh, like I'm going to learn about bats and then write a report? Give me a break."

The story goes on for seven more panels as Calvin works through the process of completing the report. Calvin shows that he understands Information Seeking Strategies through Synthesis—trying to get Susie, who is going to the library, to research bats for him, make copies of the

> *He really does understand what it takes to do well—he's a natural Big6er—but he'd prefer to get others to do it.*

information, underline the important parts, and outline the paper. From a Big6 perspective, he's got the right idea, but he just doesn't want to take too much time or effort (Big6 #6—Evaluation). He knows what the paper should look like—an introduction, body, a couple of pictures, and a conclusion—and he's got a sure-fire way to get a good grade: a professional-looking, clear plastic binder. Works every time, right?

Folks in South Dakota once told me that they use this and other Calvin stories to teach Evaluation—Big6 #6.2 evaluate the process. They share the cartoons with students and have them identify which Big6 stages Calvin is trying to accomplish. The students can then state what Calvin is doing wrong, and how he might improve because he doesn't quite do things the way we'd want to see it done.

I've used another Calvin cartoon strip in the same way—the one about making a diorama of a desert scene. My favorite line is when Calvin asks his mother, "Where do we keep the papier maché?" When his mother answers that they don't have any and that it's his problem, Calvin states, "If I get a bad grade, it'll be your fault for not doing the work for me." Again, this leads into a great discussion about what not to do from a Big6 perspective.

Know of any other useful comics or stories? Send them to us, and we'll let everyone know in a future issue of the Big6 Newsletter.

Using Big6 Glasses

v2 n6 p7

By Kathy Spitzer

A very graphic way of demonstrating the Big6 to students is to tell them that we look at the world through Big6 glasses. We've all heard of a person who looks at the world through rose-colored glasses. Well, how about Big6 glasses?

We asked an art teacher to come up with a design for a pair of Big6 glasses because we wanted to graphically illustrate to the audience how to view the world through Big6 glasses. The glasses were made out of pink fluorescent cardboard with silver sparkles (think Elton John) and forced the wearer to look out through the B and the g (See the illustration for a design that you can copy). The Big6 design was then attached to the front of a pair of old glasses frames.

They certainly were and are an attention grabber. In fact, Mike Eisenberg liked these so much, he "borrowed them" for a presentation…and still has them!

Why not create your own Big6 glasses, put them on and then challenge your students to come up with problems that they are facing? While wearing the Big6 glasses you can brainstorm some ideas using the Big6 process and illustrate them on a large chart. This will help students see the applicability of the Big6 to more than just their schoolwork.

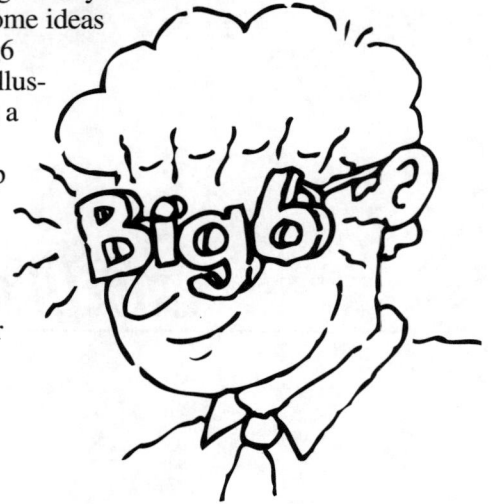

CHAPTER 11

The BIG6

Task Definition

Task Definition - Turning the Tables

v1 n2 p15

By Mike Eisenberg

Here's a tip for classroom teachers concerning communicating assignments to the home—relaying tasks and objectives to parents. There are a number of ways to do this including the traditional method—sending home notices with students. More recently, schools are using voice-mail systems or Web sites—"homework hotlines" where parents can call or search to find out about their child's various homework activities and assignments. We certainly support the idea of students working with parents, but are a bit uneasy about placing the homework or assignment burden on the parent.

With parent-oriented homework hotlines, who becomes responsible for knowing what the assignment is? The parents! As educators and parents, we want just the opposite! We want the students to be fully responsible for their tasks. We want to encourage students to focus on Task Definition, to be the ones calling or e-mailing homework hotlines, to be the ones making sure they fully understand what they are to do.

So, let's turn it upside-down. Teachers—don't spell out some of your assignments at all! Make it a game. Just give a vague, broad description of what you want the students to do on a project, homework, or

even for a test. Be willing to answer any and all questions about the assignment, but put the burden on the students to find out exactly what is expected. We noted in the first issue of the Big6 Newsletter about encouraging students to do "brain surgery" on their teachers (without actually opening up the skull). Students need to get inside their teacher's head—to figure out exactly what the teacher has in mind—because the students will suffer the consequences if they don't. So, help your students out—by giving little or no direction!

E-mail For Task Definition

v1 n4 p11

By Mike Eisenberg

This tip focuses on baseline communications technologies. See Virtual Dave's column for insights into what's coming next!

Yes—we all readily acknowledge the importance of Task Definition. It's common sense: if students don't understand what's being asked of them, if they don't realize the specifics of the problem as well as the nature of the information required by the task, it's doubtful that they will succeed. Yet, since everyone is so busy in school, it's difficult to find time for meaningful one-on-one discussions between students and teachers about tasks. Some students and teachers have trouble communicating—particularly in the upper grades.

Technology can help. We now have a range of technologies at our disposal to facilitate communications. E-mail, for example, is a basic, but powerful tool. Students can e-mail questions or their interpretations of assignments and get back comments from teachers. In work with undergraduate students, we receive messages on a regular basis asking for clarification on assignments. Oh certainly, there are full instructions posted on the class Web site, and I also communicate with the entire class via a listserv—an electronic discussion group. But, neither of those is personal and direct. And e-mail saves me time compared to a long conversation. I can get right to the point, and even copy and paste from the assignment if necessary. So, even though you may see your students all day long, think about setting up some e-mail capabilities for Task Definition.

p.s. – We also use e-mail for feedback and evaluation. Students can submit short examples of their work, and we can provide some comments.

Task Definition for Those Vague or Confusing Assignments

v2 n1 p7

By Mike Eisenberg

You know about the "vague assignment" problem, don't you? It happens when teachers think they are being clear, but their students don't really understand what's expected of them. It also happens when teachers give students free reign on a report or project— "choose any topic you want, one that interests you"— but many students don't have a clue as to what they are really supposed to do. It's true, teachers think they are motivating students by allowing them to choose something that interests them, but it can just as easily terrify even a conscientious student. And the confusing assignment problem can also happen when teachers do give clear and unambiguous directions, but for some reason the students just don't get it.

For example, in the Helping with Homework (1996) book, we describe an interview with a class about a test they were supposed to take on the following Monday. Only about one quarter of the class really knew what was going to be on the test, what material they should study, or what type of test it would be. Yes, the teacher had gone over the directions, but the students hadn't really "heard" it. Perhaps they were daydreaming, had something else on their minds, or truly didn't understand the directions.

The solution to all these types of problems is not for the teacher to go over the assignment again or strive for more detail and clarity. Rather, we should strive to help the students assume responsibility for their own tasks. We want to move the focus of responsibility for the assignment from the teacher to the students.

For example, we talk to students about doing "brain surgery" on their teachers: "Get inside your teacher's head—quiz the teacher on expectations, criteria for assessment, and key elements. Don't let the teacher move on to something else until you fully understand all aspects of the assignment."

Another tip to encourage student responsibility is to purposely give assignments without much explanation. "You are to create travel brochures on countries." Those are all the directions you need to give. This forces the students to find out the details and can lead to a stimulating exchange on options, key aspects, and grading. Leave time for discussion, but be clear that it's their job to find out what's to be done, not yours to tell them in advance. There may be some difficulties at first, but in the long run, this helps to shift the focus from the teacher to the student.

That's the bottom line—to get the students to take responsibility by thinking Big6. It means starting with Task Definition and not moving on unless they fully understand the task, what it will take to succeed, and the information requirements of the task. Students who use the Big6 in this way, on a regular basis, won't panic when faced with vagueness or ambiguity. They will succeed and thrive.

Focus on Task Definition

v2 n1 p16

By Mike Eisenberg

"Understanding exactly what is expected on homework, assignments, or tests is a key to student success."

In Big6 terms, that's Task Definition—Big6 #1. However, teaching Task Definition is often ignored or overlooked in terms of specific, formal instruction.

Most of the time, teachers do give directions concerning an assignment, but communication about the task is mostly one-way and informational rather than instructional. The assumption is that students will then know what to do and how to do it. But we've found that even students in upper grades really don't understand what is meant by such aspects of assignments as: compare and contrast, cite your sources, summarize, choose among, outline, or describe.

Figure 1: Flash Cards: Eight Common Words in Essay Questions

FRONT	BACK
Compare	Tell about both the similarities and differences
Contrast	Tell about the differences
Define	Explain what it means
Describe	Tell all you can, in an organized way
Discuss	Determine what the different sides are and tell about them
Explain	Clearly tell the details, or reasons or causes
Relate	Tell how things are connected, what they have in common
Summarize	Present your information in as few words as possible

Bob Berkowitz has worked closely with students and their teachers on helping to recognize and understand key terms in assignments and on tests. One technique that Bob uses is to give students an assignment and have them highlight or underline what they think are the key words. Bob and the teacher then go over what is meant by each term, and students make flash cards to help them remember.

To create the flash cards, Bob takes the eight most common words that start essay questions (see Figure 1) and has the students put a key word on one side and the definition on the other side of a card.

Based on their understanding of the assignment or exam question, the students discuss what a successful assignment or exam answer would look like. They do this before actually completing the assignment or answering the question. They key is to get the students thinking about the nature and aspects of the assignment, not just to jump in and do it.

The Big6 Applied to Everyday Situations

v2 n2 p16

By Mike Eisenberg

Successful task definers apply the Big6 skills to everyday tasks and situations:

- Deciding what movie to go to on Saturday night.
- Preparing for a basketball game.
- Picking out a birthday present for a friend.
- Choosing a college to attend.

The "birthday present" problem is one that really grabs the students' attention. Tell the class that you need to buy a birthday present for a niece or nephew who just happens to be about their age. They will immediately make suggestions, so explain that you'd like to use this as an example of solving information problems using the Big6. Eventually go through each stage, but make sure you spend plenty of time focusing on the aspects of the task—what is the problem (Big6 #1.1) and what are the information aspects of the problem (Big6 #1.2).

I also like to organize students in triads—where students assume one of three roles:

- A talker who explains a problem
- A listener/questioner who probes for detail, and
- A recorder who writes it all down.

Later the students switch roles so that each one has a chance to do all three. Finally, the students report back on the problem they recorded (not on their own)—orally to the whole class, in writing to the teacher, or both.

Another technique is to have students keep a "Task Definition Log" for a week or so. Work with the students to develop:

- The criteria for what makes a task or problem
- What data they will record, and
- A chart for recording the data.

The logs can be discussed each day as well as summarized in final presentations that delve into the nature of tasks and problems, and how information, the Big6 Skills, and technology relate to them.

Using everyday situations and problems to teach the Big6 have proved extremely motivating. Students become animated and engaged in the problem at hand. They also begin to see the transferability. That's right—the Big6 is not just for school assignments. As one student said, "It's for fun things too."

CHAPTER 12

The BIG 6

Information Seeking Strategies

TIPS #3: Teaching Information Problem-Solving Brainstorm/Narrow to Set an Information Seeking Strategy

v1 n2 p16

By Bob Berkowitz

Brainstorming all possibilities and then selecting the best for a particular situation is a technique that we use continually in the Big6 approach. For example, in Task Definition, we encourage students to brainstorm possible topics and then select one which best meets the task. We also have students consider various possibilities for presenting information (Synthesis) and select one that will best communicate their information.

Brainstorm/narrow is also valuable in Big6 #2—information seeking strategies. Here, we want students to think of all possible sources that might be relevant to the topic or task, and then to select the best sources. However, the best sources aren't always the ones that are the highest quality or have the most information. Sometimes cost, availability, or ease-of-use (including readability) are the basis for our choices.

So, when teaching Information Seeking Strategies, first have students brainstorm all possibilities. Let them open their minds—even get outrageous. For example, if they are studying space, they might brainstorm "visiting the Kennedy Space Center" or even "traveling on the space shuttle" as possible sources in addition to books, CD-ROMs, encyclopedias, magazines, and Web sites. The Internet and other technologies may just make it possible to use some of these previously unreachable sources. Our challenge is to get students to think—creatively and broadly. Then, in Big6 2.2, they can think critically—evaluating sources based on certain criteria (see chart below) and then narrow. Once they've done this, they now have a plan—an information seeking strategy.

POSSIBLE SOURCES	RELIABLE/ AUTHORITATIVE	VALID (ON THE TOPIC)	ACCURATE	PRECISE	COMPLETE	EASY TO USE	AVAILABLE	CURRENT	COST	FUN

TIPS #2: Information Seeking Strategies: Spying in Sports Via the Internet

v1 n4 p16

By Mike Eisenberg

Articles in the previous two issues explain how sports can be a highly useful context for teaching the Big6. Here are some additional examples that were described in Sports Illustrated, September 29, 1997, pp 78+.

So—here's the task: to find out about an opponent for an upcoming game. What are all the possible sources of information? There's live scouting, videotapes of previous games, magazine articles on the team, interviews with former players and coaches, and press guides. And now, there's information on the World Wide Web as well!

Here are some examples from college football as described in the Sports Illustrated article:

University of Southern California used to have open practices so that Trojans' fans could get more involved. But no more. This season the coach decided to close practice—due to the Internet. Details of the formations and plays that USC worked on in practice in August appeared on some independent Web pages devoted to the Trojans.

In 1996, a detailed practice report about Boston College appeared on the Web before Boston College was to play Virginia Tech. The Boston College coach was quoted as saying it included "things about our practice I didn't know." For example, the report noted some problems with the hike in punt practice and that one of the defensive players had trouble covering the receivers. Did Virginia Tech use this information? No one knows, but they were aware of the report on the Web. Virginia Tech won 45-7.

Many teams now regularly check the Net to see what's there about them and about their opponents. The University of Utah's football team has a designated Web surfer. According to Sports Illustrated, he looks in local Web sites of Utah's opponents for information about player injury and team strategy that doesn't reach the mainstream press. Apparently, he finds quite useful information. For example, before Utah went to play Louisville on Sept. 6, he learned through the Internet that a key Louisville defensive player had a shoulder injury. Utah used this information in setting their strategy. Did it make a difference? Who knows? But Utah did won 27-21.

So, have the students search for information about their favorite teams and favorite sports. See if they can uncover any unique or special information for that competitive advantage.

CHAPTER 13

The
BIG6

Location and Access

TIPS #2: Teaching Information Problem-Solving

v1 n1 p14

By Bob Berkowitz

Here's a tool for location & access—to use when teaching students keyword searching.

Often, students have trouble thinking of terms to use—or they haven't considered how various terms relate to each other. This "bubble chart" provides a framework for helping students to think through their topics, relevant keywords, and connections among the words. Developing skills with keywords is especially important when using the World Wide Web because the various search engines do not have a controlled vocabulary for more precise searching. The bubble chart can be used with other techniques, for example, to organize keywords after "open brainstorming" of possible keywords.

Access: Keyword Searching

The key to access within a resource is the <u>vocabulary</u>. The following exercise will help to develop a rich vocabulary for searching on a particular topic.

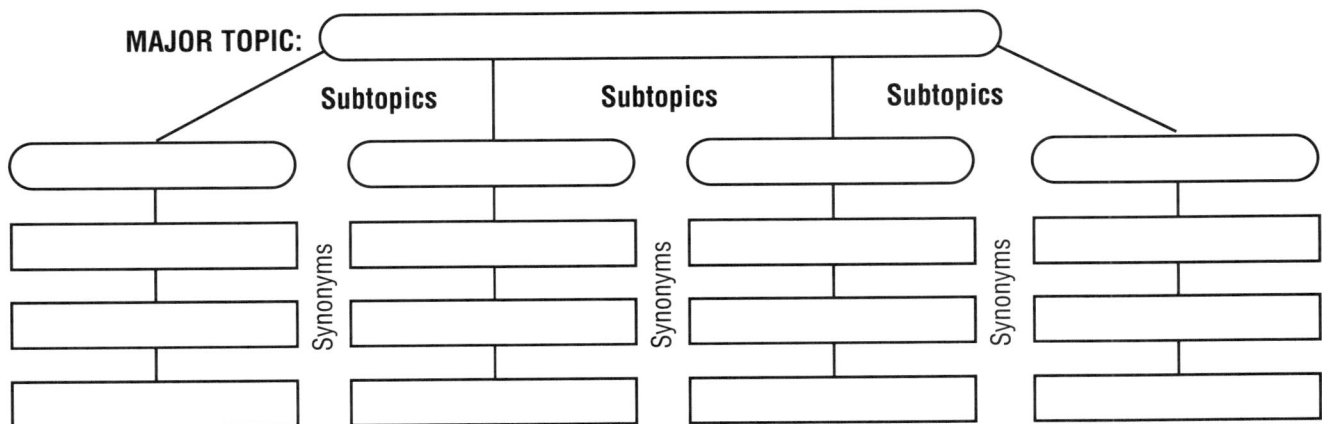

MAJOR TOPIC:

Subtopics   Subtopics   Subtopics

Synonyms   Synonyms   Synonyms

Of course, teaching keyword searching (or any other Big6 Skill™) should only take place in the context of real curricular needs. Some examples include:

- a 4th grade class searching CD-ROM encyclopedias for information on planets for their science reports.
- 8th graders using the WWW for information to write biographies of current newsmakers.
- 11th grade students working on a unit about "war"—using a variety of print, electronic, and online resources to study the causes, nature, and effects of particular wars.
- undergraduate business majors developing profiles of companies in various business sectors.
- adult students learning to use electronic and print reference materials to compile consumer product reviews.

CHAPTER 14

The BIG 6

Use of Information

TIPS #1: Teaching Information Problem-Solving

v1 n1 p13

By Mike Eisenberg

Want to really help your students? Help them to learn to cite their sources—all the time. If you are a classroom teacher, require it—and not just for papers, reports, or projects. We promote citing sources all the time—for every answer to every question on every assignment. Two quick examples:

- Students working on homework questions from their history textbook? Include the page number(s) from the textbook (e.g., p. 165-166) or the citation if another source is used, (e.g., Random House Dictionary, 1992, p. 72).

- Kindergarten students are making pictures of animals? On the back, they can note with a word or symbol whether they used a book themselves (their own knowledge) or if they visited the zoo.

Citing sources is for much more than just "intellectual honesty." Citing adds credibility to students' work, and they learn that we value their work even more when it includes cites.

Citing is also an important tool for assessing where students might be having problems—from a Big6™ perspective. If a student has the wrong

answer to a question is it because he or she was:

- in the wrong section of the book—which might indicate a possible Location and Access problem,
- on the right page but couldn't find the right answer—possibly due to a Use of Information (comprehension) problem, or
- using an inappropriate source—due to difficulties with Information Seeking Strategies.

So, help your students out—get them in the habit of continually citing sources.

The Trash-N-Treasure Note-Taking Technique

v1 n2 p13

By Barbara A. Jansen

Selecting information from sources without copying sentences verbatim is a challenge for most students. This "use of information" (Big6 #4) is a high-level task that requires students to evaluate content in relation to a topic or question. Here's a useful technique that relates note-taking to a pirate's treasure map (show one if possible).

Explain that the pirate's map itself is like the article or chapter of a book containing information about the topic. The X on the map, which marks the exact location of the buried treasure, is the section of the text containing needed information, or an "answer" for specific questions defined in the task.

A pirate must dig for the treasure, tossing aside dirt, weeds, rocks—all the trash. A researcher must dig to find words that help answer the questions—treasure words. Of course, these words are not trash to the original source, only to the researcher because they do not answer the questions defined in the task.

You can demonstrate this concept using an overhead transparency and copies of an encyclopedia article or section. Show a prepared question—with underlined keywords and a list of related words. Scan the article until the appropriate heading is located. Place a slash at the end of the first sentence and read it. Ask *"does this sentence answer the question?"* If the answer is no, tell the students that that sentence is "trash" to them. Go on to the next sentence, placing a slash at the end. Ask the same question. If the answer is yes, underline the first phrase and ask if that phrase answers the question. If the answer is no, underline the next phrase and repeat the question. If the answer is yes, read that phrase word-by-word, asking which words are needed to answer the question—these are treasure words. Circle those words, then write them in the appropriate place on the overhead data chart—or whichever organizer the students are using. Continue phrase by phrase and word by word until coming to the end of the sentence.

Count the words in the sentence and then count the treasure words. Students are very impressed when you say, "The sentence has 17 words and I only needed to write 4 of them. I don't know about you, but I would rather write 4 than 17!"

Demonstrate the process again, allowing the students to practice, using copies of the article. Allow students to independently practice a few times before they begin their own research. Monitor each student's work, re-teaching as necessary.

For more information on this, see Jansen's "Reading for Information: The Trash-n-Treasure Method of Teaching Notetaking" *School Library Media Activities Monthly,* February 1996.)

TIPS #1: Active Listening Strategies

v1 n5 p8

By Bob Berkowitz

Okay–listen up! Time to discuss listening skills.

Listening skills are part of Big6 Skill 4.2 Use of Information: extracting information from a source.

Active listening involves listening for a purpose, selecting main ideas, and mentally or physically noting important information.

Active listening is a necessary skill when attending lectures, listening to speeches, using multimedia presentations, watching instructional television, participating in interpersonal relationships, getting along in the world of work—in other words, for life in general. It is important to provide opportunities for students to analyze presentations and to discover the organizational patterns of information. Some patterns include lists, general-to-specific, cause-and-effect, compare-and-contrast, advantages and disadvantages, or question and answer. By using effective listening strategies, students learn to focus their attention on important points and take notes.

Oral reports provide a perfect occasion to practice effective listening. Instead of merely listening (or pretending to listen), students in the audience can be involved by completing a data collection sheet,

Figure 1:	Immigrant Group

I. Time Period

II. Region

III. Reasons for Immigration
   A.
   B.
   C.

IV. Areas of Settlement
   A.
   B.
   C.

V. Laws and Restrictions
   A.
   B.
   C.

IV. Problems Encountered
   A.
   B.
   C.

VII. Contributions
   A.
   B.
   C.

Figure 2: **U.S. History**

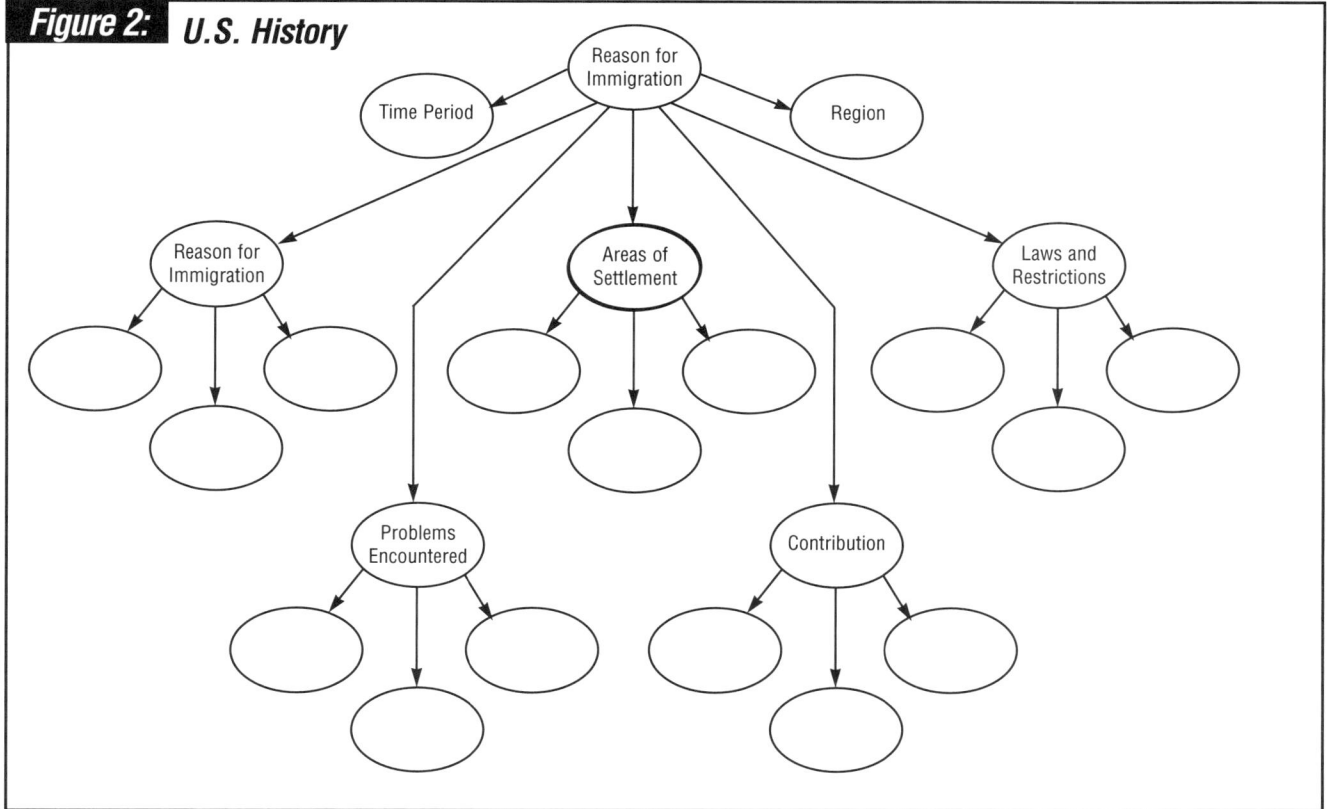

mind map, or outline. To guide students in listening to and extracting information, the teacher can create templates ahead of time for the class to complete. Figures 1, 2, and 3 provide examples of three kinds of templates for recording notes about immigration.

Active listening skills are necessary information survival skills, particularly when you consider that one day your computer may be talking to you and asking you questions. Extracting specific information in an organized manner requires practice. Practicing guided note-taking before moving to independent

Figure 3: **U.S. History**

Immigrant Group   Name:
Region

TIME PERIOD/ DATES	REASONS FOR IMMIGRATION	AREAS OF SETTLEMENT
LAW RESTRICTIONS	PROBLEMS ENCOUNTERED	CONTRIBUTIONS

note-taking enhances the learners' confidence levels and promotes success.

TIPS #1: Structured Note-Taking–A Technique For Coping with Information Overload

v2 n2 p9

By Bob Berkowitz

Quite often, we've observed students who are overwhelmed when they are given an assignment or project requiring them to locate, identify, and use information from a range of information sources. The problem—and we've seen this in grades K through college—is that they aren't able to recognize and pull out relevant information. The challenge for teachers and library media specialists is to help students develop the skills to identify and extract important information so that they will have confidence in their own abilities to tackle these assignments or projects.

The Structured Note-Taking strategy is a simple yet effective Big6 tool that is easily adapted for use in all content areas as well as grade levels. It has been successfully used with social studies, science, and language arts students. For example, it was used extensively with Mr. Hopsicker's students who performed so well on the New York State Regents Exam in U.S. History (see lead article, page 126).

To create a Structured Note-Taking strategy, the teacher or library media specialist must first analyze the content objectives of the assignment, then identify

Teachers can use structured note-taking as a springboard for more elaborate assignments.

a few clear, central areas to help students focus their attention on the materials they will be using.

For example, in an American History class, students had to determine which historical events are important to U.S. foreign policy, who the key people are and how they were involved, and what was the purpose and impact of the U.S. foreign policy. All students were given structured note-taking charts on six foreign policy topics (see Figure 1). Students were then divided into small groups, and each group worked to complete a chart on only one of five foreign policy topics. Later, each group presented their chart to the entire class, and the students were able to practice taking notes from oral presentations. During these group presentations, the teacher had a chance to discuss and correct any misleading information and add any missing information.

Teachers can use structured note-taking as a springboard for more elaborate assignments. Using the example above, the teacher could ask students to refer to their structured notes to:

- Answer an essay question
- Participate in a debate
- Create a combined chart that will help review key concepts, people or events
- Further examine a particular issue.

Since all of the charts were discussed in class, the teacher can be assured that students will be using accurate information to complete these assignments.

Students benefit from the process of completing a structured note-taking information organizer since the process is transferable to other situations—in real life and in school.

Figure 1: The U-2 Incident	
Why was this event important to U.S. foreign policy?	**Who were the significant historical people involved, and how were they involved?**
What was the purpose of this U.S. foreign policy?	**What was the impact of this foreign policy on the U.S./World?**

TIPS #1: Note-Taking 101

v2 n5 p15

By Verna LaBounty

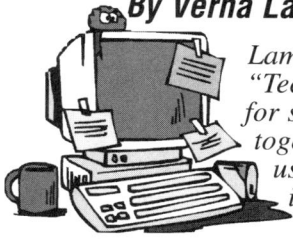

Lament heard in the teachers' room: "Technology just makes it easier for students to copy. They can put together an entire report just by using cut and paste. No thinking is required."

It is all too true that some students will turn in reports that contain none of their own thoughts and analysis. However, it is possible to model a technique for using technology to improve both the content and the originality of students' work. Using a computer to gather and organize information is a natural extension of students' skills beyond searching for information. Students will work with enthusiasm when technology becomes a tool in the note-taking and organizing process. The steps for using technology for note-taking and Synthesis include:

STEP #1: TAKE ELECTRONIC NOTES

Students take "electronic notes" by copying and pasting from encyclopedia and periodical databases and from the Internet. They add to these notes by using word processing to include information they find in books. For each item, they include the bibliographic citation information as part of the notes.

STEP #2: REFINE ELECTRONIC NOTES

A keystroke and a mouse click replace the shuffling and organizing of paper and pencil note cards. Students choose the main ideas, the "treasure," by highlighting facts, terms, quotes, and definitions.

STEP #3: ANALYZE INFORMATION AND CREATE TOPICS

Students analyze their information and create topics and sub-topics. This helps them organize the information in a logical fashion. Students include these topics and sub-topics by word processing their ideas and by choosing a different text color for each. For example, in creating a biographical report, a student could use red text for personal information, blue for career highlights, and orange for accomplishments.

STEP #4: REVIEW NOTES

Students go back through their notes and go through a process of highlighting the information fitting in a topic or sub-topic and changing the text color of that

Students will work with enthusiasm when technology becomes a tool in the note-taking and organizing process.

information to match the topic's or sub-topic's chosen text color. When this step is complete, the students end up with multi-colored notes.

STEP #5: REARRANGE MATERIAL

Students rearrange the colored material using the process of cut and paste to organize information by topics and sub-topics. They add appropriate topic headings. Other possibilities for completing this step include copying pertinent information to a database file, using a spreadsheet with columns, or copying information to various kinds of graphic organizers. When students have finished this step, they can see the leftover, unneeded information and can analyze the chosen information, "the treasure," to identify any gaps they need to fill.

STEP #6: INDIVIDUAL CONFERENCE

The teacher holds an individual conference with each student to review the organizational plan for their papers and to help them identify gaps.

STEP #7: DELETE THE TRASH

Students delete the "trash;" the leftover irrelevant information and do further research to fill any gaps they identified.

STEP #8: USE ELECTRONIC NOTES

Students use their electronic notes to write a report using their individual prose style.

STEP #9: CREATE BIBLIOGRAPHY

Students create a bibliography using the citation information they saved in the note-taking process.

STEP #10: TURN IN PAPER

Students turn in an original paper.

TIPS #1: Like To Use Textbooks? Here's a Big6 Option For You

v2 n3 p16

By Mike Eisenberg

In the interview with Scott Hopsicker (see page 129), Bob Berkowitz advised Scott to improve his presentation of information by concentrating on important facts rather than getting bogged down in teaching every small fact included in the textbook. This brought to mind the subject of textbooks and review books.

Schools need to provide students with information resources that explain the basic curriculum. The problem is, schools generally fulfill this need by spending a small fortune each year on elaborate, glossy, expensive textbooks. But textbooks often cover only part of the school, district, or even state curriculum. Textbooks include many other topics as well as "enrichment" activities and sections that teachers and students never use. Even more importantly, enrichment is better handled through a broad resource-based learning approach anyway. We don't want to spoon-feed students when they go beyond the specific curriculum. We want them to explore on their own and learn how to find and use the full range of digital and print resources.

So, here's an alternative to contemplate. Why not save some money by using inexpensive review books instead of textbooks for the core curriculum? Then, use outside resources to flesh out the core as well as to go beyond the core. In New York State, for example, there are Regents Review books for every state-wide curriculum. There are similar books for almost every subject area—even at the university level, especially in law and medical schools. Review books identify the key aspects of a curriculum, present the material in a succinct, well-organized manner, and provide opportunities to practice responding to sample exam questions.

Teachers, parents, and students already turn to review books in the few weeks preceding exams. Why wait until the end? Why not start earlier—say on the first day of school? Review books are particularly valuable for Use of Information—Big6 Skill #4 because they provide straightforward explanations of course material. Further, these explanations are usually presented in the same format using the same vocabulary that is found on the tests. Considering the difficulties we all face with information overload, review books are a welcome relief.

So, the Big6 tip is to find a good review book and use it early in the year. You might even consider using review books instead of textbooks. You'll be helping students to learn the course material and succeed on tests. You'll save money and have time to extend students' learning with resource-based activities as well.

CHAPTER 15

Synthesis

TIPS #2: Synthesis Ideas that Make Dollars and Sense

v2 n6 p16

By Bob Berkowitz

Does your school teach business or basic economics as part of the curriculum? Here are some Big6 ideas for high school related to teaching business and economic concepts to capture your students' interest and create excitement. These six Synthesis ideas are also applicable to other situations:

1. Take a survey to find out how different students would spend $20, $200, $2,000.

2. Show the differences and similarities between getting money from a pawnshop, a bank, a credit card, or a loan company.

3. Make a dictionary of "money" words, such as: collateral, interest, withdrawal, debit, asset, liability, etc.

4. Make a chart to show how prices of goods have been affected by war, scarcity of materials, strikes, interest rates, etc.

5. Make a scrapbook of newspaper, magazine and Internet advertisements that encourage people to shop or buy on credit.

6. Using percentages that equal 100, make a budget for a family's expenses, and show how this budget would change if more people were added, if a family member were to go to college, or if one of the main income earners became unemployed.

> *...In order to turn a good idea into a good instructional activity you need to consider the purpose for the instruction, the goals and objectives of the unit, and how the unit fits into the overall curriculum plan.*

Each of these ideas can act as the starting point for creating high quality instructional units that reflect authentic learning. However, in order to turn a good idea into a good instructional activity you need to consider the purpose for the instruction, the goals and objectives of the unit, and how the unit fits into the overall curriculum plan.

In planning the instructional unit, answer these basic questions:

- Is this unit really necessary?
- What are my students' basic skills?
- What assumptions am I making regarding students basic competencies concerning the unit content and the Big6 Skills?

- What will the students' next step be after they complete the unit?
- How will the significance of this unit be conveyed to students?

To improve the quality of learning, keep in mind that students learn better if they:

- Understand the reasons for doing the assignment
- Know what they are trying to learn

- Find the assignment challenging, but not impossible
- Have the resources to complete the assignment
- Enjoy what they are doing
- Receive positive comments when they are done.

We invite you to add to this list and use it as your own yardstick to measure the effectiveness of your instructional activities.

CHAPTER 16

Evaluation

TIPS #1: Evaluation - Recognizing Nonlinearity in the Process

v1 n3 p11

By Mike Eisenberg

While the Big6 process is often presented in a stepwise fashion (from #1 Task Definition through #6 Evaluation), people do not generally work that way. From experience, we find that successful information problem-solving requires successful completion of each of the Big6 stages at some point. But, in any given situation, individuals may jump around, branch off, or loop back. Therefore, we emphasize that the Big6 approach advocates developing competence in each of the Big6 areas, but does not require a lock-step marching through the process. The graphic on page 56 also illustrates this point.

One way to demonstrate this to students is to have them compare their own problem-solving process to the Big6. Here's an exercise that does this:

Choose a recent homework or class assignment, and have the students recall what they did.

> *From experience, we find that successful information problem-solving requires successful completion of each of the Big6 stages at some point. But, in any given situation, individuals may jump around, branch off, or loop back.*

Ask the students to write on index cards the steps that they took to complete the homework, step-by-step, one step to a card. For example, what did they do first? "Read all the questions." Next? "Skimmed the chapter." Third? "Re-read the first question." And so on.

Give them plenty of opportunities to create additional cards and to change the order until they are satisfied that they have reasonably described their process. Number the cards in order.

Next, have the students match each of their cards to the Big6. They can do this by writing the corresponding Big6 number on their index cards. If more than one Big6 skill seems to apply, have them select the one that best describes their step.

Finally, have the students compare the order of their process to the Big6 order. Have them sort the cards two times—once in their step-by-step order and then according to the Big6. Or, have them create two tables—one in Big6 order and the other in their order. Older students can also create time sequence graphs that do the same comparisons.

Students will get the point—that while they mostly do all the Big6 stages, they don't generally do them in a linear Big6 order. And that's just fine!

CHAPTER 17

The BIG 6

Conclusion

TIPS #2: Big6 With a Country Twist

v2 n1 p14-15

By Bob Berkowitz

More and more teachers, library media specialists, and technology coordinators are providing Big6 in-service sessions or Big6 orientation programs for their faculty. As a wrap-up to these sessions, it's nice to have a group activity that will reinforce the Big6 stages. Here is a group activity (for adults) that will catch your audience's attention and provide a laugh or two.

After the entire Big6 session try this closing activity with your faculty:

■ Divide the faculty into 10 small groups. Give each group one of the sets of country and western phrases (see Figure 1 on page 114), a piece of poster board or large piece of newsprint paper, and a wide tip marker.

■ Direct each group to choose one phrase and write it on the poster board. Later in the activity, the poster board will be used as a cue card.

■ Invite one member of each group to come to the front of the room with that group's cue card.

■ Position these volunteers in a row, from 1 to 10, facing the audience, and ask them to hold the cue cards so that no one in the audience can see the written phrases.

■ Using the overhead projector, show the "Do-it-Yourself Country & Western Song" (see Figure 2 on page 114) to the faculty audience.

■ Tell the volunteers that they will need to reveal their numbered phrase in time for the rest of the faculty to sing the song.

■ Invite the faculty to sing the song to the tune of "Red River Valley," filling in the blanks as the cue cards are revealed one at a time.

After singing (and laughing), you can review the activity from a Big6 perspective by focusing on any or all of the Big6 stages. For example, you can prompt the audience to tell you how each of the Big6 stages could be defined in terms of the activity:

■ **TASK DEFINITION:** What was the task? Ask audience members to define the task. This provides an opportunity to point out that it isn't always easy to follow verbal directions.

■ **INFORMATION SEEKING STRATEGIES:** What were the possible information sources?

■ **LOCATION & ACCESS:** Where were the information sources?

■ **USE OF INFORMATION:** How was the information engaged?

■ **SYNTHESIS:** How were information sources organized and presented?

■ **EVALUATION:** Was the task carried out successfully? Did they laugh?

However you use or expand on it, using the "Do-it-Yourself Country & Western Song" can provide an interesting and humorous context for reinforcing the Big6 skills approach.

NOTE: *This instructional activity is based on:* Do-it-Yourself Country & Western Song Kit *which is located at* **www.nzso.co.nz/fun/cw-kit.html.**

Figure 1: **Country and Western Phrases**

1.
on the highway
in Sheboygan
outside Fresno
at a truck stop

2.
in September
at McDonalds
ridin' shotgun
wrestlin' gators

3.
that purple dress
that little hat
those training pants
that creepy smile

4.
sobbin' at the toll booth
drinkin' Dr. Pepper
weighted down with Twinkies
crawlin' through the prairie

5.
in the twilight
but I loved her
by the off-ramp
near Poughkeepsie

6.
no guy would ever love her more
she'd bought her dentures in a store
that she would be a crashing bore
that she was rotten to the core

7.
I promised her
She asked me if
I told her shrink
The judge declared

8.
stay with her
swear off booze
have my rash
hate her dog

9.
our love would never die
there was no other guy
man wasn't meant to fly
that Nixon didn't lie

10.
run off
wind up
boogie
yodel

11.
with my best friend
in my Edsel
on a surfboard
with her dentist

12.
You'd think at least that she'd have said
I never had the chance to say
She told her dumb friend Grace to say
I watched her melt away and sobbed

Figure 2: **Do-it-Yourself Country & Western Songs**

I met her _____; _____; I can still recall _____

she wore; she was _____ _____,

and I knew _____; _____ I'd _____ forever;

She said to me _____; But who'd have thought she'd _____

_____; _____ goodbye.

TIPS #1: Big6 Booktalking

v1 n6 p9

By Mike Eisenberg

Booktalking from a Big6 perspective means promoting literature and reading in two contexts: (1) the context of student needs and (2) the context of the Big6 process. To guarantee success, booktalk in context and following these guidelines:

- Link your booktalks to an assignment or real student need.
- Select 15-20 books that meet the assignment.
- You don't have to talk about all the books you bring.
- You don't have to bring a book for every student.
- For each book, talk about something that will grab the students' attention: plot, theme, characters, a story about the author, other books by the author that you have read.
- Always be honest with the students. If you haven't read a book, say so. Never tell them you think a book is good if you really don't know.
- Be prepared to sign out the books on the spot.
- As soon as a student indicates he or she wants a book, stop talking about it and pass it to that student.
- If students appear uninterested, pass each book around after talking about it.
- Keep the booktalk moving.
- Follow-up the booktalk with a display including any books not selected in the class and other books that meet the criteria of the assignment.

TIPS #2: Motivation in Teaching the Big6

v1 n5 p16

By Mike Eisenberg

Want to create Big6 excitement? Make the Big6 relevant to the needs of an individual or group. We have worked with audiences on using the Big6 in relation to:

- Winning at sports,
- Completing a project,
- Buying and selling stocks,
- Doing well on a standardized test,
- Buying a birthday present for someone, and
- Selecting a college.

We also find that it is important to emphasize specific Big6 Skills within the overall process. We don't just talk about learning to search the Web. We talk about searching the Web as a Location & Access skill within the overall Big6 process. This allows learners to place the skill within context.

Making the Big6 relevant to individual and group interests actually relates to a more general model of instructional motivation—John Keller's ARCS model:

A-ATTENTION: Get and sustaining attention. It's essential to immediately grab attention, but it's also important to keep their attention over time. Of course, getting and sustaining attention by itself is simply entertainment, and that isn't enough for a learning situation.

R-RELEVANCE: Make the learning relevant to an individual's or group's academic, professional, or personal needs and interests. Relevance is a clear key to success.

C-CONFIDENCE: Use instructional strategies that build confidence in the learners. This involves analyzing the learners and creating instruction that will lead to their success. It is important that students feel capable of doing well.

S-SATISFACTION: Finish with a positive feeling. What was learned was worth the time and effort.

These four motivation elements are easily applied to teaching the Big6 Skills. We can capture attention by selecting topic like technology, the information age, success, and the future. Most audiences are interested in these topics. Relevance, as noted above, means teaching the Big6 in context. Confidence requires us to make sure that we aren't trying to do too much at one time and that we analyze our instruction in terms of students' abilities to succeed. Satisfaction means paying attention to audience reactions and being willing and able to make adjustments.

ARCS works! If you gain, grab, and sustain attention, make the instruction relevant to needs, give students confidence that they can do it, and have them walk away satisfied with the experience, then you are guaranteed a successful learning and teaching experience.

For more information, see Small, Ruth V. Designing Motivation into Library and Information Skills Instruction, *School Library Media Quarterly Online,* **http://www.ala.org/aasl/SLMQ/small.html.**

The BIG 6

Teaching Technology & Information Skills

PART V

Assessment

Student Self-Assessment Skills: Focus on Success

v1 n1 p6-7

By Bob Berkowitz

This article will appear in two parts. Part one explains the importance of student self-assessment skills and how, by sharpening these skills, students and teachers can see excellent results, both in and out of the classroom. Part two (in the next issue) provides specific techniques and tools to help students improve their self-assessment skills.

Self-assessment

Students who are truly active learners continually self-assess. Self-assessment is personal, constructive feedback that can motivate and excite students to higher levels of achievement. Through self-assessment, students learn to translate expectations into action—to build on their accomplishments and work on weaknesses.

Self-assessment is the central part of Big6™ #6 - Evaluation. Through self-assessment, students assume responsibility for their own learning and success. From the Big6™ perspective, evaluation is defined as making judgments based on a predetermined set of criteria. Students learn to assess the results of their efforts by analyzing the effectiveness of their product and their efficient use of the information problem-solving strategy.

We believe it is crucial to help students learn to:

- value and recognize quality work,
- reflect on the ways they go about tackling assignments and tasks,
- determine how they can improve,
- recognize the relationship between self-discipline and achievement, and
- gain self-confidence in solving information problems.

Students are able to examine their own progress as well as strengths and weaknesses. Even young children can determine if they are effective (having done a good job or worthy of a good grade) or efficient (not wasting time and effort). As students get older, they can assume more and more responsibility for their own achievement and assessment of that achievement. Teachers can reinforce self-assessment by involving students in developing criteria, grading schemes, and rubrics. Teachers can also help students to generalize from "schoolwork assessment" (on projects, tests,

> *"In order for students to do their best in school they must be able to judge the quality of their own work—their product and processes."*

assignments) to success in areas of personal interest (sports, art, music, hobbies), and ultimately at work (job satisfaction, salary, making a contribution).

Good information problem solvers are good at self-assessment. In order for students to do their best in school they must be able to judge the quality of their own work—their product and processes. It is difficult, if not impossible, for students to do their best if they don't know how to recognize it when they see it. All too often students are left to guess at such things as whether they are finished with an assignment or whether they have done a good job on an assignment. Students should be able to compare their efforts against teacher expectations and established standards, and when necessary, revise or redirect their effort.

Student Encouragement

Students don't often take the initiative to self-assess because they haven't been encouraged to do so, may not see the value in self-assessment, or may not know how to do so. That's where the Big6™ approach comes in. The Big6™ reminds us that evaluation is essential to the process. As teachers, we must provide students with opportunities to learn self-assessment in the context of curriculum, personal, or work situations.

Feelings are an important part of self-assessment. Students may lack confidence and pride in their work because they don't really know whether or not they have done a good job. Or, feelings of confidence and pride are replaced with frustration and disappointment when they get their assignment back with a poor grade when they expected to do well. Self-assessment helps students to apply the same evaluation criteria as teachers do to their work. They learn to look at their work through their teachers' eyes. In this way, students can build on strengths and identify areas for improvement. Students gain insight into specific areas to improve their performance. This can boost confidence, pride, and a higher level of academic success.

We often assume that students are able to rate the quality of their products or the effectiveness of their approach to solving information problems, but of course, this is not always the case. Self-assessment skills should not be assumed—they should be part of the instructional program. Students need to be taught what the standards of excellence are and how to recognize and apply them. Again, it's helping students to learn to view themselves in the ways that teachers do. In this vein, we see two key areas of self-assessment as part of the Big6 Skills™ approach: assessing effectiveness of the product (Big6™ #6.1) and efficiency of the process (Big6™ #6.2).

In effectiveness, students learn to judge their products. Students can learn to diagnose the result of their effort when they learn to do such things as:

■ compare the requirements to the results

■ check the appropriateness and accuracy of the information they use

■ judge how well their solution is organized

■ rate the quality of their final product or performance compared to their potential (i.e., Did I do the best that I could?)

■ judge the quality of their product to a predefined standard.

Assessing Efficiency

Assessing efficiency involves students in evaluating the nature, tendencies, and preferences of their personal information problem-solving process. This is sometimes referred to as, "meta-cognition" — recognizing how we learn, process information, and solve problems. From a Big6 perspective, we can help students to learn how to assess the efficiency of the process they use to reach decisions and solutions. Some techniques to facilitate this include:

■ keeping and evaluating a log of activities

■ reflecting back on the sequence of events and judging effort and time involved

■ reviewing and analyzing the areas of frustration and barriers they came up against

■ rating their abilities to perform specific information problem-solving actions. (i.e., locating, note taking, skimming, scanning, prioritizing).

In Summary

For self-assessment to be useful, students must be able to make judgments about both the quality of their decisions and products as well as the process they used to get there. Self-assessment, for both content and process, should be based on predeveloped and understood criteria. Whenever possible, establishing criteria should be a cooperative effort among classroom teachers, library media and technology teachers, and of course, students.

Self-assessment leads to academic success. It is difficult, if not impossible, for students to do their best if they don't know how to recognize it when they see it. All too often students are left to guess at such things as whether they are finished with an assignment or whether they have done a good job on an assignment.

The next installment of this article will discuss specific techniques and tools to help students improve their self-assessment skills.

Student Self-Assessment Skills: Focus on Success, part II

v1 n2 p4-5

By Bob Berkowitz

This article is a continuation from the September 1997 issue. Part I explained the importance of student self-assessment skills, and how by sharpening these skills, students can improve their performance. Part II provides specific techniques and tools to help students improve their self-assessment skills.

Ask & Answer

There are many techniques to help students learn self-assessment. For example, a practical, easy-to-implement technique that provides meaningful information to students about their own work is a simple "Ask & Answer" sheet (see Figure 1). "Ask & Answer" leads students to evaluate their own product and process and to reflect on how they might improve in the future. While the sample provided is aimed at middle-elementary age students, it could be easily adjusted for various ages.

The key to the "Ask & Answer" format is to pose meaningful questions that provide insight into both the content knowledge and information skills abilities. Some typical target questions on specific aspects of the Big6 process include:

TASK DEFINITION:

■ Did I do what was asked?

■ Did I have enough information?

INFORMATION SEEKING STRATEGIES:

■ Were my information sources helpful?

■ Should I have found and used other sources?

LOCATION AND ACCESS:

■ Was it easy to find sources and information within sources?

USE OF INFORMATION:

■ Did I have trouble understanding the information in sources?

SYNTHESIS:

■ How well is my project organized?

■ Did I have a good plan to organize my information/project?

■ Does my project include all the appropriate information I found?

Figure 1: Ask & Answer

How will I know I did a good job? (How will my teacher grade the assignment?)

1. _____

2. _____

3. _____

4. _____

Did I do the best job I could do?

How proud am I of my project?

How proud am I of my effort?

To get a better result next time, I could:

1. _____

2. _____

3. _____

4. _____

Figure 2: Group Participation Assessment

Name: _____ Date: _____
Assignment: _____

Now that you have finished your group assignment, take time to think about what you have accomplished. Write a self-evaluation of this experience.

1. Briefly describe the steps that you and your group took to complete the assignment. What happened first, second, and so forth? Did the group divide up the tasks? If so, how was this decided and how was it done?

2. Reflect on the steps outlined in (1). What do you think worked well? What could use improvement?

3. Consider the steps taken in relation to the Big6? Are there Big6 skills that you and your group did particularly well? Are there steps that need improvement?

4. Assess your own effort. Comment on:
   - the nature and quality of your contribution to your group's final product.
   - the nature and quality of your participation as a group member and group leader.
   - what you learned about the subject and, more importantly, working with others.
   - what you did well.
   - what you would do differently the next time you have to work with a group on an assignment.

Figure 3: Formative Self-assessment

Directions:

Each day, use this form to record short descriptions of your feelings as you work through your assignment. Also note any successes or concerns you have. For any negative feelings or for concerns, note possible actions you might take to resolve them.

DATE	BIG6 STAGE	FEELINGS	SUCCESSES/CONCERNS	ACTION

EVALUATION:

- Is my project good; how do I know?
- Am I proud of my project/effort?
- What could I do better next time?

Raising self-assessment questions allows students to take time to reflect on what they have learned, their accomplishments, and areas for improvement. Students become comfortable with reflecting on their own abilities. Rather than passive reactors to teachers' assessments, students are active participants in judging their knowledge and skills. Figure 2 provides additional examples of how to do this.

When students consider and answer these kinds of questions, they gain insight into their own skills and abilities as Big6 information problem-solvers. The goal is to help students become independent self-assessors.

Assessment

Self-assessment can also take place during an assignment. This is formative assessment as opposed to after-the-fact or summative assessment. In formative self-assessment, students reflect on their skills and progress as part of working on an assignment. This may result in students redefining the task, changing an approach, or realizing that they need help. Conversely, students may recognize that they are right on target and should continue.

Figure 3 is an example of guiding students through formative self-assessment. The students are asked to make daily notes of their feelings and successes and concerns as they work through an assignment. There's also an opportunity to brainstorm possible actions to take to improve a situation.

Scoring Guides

Another useful technique that can be used for formative or summative assessment is to provide students with an "assessment scoring guide." Sometimes called "rubrics," scoring guides designate specific levels of performance related to stated criteria. For example, for a scientific experiment, a criteria for Big6 #5 (Synthesis) might relate to the completeness and accuracy of data tables and graphs.

Students can use criteria and scoring ranges such as: "highly competent, competent, and not yet acceptable." For example, "complete and accurate

"Rather than passive reactors to teachers' assessments, students are active participants in judging their knowlege and skills."

data tables and appropriate and complete graphs" would score Highly Competent. Whereas, "incomplete but accurate data tables and appropriate but incomplete graphs" would score Competent. Furthermore, "no data tables or graphs" would score Not Yet Acceptable.

These scoring ranges allow students to assess themselves or to compare their judgments with those of their teacher or library media specialist. Students can also develop their own criteria—actively participating in creating the scoring guide. See the next issue of the *Big6 Newsletter* for examples and more on scoring guides.

Self-assessment is a crucial component of the Big6 process—stage #6, evaluation. approach. From experience, we have found that successful self-assessment activities should:

- connect to meaningful assignments.
- engage students in concrete tasks of reflecting and responding to a predetermined criteria.
- involve students in sharing their insights with classroom teachers, library media specialists, technology teachers, and other instructional staff.
  - be sustained and ongoing.
  - be an integral part of the assignment and "count" as part of the grade.

Self-assessment is central to information problem-solving because it teaches students to:

- determine the strengths and weaknesses of their solutions.
- justify decisions based on criteria.
- understand the value of using a process to solve information problems.
- become self-directed/self-motivated to produce quality work.

Focusing on student self-assessment fosters the role of teacher as guide, coach, and facilitator rather than center of all knowledge and ultimate arbitrator. Students assume control and responsibility for their own work and become active participants in their learning.

The "life-span" of teaching students to self-assess goes beyond a single experience. The skills build over time and the impact will linger a lifetime.

Assessment: Big6 Scoring Guides for Diagnosis and Prescription

v1 n3 p4-5, 14-15

By Bob Berkowitz

Articles on assessment in the previous two issues focused on student self-assessment and introduced various techniques for conducting assessment. With all that's going on in schools, it's unrealistic to expect teachers, librarians, and even students to be able to add elaborate information skills assessment activities to what they already do. We need an effective and easy-to-use tool to help with assessment. Here it is: the Big6 Scoring Guide.

Big6 Scoring Guides are designed to communicate expectations for students' work and achievement in ways that students can understand and use. Big6 Scoring Guides focus on the process of solving information problems as well as the final result. Therefore, guides are useful both during and after working on assignments—for both formative and summative assessment.

Formative assessment, as explained in previous articles, involves diagnosing students' performance during learning so that adjustments can be made before students turn in their work. Adjustments may include:

■ redirecting planned instruction to focus on areas where students are having trouble

■ providing special learning activities not previously planned

■ helping students to apply relevant technology tools

■ redefining the problem or returning to a previous Big6 stage

■ offering one-on-one tutoring

■ brainstorming alternative approaches.

These types of adjustments are prescriptions for improving learning. Of course, Big6 Scoring Guides can also be used to assess final products: summative assessment. In working with teachers, we find that post-assignment debriefings—built around Big6 Scoring Guides—are effective ways of involving students in the assessment process.

To create Big6 Scoring Guides

1. Define the curriculum objectives within a Big6 context.

2. Determine which Big6 Skills are important (the focus) for this particular assignment.

3. Develop criteria across a scale (from "highly competent" to "not yet acceptable"). There may be more than one aspect to each criteria. Consider which aspects are essential.

4. Determine what evidence will be examined to determine student performance for each Big6 skill.

5. Conduct the assessment.

6. Share the assessment with students.

7. Revise as necessary.

Figure A: *Muscular Action Worksheet*

Your task is to design a controlled experiment to test the hypothesis below. Your experiment should be designed so that it can be conducted in a 15- to 20-minute period.

HYPOTHESIS:
When there is an increase in muscular activity, there is a corresponding increase in the energy used by muscles. This energy increase causes heat as well as a corresponding increase in oxygen consumption.

MATERIAL:

PROCEDURE:

RESULT: (tabulate data and represent in an appropriate graph)

CONCLUSION:

QUESTIONS:
■ What variable(s) did you test?
■ What are the constants?
■ What was the experimental control?
■ Evaluation/Scoring Guide

For example, assume that completing Figure A is the task for students in ninth-grade biology studying "muscular activity." Figure B is the Big6 Scoring Guide designed to assess students' performance. This guide is designed to include multiple assessments—by student (S), teacher (T), and library media specialist (L). This allows students and teachers to quickly identify gaps in their views of perceived performance. Focusing on gaps can lead to clarification of misunderstandings and highlighting the need for further instruction.

The column labeled "Evidence" indicates the products or techniques used to assess specific skills. Examples of evidence include written, visual, or oral products, assignments, homework,

projects, tests, observation, or even self-reflection. This is an essential piece of the Scoring Guide since it identifies the specific context for assessing student performance.

The last column, "Focus," relates to the relative importance of each skill being evaluated. It is not necessary or desirable to assess all Big6 skills equally in every learning situation. The assigned focus should be based on the goals and objectives of the unit in terms of Big6 skill development and content learning. For example, in the muscle example, a percentage of emphasis is assigned to each of the Big6 skills. Location & Access is not a skill emphasized in this situation while Task Definition, Information Seeking Strategy and Synthesis are.

Figure B: Big6 Scoring Guide for Muscular Action

Big6™ Assessment Scoring Guide

Big6™ Skills		Criteria							Evidence	Focus
		Highly Competent		Competent		Adequate		Not Yet Acceptable		
Eisenberg/ Berkowitz © 1997		10 points		8 points		7 points		5 points		
1. Task Definition 1.1 Define the problem. 1.2 Identify the information needed.	S T L	Experiment meets 15-20 minute requirements. Procedure tested: oxygen consumption & levels of heat.	S T L	Experiment limited to 15-20 minute requirements. Procedure tested: oxygen consumption or level of heat, but not both.	S T L	Experiment did not meet time requirement. Procedure tested: oxygen consumption or level of heat, but not both.	S T L	Experiment did not meet time requirement. Procedure did not test for either; oxogen consumption or levels of heat.	Experiment	20%
2. Information Seeking Strategies 2.1 Determine all possible sources. 2.2 Select the best sources.	S T L	Procedure can be repeated exactly and produce the same results. Procedure tests the hypothesis.	S T L	Procedure tested the hypothesis, but is not easily followed.	S T L	Procedure tested the hypothesis, but is not easily followed, and does not give the same results.	S T L	Procedure does not test the hypothesis. Procedure cannot be repeated at all.	Procedure	40%
3. Location & Access 3.1 Locate sources. 3.2 Find information within sources.	S T L		S T L		S T L		S T L			
4. Use of Information 4.1 Engage (e.g., read hear, view, and touch). 4.2 Extract relevant information.	S T L	Complete and accurate data tables. Complete and appropriate graphs.	S T L	Accurate data tables. Appropriate but incomplete graphs.	S T L	Incomplete data tables. Incomplete and inaccurate graphs.	S T L	No data tables. No graphs.	Results	10%
5. Synthesis 5.1 Organize information from multiple sources. 5.2 Present the result.	S T L	Appropriate conclusion. Answers all questions completely.	S T L	Appropriate conclusion. Answers all questions poorly.	S T L	Conclusion attempted, but inappropriate. Questions poorly answered and/or only some questions answered.	S T L	No Conclusion. No questions answered.	Conclusion Question	20%
6. Evaluation 6.1 Judge the result. 6.2 Judge the process.	S T L	Scoring Guide thoughtfully completed	S T L		S T L		S T L	Scoring Guide not completed.	Scoring Guide	10%

Figure C: Blank Big6 Scoring Guide

Big6™ Assessment Scoring Guide

Big6™ Skills	← Criteria →				Evidence	Focus
	Highly Competent	**Competent**	**Adequate**	**Not Yet Acceptable**		
Eisenberg/ Berkowitz © 1997	10 points	8 points	7 points	5 points		
1. Task Definition 1.1 Define the problem. 1.2 Identify the information needed.	S T L	S T L	S T L	S T L		
2. Information Seeking Strategies 2.1 Determine all possible sources. 2.2 Select the best sources.	S T L	S T L	S T L	S T L		
3. Location & Access 3.1 Locate sources. 3.2 Find information within sources.	S T L	S T L	S T L	S T L		
4. Use of Information 4.1 Engage (e.g., read hear, view, and touch). 4.2 Extract relevant information.	S T L	S T L	S T L	S T L		
5. Synthesis 5.1 Organize information from multiple sources. 5.2 Present the result.	S T L	S T L	S T L	S T L		
6. Evaluation 6.1 Judge the result. 6.2 Judge the process.	S T L	S T L	S T L	S T L		

S-Student, T-Teacher, L-Library Media Specialist

The hardest part of creating Big6 Scoring Guides is writing the specific statements of performance under each criteria and Big6 skill. We find that people get much better at this over time. Figure C is provided as a template to help you practice.

We also find that collaboration helps. Try working with library media specialists, other teachers, and even students. In fact, having students participate in creating their own Big6 Scoring Guides is an excellent technique for teaching the Big6 Skills of Task Definition and Evaluation.

The Big6 and Student Achievement: Report of an Action Research Study

v2 n2 p1, 6-7, 15

By Mike Eisenberg & Bob Berkowitz

This article describes one of the most exciting Big6 developments ever. We are constantly asked, "Do you have proof that the Big6 makes a difference? We know that it feels like the Big6 helps students to succeed, but do you have any evidence of impact?" Until recently, our response would be, "No, but we are working on it." Well, wait no longer! With this article, we are finally able to report the results of an action research effort on the impact of the Big6 in a specific curriculum situation. Yes! The Big6 makes a difference, and here's a dramatic example of how and how much.

Setting the Scene

Scott Hopsicker is a social studies teacher at **Wayne Central High School** in 1997-1998. Wayne Central is located near Rochester, New York. Even though he had been a teacher at Wayne Central for only two years, Mr. Hopsicker was a very active and popular teacher—he was involved in coaching as well as teaching, and was well-liked by his students. But Mr. Hopsicker had a problem. In his first year as a teacher, his students did not perform well on the New York State Regents Exam in American History. Only 53% passed the Regents exam, a standardized test that most New York State students must take. Needless to say, Mr. Hopsicker was concerned about his students, and wanted to do something to help them improve their scores. He spoke to the Assistant Principal, who suggested that Hopsicker discuss the situation with Bob Berkowitz, the library media specialist. Bob has had success with helping students on Advanced Placement tests in various subjects. Maybe he could help Mr. Hopsicker. Mr. Hopsicker saw

himself as a conscientious, well-prepared teacher. He obviously needed a new strategy.

The students at Wayne Central are a heterogeneous group. In 1997-98, Mr. Hopsicker had a total of 59 students in three sections of American History. This group was similar to the previous year's students—nothing made the students stand out. Last year, only 53% of his students passed the American History Regents Exam. There was no reason to expect this situation to change unless Mr. Hopsicker changed his approach. He went to see Bob.

The Big6 Intervention

Bob Berkowitz began working with Mr. Hopsicker in Fall 1998. Bob explained the Big6 approach—how the process focuses on helping students solve information problems—and the philosophy—how the process can put kids in a position to succeed. Together, they analyzed the American History curriculum and Regents Exam from a Big6 perspective. Bob served as Mr. Hopsicker's information consultant, using the Big6 and his understandings of information processes to design a series of instructional strategies to help students learn American History content and to be able to demonstrate their knowledge through the New York State Regents Exam.

The approach taken was not a one-shot or even a few Big6 lessons. Bob and Mr. Hopsicker decided to use the Big6 as a framework for teaching the course content. They analyzed the curriculum from a Big6 perspective and designed Big6 strategies to help students learn the content of the course and express their knowledge through writing, projects, and exams. Examples of some of the Big6-related learning activities included:

■ Learning the nature of the Regents exam including key words in essay and multiple choice questions (Big6 #1–Task Definition).

■ Developing techniques for organizing and presenting information, for example, "Bob's Boxes," which involves analyzing the components of an essay question and creating a graphic chart to organize the information and ensure that each part of the essay question is addressed (Big6 #5–Synthesis).

■ Using self-assessment tasks to help students recognize their own strengths and weaknesses and how to learn skills and strategies to address their weaknesses (Big6 #6–Evaluation).

The main differences between Mr. Hopsicker's approach in 1997-98 and the previous year were the use of the Big6 model and Bob Berkowitz. The approach was "information-centered"—based on the

Big6 model of information problem solving. Bob Berkowitz acted as an "information consultant." Students learned to apply Big6 skills to every aspect of the course. Therefore, the Big6 served as the basis for analyzing the course curriculum and for the students' activities and strategies.

To summarize the intervention, the Big6 approach allowed Mr. Hopsicker's students to approach the Regents exam as they would any other information problem; this increased students' confidence, since they knew going into the test that they had the tools to succeed. And succeed they did.

Action Research

Action research is an important tool for practitioners like teachers and library media specialists. Action research studies allow researchers to measure the impact that changing the way something is done in real life affects the way an organization operates. In the case of Mr. Hopsicker's class, it was possible to measure the results Mr. Hopsicker got from changing his approach to preparing students for the Regents exam.

The nature of Mr. Hopsicker's class made an action research study very easy to design and carry out. As was mentioned before, there were no substantive differences between Mr. Hopsicker's American History classes in 1996-97 and 1997-98. Both groups faced the same task at the end of the year—to take the Regent's exam. No other aspects of the learning process changed—except for the Big6 intervention. The class structure, grouping, scheduling, curriculum, and textbook were the same.

And, at the beginning of the year, Mr. Hopsicker himself was no different in 1997-98 than the year before. But this began to change with his regular interaction with Bob Berkowitz and the Big6. This interaction began in Fall 1997. Bob and Mr. Hopsicker met one to three times a week during Mr. Hopsicker's preparation period. Mr. Hopsicker learned to view his course (both content and the processes involved) from a Big6 perspective. He saw how the Big6 process could be used to structure content for better student learning as well as help students to show what they knew on assignments and exams. Over the course of the year, Mr. Hopsicker did change—he was able to restructure his course and teaching approach from a Big6 perspective.

Since the students involved were essentially the same and no other variables were different except for the Big6 influence, it is reasonable to compare the students' performance from one year to the next. In essence, Mr. Hopsicker tried two differ-

ent approaches to preparing students for the American History Regents Exam: (1) a traditional, content-driven approach and (2) a Big6, information process-driven approach. Thus, Mr. Hopsicker provided a test of the difference the Big6 approach can make for students.

Results

In 1997-98, Mr. Hopsicker's students, 59 of them, comparable to the students from the year before in almost every way—took essentially the same standardized test as the year before. But this year, the results were very different. In 1996-97, only 53% of Mr. Hopsicker's students passed the American History Regents Exam. This year, armed with the Big6, 91% of Mr. Hopsicker's students passed the Regents exam! Needless to say, this is a dramatic improvement.

The main difference between Mr. Hopsicker's approach...were the use of the Big6 model and Bob Berkowitz.

Of the 59 students in Mr. Hopsicker's class, 54 of them passed the Regents exam (note that a score of 65 is required for passing on all New York State Regents Exams). Of Mr. Hopsicker's students, 83% passed with a score of 70 or more. The scores were distributed as follows[1]:

SCORE (PERCENTAGE)	NUMBER OF STUDENTS
100	1
90-99	10
80-89	15
70-79	23
65-69	5
Less than 65	5

There were five students in the class designated as learning disabled (i.e., having school developed "independent education plans.") Typically, these students do not pass the New York State Regents Exam in American History. In Mr. Hopsicker's group this year, two of the five students passed.

Discussion—What All This Means

Such a dramatic improvement in students' scores would be big news for any teacher. The fact that the improvement relates to Mr. Hopsicker's use of the Big6 with his students makes these results especially exciting for us.

The Big6 process clearly made a difference in

this situation, both for Mr. Hopsicker and for his class. In terms of Mr. Hopsicker's use of the Big6, he was able to redesign his curriculum with a Big6 perspective, to create a more focused, effective curriculum. In discussions with students, it was evident that they came away from the experience with a different attitude towards American History, as well as toward tackling information problems. They learned that it is important to remember the process, not just the knowledge.[2]

There are other possible explanations for the students' success besides their use of the Big6, for example, the Hawthorne effect or the collaboration itself.

The Hawthorne effect (named after a Western Electric company plant) refers to a study that found productivity increased due to the attention that the subjects received rather than the intervention itself. In this case, one might argue that the that the extra time and effort that Mr. Hopsicker spent with the students had more of an impact on them than the techniques that he employed. Mr. Hopsicker is a highly conscientious teacher—he spends a great deal of time and effort on his students. The fact that Mr. Hopsicker is a caring, dedicated teacher with contagious enthusiasm might account for some of the improvement. However, Mr. Hopsicker was no less enthusiastic or caring during the previous year. It seems unlikely that the dramatic difference in results was simply due to the attention given and Mr. Hopsicker's personality.

We all know that some of the best teaching that can be offered to students is through collaboration with colleagues. Perhaps Bob Berkowitz and Mr. Hopsicker working together with this class made the difference. This is true to some extent, because Bob brought his expertise to bear on his colleague's problem. Hopsicker himself acknowledged that his change related to working with Bob and the Big6. However, while collaboration might account for some of the differences, the collaboration was based on viewing, analyzing, and restructuring the curriculum from a Big6 perspective. Therefore, it seems highly unlikely that the collaboration alone accounted for the dramatic improvement in student achievements.

In discussions with students, it was evident that they came away from the experience with a different attitude towards American History, as well as toward tackling information problems.

Next Steps

This article represents only a preliminary report of the results. We intend to complete a more thorough comparison to previous classes in Wayne Central and to others taking the American History Regents Exam in 1997-98. There are also data concerning student attitudes to analyze and report. We also will attempt to track the performance of Mr. Hopsicker's students on other Regents exams to determine if there was any carry-over effect. That is, from discussions, students explained that they applied the techniques learned in Mr. Hopsicker's class in other subjects. It may be possible to explore whether this actually was the case.

Beyond this study, we recognize the importance of replicating this study in other settings. Replication is the strongest form of research evidence, and we will be conducting other studies of Big6 interventions and measuring the impact on assignments, projects, and exams.

We also encourage others to conduct their own action research studies—to focus on the use of identifiable Big6 applications within a subject area and to compare similar assessments across time and groups. We continually hear from teachers and library media specialists about their positive experiences with the Big6 and how they have observed how valuable it is in working with students. We hope you will consider carrying out your own study on the impact of the Big6 on student learning.

Finally, as noted, we will present more on this study in future issues of The Big6 Newsletter. As a first follow-up in the next issue, we will offer an extended interview with Mr. Hopsicker explaining what took place from his perspective.

[1] As of this writing, we do not have a comparative breakdown of scores from the previous year's class or from other classes in the school or state. We hope to report these in a future article.

[2] We also hope to offer a more detailed presentation and analysis of students' attitudes and reactions in the future.

Interview with Scott Hopsicker - Big6 Success Story!

v2 n3 p1, 4-7, 14-15

By Mike Eisenberg

In the last issue of *The Big6 Newsletter*, we reported on an exciting field-based study of the impact of the Big6 on student learning. The article explained how more than 90% of the students in Mr. Scott Hopsicker's U.S. history classes passed the June 1998 New York State Regents Exam. In 1997, only 53% passed. This is a striking and impressive finding. The major intervention—the difference between 1997 and 1998—was Hopsicker's use of the Big6 and his interactions with Bob Berkowitz, the library media specialist in the school.

As part of the study, I interviewed Mr. Hopsicker about one month before the students took the Regents Exam. The first part of the interview focuses on how Mr. Hopsicker changed his teaching style and how his students learned to be successful at writing essays. Mr. Hopsicker also discusses strategies for multiple choice questions, parental involvement, and his analysis of the changes he's seen in his students.

The interview reflects Hopsicker's enthusiasm for working with Bob and for using the Big6 approach. Scott has a confidence in how well his students will perform on the exam. The interview is abridged due to length, but Mr. Hopsicker's words are presented verbatim.

Mr. Hopsicker was lured away from Wayne Central and now teaches in the Brockport (NY) Central School District.

MIKE: Scott, why don't you tell us a little about yourself and what you teach?

SCOTT: I teach at Wayne Central High School and this is my second year. I teach U.S. history and government, and I also teach a Regents course for seniors. My first year here, I taught global studies I, which studies Asia, Africa and Latin America, and I taught U.S. history. During summer school—I teach global studies II, a Regents course which studies Europe and the Middle East. I also taught an economics course and history for the 8th grade.

MIKE: So you've really taught the whole gamut across the social studies curriculum?

SCOTT: Except AP history.

MIKE: You're pretty familiar with what is expected of the kids. The one thing you taught both last year and this year was U.S. History and Government. And what grade is that?

SCOTT: That's for eleventh grade.

MIKE: That ends with the New York State Regents Exam?

SCOTT: Yes.

MIKE: Has the Regents Exam been pretty much the same over the past few years?

SCOTT: Yes, you can pretty much figure out patterns.

MIKE: Why don't you tell me a little bit about your students?

SCOTT: They're a heterogeneous group— across the board. Everybody takes the Regents. We have learning disabled kids, as well as kids who dropped out of Advanced Placement for one reason or another. It's a mostly rural community.

MIKE: What percent of students in your eleventh grade classes will go on to some form of higher education?

SCOTT: Personally, I think it will be somewhere around 60%.

MIKE: So that's really not that high of a percentage compared to the general Rochester area. Why don't you tell me a little bit about last year, about your experiences, what you taught, and how you found it? In your own words, how did you come to work with Bob and the Big6 stuff?

SCOTT: At the end of the first year, I finished with 53% of the students passing the Regents. I was horrified. I looked at myself first—I didn't blame the kids. I went to Bob soon afterwards.

MIKE: What made you go to Bob?

SCOTT: I was referred to him by the vice-principal. He said Bob had worked with people in the past and had tremendous results. So I went to Bob. First thing, when I dropped off a couple of binders, he said, "I can tell you right now—you probably taught every small fact, being a first year teacher, and you didn't actually teach concepts or themes." I was more of an instructor than a teacher. I presented information and then expected the students to keep up to date on it—I was assuming things.

> They hated essays. When I asked at the beginning of the year that's what they would tell me. Now, they write them and they're motivated because they're getting 100s.

MIKE: So, Bob helped you look at the way you organized and presented the information.

SCOTT: Yes. We didn't make it less, but we did simplify it using various techniques based on the Big6. We tried not to assume anything. One of the problems students in high school have is writing essays. So we created a new essay strategy for them—how to find, organize, and present information for essays. We used something called the "perfect chart" which helps the students to outline the essay first. The students develop charts, and I develop one too. My chart is the perfect one—it includes all the information needed to get a perfect 100 score on the essay. So, there is no guessing game. The students know exactly what it takes to get a 100.

Figure 1: *Perfect Chart*

CASES AND ISSUES

McCulloch v. Maryland (1819)—federalism
Dred Scott v. Sanford (1857)—property rights
Plessy v. Ferguson (1896)—civil rights
Korematsu v. U.S. (1944)—Presidential power
Engel v. Vitale (1962)—freedom of religion
Miranda v. Arizona (1966)—due process

Choose all cases from the list. For each one chosen: (1) Show how the constitutional issue listed was involved in the case, (2) State the Supreme Court's decision in the case, and (3) Discuss an impact of the decision on United States history.

	HOW CONSTITUTIONAL ISSUE WAS INVOLVED	SUPREME COURT DECISION	IMPACT OF DECISION
McCulloch v. Maryland	*Federalism = The division of power between state and national government* *Issue: Whether the state of Maryland could tax the National Bank*	*Maryland could not tax the bank because it was created by the federal government*	*Federal agencies are immune from control by the states.* *Federal laws are supreme over state laws.*
Dred Scott v. Senford	*Issue: Wether Dred Scott could sue for his freedom because he was a slave.*	*Slaves are property, not citizens. Therefore, slaves can't sue for their freedom.*	*Greater distrust between abolitionists and pro-slavery citizens, making compromises worthless to avoid the Civil War.*
Plessy v. Ferguson	*Issue: Whether seperate facilities for blacks and whites was constitutional.*	*Seperate, but equal is constitutional and it does not violate the 13th and 14th Amendments.*	*Seperate facilities were not equal for blacks and the decision was later reversed by Brown v. Board of Education. Seperate was not equal; segregation ended.*
Korematsu v. U.S.	*Issue: Whether the war powers of President FDR justified placing Japanese-Americans in internment camps.*	*Internment camps were justified because Presidental powers expand during war or national crisis.*	*Rights of citizens can be suspended during war or national crisis.*
Engel v. Vitale	*Issue: Can schools force students to say a school prayer to start each day.*	*School prayer was contrary to the 1st Amendment because the Amendment provides for religious freedom but prevents government from establishing a religion.*	*A couple of Presidents since have called for a constitutional amendment allowing school prayer.*
Miranda v. Arizona	*Issue: Can the police deny you your right to an attorney during questioning.*	*The 15th Amendment protects from self-incrimination and the 6th Amendment provides a right to an attorney was violated by the police when questioning Miranda.*	*All suspects must be read their rights when questioned and have the right to an attorney.*

MIKE: So now the students have a model of what the perfect content for the essay would be. What does the chart look like?

SCOTT: What I did is—I created these charts (see Figure 1). A lot of times the Regents Exam will give you essay questions where you can't even find the information in the text book. So then how can you ask the students to do that [use the textbook]? So what I did was to copy the information from the Barron's Review Guide and we give that to them now.

MIKE: So, you're giving the students the content—the correct answers?

SCOTT: Yes. Then they have to write an essay. We work with them first on rewriting the question in their own words. They then make sure that they include all the factors—the parts—called for in the essay. The Regents Exam usually requires students to write about three factors (for example, three causes of the Revolutionary War). But, we never know how many are required, so in practice we make them do all of them.

MIKE: Anything else?

SCOTT: We also focus on difficult vocabulary words in the essay instructions. Instructions such as, "identify and discuss" are different than "compare and contrast." Even in high school, students still won't know what those words mean. We quiz them on the words and continually reinforce their correct use.

MIKE: These are vocabulary words in the essay questions, right? Not the vocabulary in social studies; just the vocabulary related to the instructions.

SCOTT: Yes. So we teach them the key instructional words for essays.

MIKE: We just assume that kids know that, don't we? Do they really know the difference between "discuss" and "outline"?

SCOTT: Or "compare" and "contrast"? Not really. Once they know what these words really mean, they are ready to create a chart outlining the essay. They do

the chart for homework and turn it in. Then, I give them a "perfect chart"—one that fully outlines the answer to the question.

MIKE: Why do you do this?

SCOTT: I want to separate the making of the chart from the writing of the essay. If they did a poor job on the chart, their essays would also be poor. But, by writing an essay based on my chart, I accomplish two things: one, they go over the correct content of the question one more time; and two, they write an essay from accurate and complete information. Later, they'll get another chance because they will see the question again on a test. So, we cover the subject content and the organizing and writing process a number of times.

MIKE: Anything else?

SCOTT: The final step we have them do is to answer two basic questions: "Did I answer the question?" and, "Did I use appropriate information to answer the question?"

Figure 2: *Mr. Hopsicker's Study Tips*

© Berkowitz & Hopsicker, 1998

1. Time Management: How much time do you spend on studying?
How much of the time is quality time?
Is the time quiet, free from distractions?
How much time is spent searching for information?

2. Extra Help: Do I need to get help from my teacher?
I can meet with Mr. Hopsicker before homeroom (starting at 6:30 am), during homeroom, during his open periods, for lunch, or after school.
Please just make an appointment.

3. LEARNING STRATEGIES:
a. Rewrite notes/review sheets
b. Redo chapter worksheets
c. Make flash cards: person/term/or event on one side; information on other side of the card: cause/effect/impact/contribution/positive/negative
d. Note blanks: cover up information in your notes, then write in missing gap
e. Use a tape recorder: talk into a tape recorder using information, or without information
f. Read chapter and take notes on most important information
g. Review with family member, friend, or classmate
h. Use a combination of techniques listed from above
i. Use any other learning strategy that enables you to achieve your best score.

FORMULA FOR SUCCESS:
E1 + E2 = E3

Engage (read) + Extract (notes, talk about it, chart) = Ensure (result = better grades)

Dear Parent or Guardian,

As a teacher, and more importantly your student's Social Studies teacher, I know that parents/guardians can be key partners in helping their children be successful in school. I am asking for your help because parents/guardians can provide an atmosphere which fosters achievement and success. However, the question is, "What can parents/guardians do to help their students that will have the biggest impact?" Answer: Assignments—especially homework.

U.S. History and Government is designed to be a conceptual course aimed at giving students an understanding of events and issues that impact social, political, economic and foreign policy concerns. The course covers such topics as: the constitution, impact of the presidents, and supreme court cases throughout America's history. Homework is assigned on a regular basis. Assignments are ways for my students to show me what they know. They are also ways for students to learn, review, remediate, or extend what is taught in my classroom. To be successful on quizzes and tests in this course, the homework must be done.

You can help your student be successful with their homework assignments by guiding, assisting, and generally making it easier for them to succeed. The attached "Homework Planner" offers a framework that you can use to guide students through assignments and homework. I think that this simple tool can make a big difference. I will make copies available for all students and encourage that they be used to help organize homework assignments. I hope you will help me by using this organizer with your student whenever he/she has homework in U.S. History and Government.

Please feel free to contact me at the high school whenever you have any concerns. If you leave a message at the main office, I will return your call as soon as possible.

Thank you in advance for your support and cooperation.

Sincerely,

Scott Hopsicker

MIKE: That's your evaluation stage. It sounds like you're identifying a number of weaknesses that students have related to writing essays that we assumed were okay. No wonder they're not doing well on the exams. You didn't do any of this last year at all?

SCOTT: Nothing. And the students hated essays. When I asked at the beginning of the year that's what they would tell me. I was hardly ever getting essays written for homework. I would have kids turn in, "I don't know, I'm dumb." And that's when I knew I was doing something wrong. I have no problems this

year. They do the essays and they're motivated because they're getting good grades.

MIKE: What I'm hearing is that the results you are getting are due to your change in approach. It's not you or Bob. The difference is the approach based on the Big6.

SCOTT: Yes, it's the approach and process. It's also the first time a lot of the students have been successful, so they keep doing it.

MIKE: Do you have any proof of this?

SCOTT: We've already seen some minor results. We applied this to the global studies Regents Exam over the summer. In summer school, the average percentage of students passing the Regents is 30-40% because you don't have your highest level of kids. This time we had 76% [passing]. I also [compared] class grades from last year and this. Last year, first quarter, 40% failed. This year, I think we had only one or two students fail the entire quarter, out of five classes, out of 125 kids.

MIKE: So you're really up around 95%! Excellent. And you sound really confident about the Regents.

SCOTT: Yes! Absolutely.

MIKE: Why don't you tell about the Regents multiple choice part?

SCOTT: We've tried to come up with study strategies for them—"Mr. Hopsicker's Study Tips" (see Figure 2). The first one is about time management—how much time is actually spent? How much is quiet time? How much is quality time? How much time is spent searching for information? How much is wasted? Another study tip is rewriting—rewriting notes or review sheets or redoing chapter worksheets.

A third study tip is developing flash cards of key terms in questions. Flash cards were very popular.

MIKE: Any others?

SCOTT: Sure. To help learn the content, tape record your notes and play it back. Or, read the chapter, take notes on it, then review it with family or friends. We also recommend using post-its to identify key areas when reading. Another tip is to underline key words in the question. We really try to get them to do that. I give bonus credit on tests if they underline key terms on every multiple choice question. With multiple choice, we also teach them to cross out the ones they know definitely aren't true, and to look closely to see if two choices are opposite—they both can't be correct.

MIKE: This sounds very exciting. What's the connection to the Big6 in all this?

SCOTT: We look at the curriculum using the Big6 and have the students follow the Big6 steps. We also invite the parents to get involved in the Big6. Often, parents don't know how to help with homework. We sent them a letter with a handout asking them to get involved and explaining how to do so. We put the Big6 information on the back of the handout, and we broke it down for the parents so they could make a checklist. (See Figure 3 on page 132 and Figure 4 on this page).

MIKE: And these are the parents of eleventh graders? Do they want to be involved and are they still involved? And are the kids receptive to this?

SCOTT: Most of the parents and kids are—yes. We surveyed the students about interaction at home. For example, how many eat dinner with their parents and how many times a week. In one of my classes, only two kids raised their hands. So our effort enables parents and kids to get together in a positive way.

MIKE: Do you have any idea of the degree of parent involvement? What percentage would you say are really involved?

SCOTT: In this district, I would say up to 60%.

MIKE: And what was it last year?

SCOTT: Last year, oh, probably down around 10% or 15%.

MIKE: That's really amazing—that kind of support. Have you had feedback from parents?

SCOTT: Yes, for example I spoke to one mother last week at the awards banquet. Last year, her daughter was a low "C" student in history and failed the Regents. Now, she has a 97 average (in the last quarter). Numerous people told us their kids hated history, but now they love it. And, last year at this time, they said their kids were panicking.

Figure 4: *Helping With Homework: A Big6 Assignment Organizer*

Assignment: _____ Date Due: _____

Complete Big6 Skills #1-5 BEFORE you BEGIN your assignment.
Complete Big6 Skill #6 BEFORE you TURN IN your assignment.

BIG6 SKILL #1: TASK DEFINITION
What does this assignment require me to do?

What information do I need in order to do this assignment?

BIG6 SKILL #2: INFORMATION SEEKING STRATEGIES

What sources can I use to do the assignment? Circle the best sources.

BIG6 SKILL #3: LOCATION & ACCESS

Where can I find my sources? Do I need help? If so, who can help me?

BIG6 SKILL #4: USE OF INFORMATION
What do I have to do with the information?
_____ read/view/listen
_____ take notes
_____ answer questions
_____ other: _____
_____ chart and/or write an essay
_____ copy and highlight
_____ properly cite

BIG6 SKILL #5: SYNTHESIS
What product does this assignment require?

BIG6 SKILL #6: EVALUATION
Student self-evaluation checklist:

_____ I did what I was supposed to do (see Big6 #1, Task Definition)
_____ The assignment is complete.

The Big6 Eisenberg & Berkowitz, 1990. Assignment Organizer © Berkowitz & Hopsicker, 1997.

MIKE: I was going to ask about that.

SCOTT: Well, I asked the kids "Are you panicking now?" They said, "No. We're concerned, but we don't feel like we did last year. We know we've practiced things and we're prepared this time."

MIKE: What about the criticism that you are just teaching to the test. That you spent the whole year preparing for it in one way or another. What's your answer to that?

SCOTT: Sure, my goal is to make them successful on the test. Yes, we use Regents essays and questions, but we really don't water down the curriculum. We also did projects that include all of Bloom's taxonomy so we're actually using high level thinking skills.

MIKE: So you do projects in addition to the essay preparation and test-taking work?

SCOTT: Oh yes. We created cause and effect projects so they can see how everything is connected together, not just little pieces and fragments. History is all one piece—all one smooth flow. It's kind of like reading a book from start to finish; everything is connected somehow. Our time line project, for example, puts it all in focus for them.

MIKE: You mentioned that you think you've covered the curriculum four times where in the past it sounds like you were struggling to get through it once.

SCOTT: Previously, we finished it once, and then reviewed just for the Regents. This year, we're not taking a review approach. We might review a couple of questions or essays, but not the entire curriculum.

MIKE: Now, have you done most of this yourself in class with Bob kind of consulting on this or does Bob come in and work with the kids or what?

SCOTT: I met with Bob two of my three prep periods a week.

MIKE: Really, that much?

SCOTT: Yes, at least two periods based on a four day rotation. Then I had Bob come in and observe me teaching. So now he can see my styles and my strengths—some of my weaknesses. He also wanted to see the kids in action and how they reacted to me. Then we came up with activities and projects. I would tell him what content things I wanted them to know. He helped decide what we wanted to base the projects on, and how often.

MIKE: So, Bob's been kind of a mentor/consultant.

SCOTT: He's also our information specialist. I come up with the content and he channels the process and helps come up with ideas for what the students should do. We work together—we mesh.

MIKE: So, you're the content person. You come up with what you want to teach. Bob is really involved with the information process and learning.

SCOTT: Yes. What I like about the Big6 is that you assume nothing and that it's really common sense. You just apply the common sense you use in everyday life to school things.

MIKE: If I were to talk to your kids, would they recognize the Big6, would they be familiar with it?

SCOTT: I don't know, but if you asked them to describe what we have done in some projects, you would know that it plugs into the Big6.

MIKE: Is there anything major I'm leaving out, anything you want to add?

SCOTT: The biggest thing that I believe the Big6 did for us. . .we took it, we broke every step down. We retaught everything. It was like reinventing the wheel, but by doing that, we have been successful. And, success has bred success. Kids actually are now pushing themselves and doing better in the classroom. I have more A's and B's than I do C's and very limited failures. That's the key, they've been successful and now they believe in it so they're willing to put some time into it. Whereas, last year—before I did the Big6— the kids said that they weren't going to do well anyway so why put any time into it?

MIKE: Do you think there is any crossover with this approach in their other classes?

SCOTT: Yes, I know they use the chart for other classes and use their study tips. They think, "If I can be successful here where I never was before, then maybe I [can] be successful with all the other [subjects]."

MIKE: One of the comments that people have about the Big6 is "Well, it's okay for elementary or middle school, but the high school kids don't relate to this or they don't need this." But according to you, it's just the opposite.

SCOTT: Yes, it clearly works with all grade levels. But, I know what you mean about some of the comments. I had someone from another school take a look at our essay strategy. She thought we were watering down the curriculum because we gave them the answers in the perfect chart. She didn't understand. It doesn't matter that we're giving them the content—it's the process that counts. We want them to actually spend more time concentrating on how to put [information] in their own words, and spend less time finding it. And, along the way, they are learning the content.

MIKE: Mr. Hopsicker, how do you feel this has helped you as a professional?

SCOTT: It's changed my whole outlook—on teaching, myself, and the way I teach. Before, I was frustrated, ineffective, and down on myself. Now I feel enthused and successful. And really able to help my kids.

MIKE: Mr. Hopsicker, unfortunately we are out of time. You do seem very, very confident that your students have learned more social studies, more history, and are able to organize their thoughts and express themselves better. I'm impressed. I can't wait to see your Regents scores! Thank you for your time.

Postscript: As was detailed earlier, Scott's and Bob's students were very successful indeed—with 91% passing the New York State Regents Exam in U.S. History.

Special thanks to Janet LaFrance for transcribing the audio tape of the interview.

The **BIG 6** Teaching Technology & Information Skills

PART VI

Teaching Aides

The Famous "Banana Split Lesson"

v1 n4 p4-5

By Tami Little

Tami Little, Library Media Specialist, Hinton Community School, Hinton, Iowa, developed this introduction to the Big6 using the context of making a banana split. It has become one of the most popular introductory exercises for helping students learn about the Big6. Also included are four variations on the lesson—by Nancy Thomas, Susan Grigsby, Earl Moniz, and Sunnie Tait. Enjoy!

Lesson: Banana Splits for Big6
Subject Area: Introduction to the Big6 Skills

Materials/Media: You will need to purchase the ingredients needed for the banana split. Be aware that some students are not able to have milk products, so additional bananas or an alternate snack may be necessary. Ingredients include bananas, ice cream, syrups, toppings, nuts, and whipped cream. Materials include dishes, spoons, ice cream scoop, knife to cut the banana, and clean-up equipment such as paper towels and water.

Aim/Objectives: This is an introduction to the Big6 Skills. The learner will experience the Big6 Skills by creating a banana split sundae.

Audience/Grade Level: This lesson was designed for adults, but can be altered to use with students of any age.

Assessment: Teacher observation and student participation in the lesson. Students will write a brief summary of how creating the banana split helped them to learn about the Big6 Skills.

The Lesson:

1. TASK DEFINITION:

1.1 Define the problem.

The information problem—You heard about banana splits, but you don't know how to make them. What does a "banana split" look like? Why is it called banana "split"?

1.2 IDENTIFY THE INFORMATION REQUIREMENTS OF THE PROBLEM.

Are you going to make them or buy them? How do you make them? How much money do you have to spend? What store will you go to? What grocery items will you need? How many banana splits do you want to make?

2. INFORMATION SEEKING STRATEGIES:

2.1 Determine the range of possible sources.

You can gather recipes from the Internet, call other ice cream places, or check cookbooks. You can go to the convenience store or a grocery store. In the store, you must find the aisles to get the ingredients. You will need to choose bananas, ice cream, toppings, dishes to put them in, spoons, and whipped topping.

2.2 Evaluate the different possible sources to determine priorities.

From the above list, prioritize the items that best fit your needs, make a grocery list of ingredients and materials needed.

3. LOCATION AND ACCESS:

3.1 Locate sources (intellectually and physically).

3.2 Find information within sources.

You are in the right aisle, in the store you chose. You must now choose the best ingredients and materials, according to the amount of money available and description of the products you need. This includes choosing the brand of the product.

4. USE OF INFORMATION:

4.1 Engage (read, hear, view, touch) the information source.

4.2 Extract the information from a source.

Time to begin making your banana splits! Organize your "information sources" (peel the bananas, take topping out of the original containers and put them in separate bowls, make all the tools available) and place them on the table.

5. SYNTHESIS:

5.1 Organize the information from multiple sources.

Place each of the items in the banana split dish in a neat order, following the recipe/directions chosen. Make sure the banana split looks "pretty."

5.2 Present the information.

Share the banana split with friends. Everyone may eat and enjoy!

6. EVALUATION:

6.1 Judge the product (effectiveness).

How did the banana split look? How did the banana split taste? Was it good? What was the quality of the ingredients? Would you choose a different banana or different spoons?

6.2 Judge the information problem-solving process (efficiency).

When making the banana split next time, would you do anything different? How did the looking for recipes and directions work? What troubles did you have when shopping? Would you go to the same store?

Variations on the Lesson as Suggested by:

Nancy Thomas, Assistant Professor, School of Library and Information Management, Emporia State University, Emporia, Kansas

"It might be useful to put all of the ingredients and materials that people will use to make the banana splits into several plain brown paper bags. Part of their job will be information seeking—(i.e., unpacking everything and then deciding what is relevant to their needs) or (choosing what items may be useful and leaving in the bag items which are not useful).

You may want to provide some items which may have little value to people, instead of providing only what is necessary for making the banana split. Sometimes we get lots more information than we need when we are researching a project. We have to decide which information is relevant and which is not. We don't necessarily use everything that we find. A monkey wrench, string, crayons, mustard, or scissors, for example, while useful tools for some purposes, may be of very little value in this exercise. You might want to provide some cookbooks that contain recipes for banana splits.

Provide some articles in the bags of ingredients and materials that force participants to make some serious choices among alternatives—i.e., choices which call for evaluation at more than one step in the overall process. This is one way to ensure that evaluation occurs at every step.

You could also redefine the task as making the most healthful banana split. Provide options (sugar-free toppings, vs. natural flavor)—thus bringing this activity to a higher cognitive level. Ask the participants to consider members' food preferences or allergies (to nuts or ice cream).

Finally, provide each group with a large sheet of paper with the Big6 steps indicated. Have one person in each group write down the steps taken and the activities or decisions made at each step. This can serve as a record of their experience and a basis for discussion after they have eaten."

Susan K. S. Grigsby, Library Media Specialist, The Epstein School, Atlanta, Georgia

"I brought in some baked beans, curry powder, muffin tins, chopsticks, etc. and had all of them set out on the table with the banana split ingredients. I started the lesson by asking if participants could figure out anything I could make with all the ingredients. Then as we went through Big6 and talked about locating relevant information, we started going through the items on the table and eliminating the unnecessary information. Thanks so much for such a great idea!"

Earl J. Moniz, Lillington Elementary School Librarian, Lillington, North Carolina

"In the event your Big6 workshop is going to be conducted in a one day session, it would not be feasible to build real banana splits the first thing in the morning or before going to lunch.

At some point in the morning, have each participant build tear-art banana splits from construction paper (colors of your own choosing). Some suggestions: blue for the container; yellow for the banana(s); white for vanilla; brown for chocolate; and pink for strawberry might be a few starting ice cream colors. You might also run an assortment of those colors through a hole punch and then through a shredder (if available) to make some sprinkles, some light brown or tan paper might indicate some caramel sauce (if you are offering any) and some black paper might represent some very dark chocolate syrup, and use red paper for cutting small circles and making cherries to go on top of it all.

The tear-art banana splits are collected before lunch. Later as they are enjoying the real banana split, the moderator has a multitude of things to explain pertaining to the Big6 process.

Interpreting the tear-art to reality (building the real one—Task Definition; Information Seeking Strategies; Location and Access to items). Individuals may also contribute their own views about how the task was accomplished—between spoonfuls."

Sunnie Tait, Librarian/Media Specialist, Wines Elementary, Ann Arbor, Michigan

"I used the Banana Split lesson with three fifth-grade classes and a fourth grade class and it was a scream. I really jazzed it up and the kids contributed along the way, telling me ways to cut the banana, etc. I had my portable phone with me and pretended to call ice cream places and asked them to deliver. At the end of one of the "shows," the kids said it was a really good play! Now, this coming week, all the classes will be getting banana split parties. I accidentally forgot to bring nuts, so I made that part of the lesson during the evaluation step. We talked about when reviewing the ingredient list should have been part of the process. They decided that should be part of Stage 1, Task Definition."

Big6 Day: The Info Show!

v2 n1 p4-5

By Sandra Gilbert

Big6 Day was designed to celebrate learning and using the Big6 process in all areas of the curriculum at **Fiest Elementary School, Houston, Texas**. On the day of the "Info Show," students heard speakers, shared products, participated in various information problem solving activities and had a great day! All curriculum areas, including PE, art, and music were included.

The Celebration

The celebration day was planned for May, since the students and faculty would be learning about and using the Big6 process throughout the school year. Previous special curriculum celebrations included Young Authors' Day, Young Scientists' Day, Math Week, and other events. One particular curriculum subject was the focus of the day with speakers, activities, and product displays. Having a Big6 Day involved all areas of the curriculum and showed how the process can be an integral part of the total curriculum.

Campus Improvement Plan

Introducing and using the Big6 in every curriculum area was a school goal that was written into our Campus Improvement Plan. That means "it SHALL be done." We used the Big6 process itself to plan how to accomplish this goal as well as to plan the Big6 Day! For example, the task became "How can the whole school celebrate Big6 Day?"

We wanted all of the staff to be excited about using the Big6 and to have common, baseline understandings of the Big6 process and how to integrate the Big6 into everyday classrooms. We invited **Barbara Jansen** from the **Round Rock Independent School District** to present an all-day Saturday workshop early in the fall. Her "Information Literacy: The Big6 Approach to Information Skills Instruction" was informative and motivational. During the day, teachers had opportunities to design problem-based instruction on specific topics for their grade level and curriculum areas. It was a great beginning.

During the school year, teachers modeled the Big6 process and planned Big6 activities along with their normal curriculum topics. For several years, students and staff had used the Big6 process in the library, but now it became a school-wide effort.

Many teachers were discovering the effective-

We used the Big6 process itself to plan how to accomplish this goal as well as to plan the Big6 Day!

ness of using the Big6 for information problem solving and designed some very creative lessons. For example, first graders were to pretend that they were getting a puppy on St. Patrick's Day. They needed to know how to take care of a new puppy. As a class, they came up with three questions to answer. One of the places selected to find information was the school library. The class came to the library to use the computer catalog to find books on puppies. Students located the books in the non-fiction area and selected a couple for the class. As the teacher read the books aloud in the classroom, the group took notes on information found that answered the questions on puppy care. After brain-storming many ideas on how to organize and share this information, the class decided that each student would create an illustrated brochure to tell how to take care of a new puppy. Everyone was pleased with the results.

Big6 Displays

Evidence of the Big6 process was seen throughout the school. The library featured a huge bulletin board in the reference area where a line of dancing bears (The Fiest Elementary mascot) tells about the Big6 in conversation bubbles. Big6 posters and bookmarks are displayed in the library and in the classrooms. Each class had a clever Big6 bulletin board reminding students of the stages. (See side bar on page 142.)

In addition, each grade level prepared a large hallway display of Big6 products or stages of the process. Also, in planning Big6 Day, each grade level had a theme:

- Academy/Kindergarten: Friendship
- Grade 1: International Cultures
- Grade 2: Whales
- Grade 3: Family Heritage
- Grade 4: Texas Cultures
- Grade 5: Colonial Days
- Physical Education: Hopscotch Around the World
- Art: Grade level theme artwork
- Music: Grade level theme music and dance.

The units or objectives were planned and presented as authentic and motivating information problems. In this way, students were seeking information to actually solve a problem, not just to study a certain topic. As a result, students moved right into Big6 #1 and defined the task to help solve the problem.

Big6 Day Activities

Each grade level also selected a speaker for Big6 Day (using the Big6 process, of course), made arrangements, and planned their own activities for the day.

Academy and kindergarten arranged a puppet show on friendship, wrote in their journals about friendship, completed a mini-poster about themselves, and shared a "Friendship snack," where students brought a piece of fruit and shared it with another Academy or kindergarten student they did not know.

First grade students experienced food and customs of various countries with an International Day. On Big6 Day, first grade students invited their assistant principal to talk to them about her hobby, deep sea fishing. She modeled the Big6 process to demonstrate how she found and used information to become successful at deep sea fishing. Students created Big6 fishing hats (a headband with six fish showing the six stages), and had a Big6 parade. They also created Tackle Box Trash (trail mix with gummy worms) and shared their international study products with third grade students. (each first grade class paired up with a third grade class.)

Students in second grade had a whale of a time! Their speaker was a librarian from another school who had been actively involved with a manatee that found its way inland to the Houston Ship Channel. She shared slides of the experience all the way to the return of the manatee to Florida. Second graders charted and mapped whale migration, measured and compared whale sizes, and had a "spouting" contest out on the playground.

Third graders heard from a genealogy expert, shared a family heritage luncheon, graphed and mapped family origins, created a pedigree chart, and shared products with first graders. Similarly, in fourth-grade, students invited speakers from the community to share their cultural heritage from Mexico, Germany, and England. Several activities focused on Texas cultures including sewing a quilt featuring family cultures.

Colonial Day activities were presented in fifth-grade. Students dressed in colonial costumes and had speakers and demonstrations. Hands-on activities featured colonial customs and events such as butter making, soap carving, potato stamping, weaving, herb uses, games, and music.

Big6 Days began with two "kick-off" assemblies. Performers from Storytime Theater worked with us to design a custom Big6 presentation in which students saw Abraham Lincoln "come alive" before their eyes and learned about this great president. Using visuals and music, the Abraham Lincoln character shared information about boyhood and early life, put on the make-up, beard, coat and hat, and recited the Gettysburg Address. The performers then demonstrated how they used the Big6 process to create the performance—they were solving a problem with information. The presentation was excellent and entertaining!

As souvenirs of the Big6 Day celebration, each student received a program of the day, a neon colored "Big6 Day: The Info Show" pencil, and a specially printed, neon Big6 Day "sticker button" to wear. Many parents reported back that the students came home excited and full of information about their Big6 Day celebration.

Great Success!

The day was clearly a success! Our school goal was met, the entire school was introduced to the Big6 process and vocabulary, and our learning was celebrated. As a result, many teachers are hooked and excited about the Big6. They realize the Big6 is

---

Big6 Bulletin Board Ideas

SOARING HIGH WITH RESEARCH: BIG6
- airplane with each of the Big6 stages on clouds.

PLANTING THE SEEDS TO RESEARCH: BIG6
- Big6 stages on flowers.

OUR RECIPE FOR RESEARCH: BIG6
- chef with Big6 stages on food items.

BIG6 RESEARCH IS HOT STUFF
- Big6 stages on red hot peppers.

GOT A PROBLEM? BIG6 RESEARCH IS THE ANSWER
- Big6 stages on books.

JUGGLING THE STAGES TO RESEARCH: BIG6
- clown with Big6 stages on balls.

ROUNDING UP RESEARCH WITH THE BIG6
- cowboy with Big6 stages on 6 boots.

GROWING WITH THE BIG6
- Big6 stages on flowers.

CATCHING THE BIG6
- fisherman with Big6 stages on fish.

INGREDIENTS TO GREAT RESEARCH: BIG6
- Big6 stages on hamburger layers.

HATS OFF TO BIG6
- Big6 stages on a variety of hats.

---

effective in meeting curriculum goals, and they have made it an integral part of their instruction. As a school, we will continue to model, learn, practice, share, support, solve problems, and grow professionally. We still have a long way to go to give our students the tools and skills they need to succeed in an information-rich world, but we have taken those first steps together. We realize, as Martha Stewart might say, "The Big6: It's a good thing!"

Big6 Bulletin Boards

v2 n1 p3,5

By Carrie Lowe

Greetings, Big6ers! One of the most important tools teachers can use to capture students' attention is a visual display. Bulletin boards are a perfect way to introduce and reinforce the Big6 to students, fellow teachers, and even parents. (Parents' Night is quickly approaching!)

Not only are the Big6 listserv (**big6@listserv.syr. edu**) participants brilliant curriculum designers and enthusiastic teachers, but they are also master bulletin board artists. There has been quite an exchange of bulletin board ideas on the listserv lately. In addition, Sandra Gilbert's article "Big6 Day: The Info Show," also in this issue, provides a number of great ideas. Try them for yourself, and see what kind of attention you can attract to the Big6.

Bonnie Hopkins of Mountain Elementary School, Los Alamos, New Mexico, has designed a great Big6 bulletin board to generate excitement at the beginning of the school year. (See Figure 1.) The bulletin board, based on an idea that Ann Gray of Pittsburg, New Hampshire, had previously sent to the listserv, features an outer space theme. It reads: "Blast off to a successful school year!" and "Use the Big6 to solve all of your information problems!" The stages of the Big6 are printed on star shapes. The first information problem that this astronaut should tackle is determining whether the alien standing next to him is a friendly or hostile life form!

Big6 Bulletin boards are especially timely when they focus on holidays or events. Gretchen Baldauf of West Seneca, New York, designed a great Halloween-themed Big6 bulletin board. In the center of the board stands Count Dracula, with gravestones all around him. The gravestones carry messages like, "Got one monster of an information problem? Use the Big6 to let it R.I.P.!" Scattered around the graveyard are cutouts of bats, spiders, and cats with the Big6 stages on them. This Halloween scene is finished off with a witch flying across a big yellow moon on her broom.

Pretty spooky!

Big6 bulletin boards can also be related to seasons. Ann Gray designed a great bulletin board to celebrate the arrival of springtime. The board features a large umbrella with "The Big6" on it. Above the umbrella are three fluffy clouds. The first cloud reads, "The Big6." The second reads, "showers you with." The third reads, "good solutions to all of your information problems." Raindrops sprinkled across the rest of the board are labeled with the stages of the Big6. The forecast calls for successfully solved information problems!

Events can be the focus of Big6 bulletin boards. Ann Gray also shared an idea for an excellent graduation-themed bulletin board with the Big6 list. Across the top, the bulletin board says, "Grads, Use the Big6 to Choose a College." The body of the bulletin board shows the silhouettes of a boy and a girl with mortar boards on their heads. Scattered around these two are six "diplomas," each labeled with one of the Big6 stages:

- **STAGE 1: TASK DEFINITION**—I need to choose a college.
- **STAGE 2: INFORMATION SEEKING STRATEGIES**—Friends, guidance counselor, WWW, college catalog guides.
- **STAGE 3: LOCATION & ACCESS**—Call friends, make an appointment with the guidance counselor, go to the library and use the online catalog.
- **STAGE 4: USE OF INFORMATION**—Talk to the guidance counselor, print information from the WWW, use the college guides and take down notes.
- **STAGE 5: SYNTHESIS**—Write to colleges.
- **STAGE 6: EVALUATION**—Did I find all of the relevant information I needed? Am I happy with my choices?

This bulletin board also reminds students and teachers that the Big6 is just as useful for solving information problems outside of school. Keep those great ideas coming! Until next time.

Big6 Poetry

v1 n2 p7

Written by Barbara A. Jansen

When I have something that needs to be done,
And I need information because I have none.
I'll use my tools that help me do
The job that I'm happy to share with you.
The Big6 will help me find what I need,
And put it together, I can do it, indeed!

When I have a task, that is something to do,
And I need information to do it because it is new,
Big6 #1 will help me succeed
By figuring out just what exactly I need.

Big6 #2 will help me choose
When I decide just what I can use.
I'll choose the ones that meet my needs best,
I may choose two or three and leave all the rest.

Where, oh, where can I find these things now?
In the library? In a book? And Big6 #3 tells just how
To find those people or print that I chose,
And get to where my information is located in those.

Read, look, and listen is what I'll do when
I use Big6 #4 to get just what I need and then
I'll write it or draw the information I find.
I'll get what I need because I'll use my mind.

Once I have found and written all that I need,
I must put it together so I can proceed
To finish the job and show it, you see.
And Big6 #5 will surely help me.

How will I know if I did my job well?
Big6 #6 will sure help me to tell
If I did it the best that I possibly could,
And do it better next time if I should.

Big6 Song

v1 n2 p11

Words by Barbara A. Jansen

(Sung to the tune of "B-I-N-G-O")

There is a process I can use and Big6 is its name-O

Refrain:
B-I-G S-I-X, B-I-G S-I-X, B-I-G S-I-X
And Big6 is its name-O.

Big6 One will help me find out just what I should do-O (refrain)
Big6 Two will help me choose those things that I should use-O (refrain)
Big6 Three will help me get those things that I will need-O (refrain)
Big6 Four helps me to take out words that I can use-O (refrain)
Big6 Five helps me finish the work that I must do-O (refrain)
Big6 Six helps me to know if I did my best work-O (refrain)

PART **VII**

Big6 in Action

CHAPTER 18

The **BIG 6**

State Wide Implementation of Big6 Skills—Utah

Introduction: The Utah Big6 Special Issue

v2 n4 p1-2

By Sharyl G. Smith

Hello to all Big6ers from Utah! I am pleased to guest edit this special issue of The Big6 Newsletter outlining the Utah experience with the Big6. In addition to my own overview article explaining the scope and nature of our efforts in Utah, we share the reports of four "alumni" teams from our Big6-based, "Information Literacy Across the Curriculum" project. These teams of teachers, library media teachers, and administrators represent all grade levels and regions in the state of Utah.

First, **JaDene Denniston**, the library media teacher at **Sunrise**, a K–2 school, demonstrates how even the youngest students can put the Big6 to work to increase learning. Her discussion details the role of each teacher, their reactions to the Information Literacy Project, the impact of the Big6 on student learning, and the enthusiastic reception of parents and school district administrators.

Roy Kanno teaches science at **Dixon Middle School.** His article takes the reader through their

project schedule, complete with assignments and results. Of special interest are the compiled data on student perceptions and achievement and the teacher's comments about the social impact on students of diverse ability working closely together for the first time.

In the final article, **Patti Harrington**, Provo District Associate Superintendent, and her committee relate a district wide plan for implementing the Big6 through an intensive technology in-service for library media teachers. Readers also will learn about a newly formed partnership among social studies teachers and library media teachers that will affect the revision of the Provo's forthcoming social studies curriculum.

As you will see, implementing information literacy through the Big6 is a statewide, long-term commitment. We hope our experiences will help you as you seek to "ensure that students are effective users of ideas and information." (AASL/AECT, Information Power, 1998, pp. 6).

EDITOR'S NOTE: An additional report, "Going for the Gold with the Big6" tells how Davis High School students in Kaysville, Utah used the Big6 problem-solving approach to study the 2002 Olympics and its impact on the state and residents of Utah. Watch for this article in The Big6 Newsletter, vol. 2, no. 5.

Information Literacy Across the Curriculum: The Utah Experience with the Big6

v2 n4 p3, 10-13

By Sharyl G. Smith

School library media programs throughout the country and especially in Utah are facing many challenges. On the one hand, there has been a decrease in funding for staffing and collection development ever since the federal budget cuts for school library media programs in the 1970s—a situation that many have struggled to reverse. On the other hand, the need to effectively teach information literacy, to impart enthusiasm for reading and to integrate information skills with classroom curriculum increases constantly. In some instances, in Utah, a general apathy toward library media programs is to blame. What is needed is a fresh, effective approach, one that builds on existing strong programs by showing the importance and potential of the school library media program to the schools' overall educational program in a way that ensures support and commitment from the entire school community. Enter the Big6.

The Big6 Comes to Utah

"Information Literacy Across the Curriculum," Utah's plan for statewide implementation of the new Utah Library Media Core Curriculum Standards (**http://www.usoe.k12.ut.us/curr/library/core/**), is heading into its fourth year. To date, 48 school teams, each composed of the school's principal, library media teacher, and classroom teachers, have participated in this Utah State Office of Education sponsored information literacy project. In short, these teams have:

- Attended a summer training institute

- Used the Big6 to write a thematic unit of integrated curriculum

- Worked with a community resource partner

- Team-taught the unit

- Held a community open house, and

- Transferred their unit into an electronic format to share on UtahLINK (**http://www.uen.org/utahlink**), Utah's educational arm of the Internet.

Most teams also have elected to revise and re-teach their units in subsequent years. The Big6 is an essential element of all parts of the plan because the Utah Library Media Core Curriculum Standards are built upon the Big6 framework created by Mike Eisenberg and Bob Berkowitz.

"Information Literacy Across the Curriculum" is also the name of the plan's training component. The title and subtitle "Teacher Team-Building Institute," emphasize not only the format of training, i.e., an institute for school teams, but also some of the basic concepts from which the institute evolved: integrated curriculum with the Big6 as "the glue;" collaboration, for both students and teachers; a focus on the roles of the library media teacher in the overall school program; "building-in," in each project school, a supportive environment for the library media curriculum; provision for student choice in assignments; and marketing the library media curriculum and the Big6 beyond the school and into the community.

Writing Curriculum Standards with the Big6

The library media curriculum standards for secondary schools were approved by the Utah State Board of Education in 1996. That approval was preceded by two years of arduous work. A six-member writing committee combed the professional literature for a research process; compiled a comprehensive list of skills they felt students need to deal with today's glut of information; spent two days with Mike Eisenberg to categorize these skills under the Big6; and turned their list of skills into meticulously written competency indicators. Field testing with students and teachers came next.

The State Office of Education selected five middle, junior, and senior high school teams to pilot the curriculum. It was designed to be fully integrated with subject area curriculum. Each team included a library media teacher and at least two classroom teachers from varying disciplines, most often English/language arts, social studies, and science. The field test revealed results related to student achievement and teacher reaction.

Elementary library media core curriculum standards developments began in 1996. The 12 committee members were charged with creating a scope and sequence of standards, objectives, and indicators that would support transition to the secondary curriculum. Early in their work, the committee met with **Betty Marcoux**, co-chair of the national writing team for *Information Power: Building Partnerships for Learning* (AASL/AECT, 1998). Betty's input helped the committee to align curriculum standards with the national standards. The elementary team created a three-part media curriculum: information literacy (based on the Big6); literature; and media literacy, i.e., standards to help students become wise consumers of media.

Once the curriculum standards were complete, both elementary and secondary writing committees felt adamantly that the curriculum could not be taught effectively in isolation. Therefore, knowing how to implement the core as an integrated curriculum became the problem. The solution was the "Information Literacy Across the Curriculum" project, in which the Big6 and curriculum integration become the twin strands that provided the focus of training and subsequent teaching in the schools. One problem was solved and project planning and funding became the next challenges.

Getting Started

As early as 1994, ideas for the form, major concepts, and details of an implementation plan took shape. Gleanings from the professional literature, conversations with colleagues, and presentations at the AASL conference in Indianapolis went into the mix. A conversation between library consultant and editor **Virginia Matthews** and **Sharyl Smith**, project director, brought the community resource partner idea into focus. **Lynda Welborn**, who was at the time Colorado's state consultant for library media, gave input and direction. Lynda had just completed a very successful training for 60 trainers-of-trainers. Ultimately all library media specialists in the state were influenced and Lynda encouraged us to apply for the same Higher Education Act (HEA) II-B (Library Education and Human Resources Development Program) Grant that made her project possible.

A grant application for HEA funding was prepared, outlining the Utah library media training model. The Utah model called for the mandatory participation of administrators and classroom teachers in training and implementation. Principals and teachers, no matter how well meaning, are able to support an idea only to the extent that they understand it. By calling on them to work with the library media teachers in using the Big6 to write thematic units of integrated curriculum, they create a built-in environment of support and personal commitment to making the "Information Literacy Across the Curriculum" project work.

After the grant proposal was accepted, a project advisory team was formed. Key players in education and related fields were invited to join an advisory council. Current advisory team members include the state's education coordinator for instructional technol-

...The Big6 and curriculum integration become the twin strands that provided the focus of training and subsequent teaching in the schools.

ogy, the directors of the Utah State Library Division, the Utah Education Network and Media Services selected school principals and district superintendents, the local PBS general manager, and higher education faculty. These members lend name recognition, endorsement, support, and publicity to the project. All are invited to attend an annual informational meeting, to take part in the selection of applicant teams, and to come to the institutes and individual school activities. Clearly, the advisory team's endorsement of the project contributes to its success.

The Institute—A Four-Day Summer Camp for Educators

The process begins each year when brochures and application forms are mailed to the schools in the spring, several months prior to the summer institute. The application forms are designed to provide the institute staff with information about prospective teams, and to guide team members in the advance planning that is crucial to later success. Applicants list the theme and concepts of the unit they wish to design, supply the names of the subjects they will integrate, and list the corresponding state curriculum standards and objectives with which they plan to work. The application also lists ideas for activities and evaluation methods. This preparation is important. The institute schedule allows no time for indecision on these basic points. However, beyond choosing a theme and subjects, teams must maintain flexibility in order that information gained from the institute presentations will shape the final unit.

Teams receive reading assignments in advance to prepare them to learn new concepts during the intensive institute schedule. Along with articles from the professional literature, more mundane information is mailed—what to bring for summer in the mountains, perhaps a swimsuit or hiking boots for those odd moments when the teams are not working. Not surprisingly, experience shows that inspiration and planning do not stop at the close of the sessions. Some of the best thinking takes place in the hot tub or on the hiking trail.

Either Mike Eisenberg or Bob Berkowitz has served as the lead teacher, with other staff coming from the Utah State Office of Education. These summer institutes are held at Solitude Resort in the Wasatch Mountains, twelve miles east of Salt Lake City. Teams arrive for an ice cream social on Sunday evening and depart after lunch on Thursday afternoon. The intervening days are long and intensive, with a "work hard, play hard" philosophy governing the schedule. The first two days feature presentations on the Big6, curriculum integration, and meaningful assessment. Each presentation is followed by a "process time," where teams adjourn to round tables to discuss concepts from the preceding presentation, come to a common understanding, and apply the new knowledge to their unit planning.

Early Tuesday, over breakfast, the library media teachers meet with the institute staff to ask questions and discuss library issues and ways to teach the Big6. Similarly, the principals meet with the staff on Wednesday morning to raise issues that pertain to their administrative role in the project's implementation.

On Wednesday, teams need less presentation time and more work time. After a morning devoted to team unit writing, a directed "super-editing" session allows for review to make sure that steps have been carefully rather than superficially undertaken. During a "museum tour," each team displays their in-progress unit and chooses a docent to explain it. The rest of the team visits the other displays, to assess and "borrow" ideas to make their own work better.

Thursday, the final day, is devoted to writing a four-to-eight month implementation plan. An alumni team presents, to assure everyone that what they are undertaking really is possible. An alumni principal talks about "making it work," sharing successful ideas for eking out planning time or creative funding. As a group activity, teams are then guided through writing their own implementation plans, including a timeline of the events— selecting and meeting with the community resource partner, teaching the unit, holding the open house workshop, hosting the open house, and entering the electronic unit into the UtahLINK database.

At some point during the week, team members may feel overwhelmed and even confused. By Thursday afternoon, although they may be exhausted, team members have in hand a unit of which they are proud, and each member has a clear idea of how they are going to teach it. The final day closes as it has every day, with participants' written reflections or assessment. Final reflections praise meaningful instruction, a real caring about participants, practical applications, and excitement and anticipation about teaching their unit to students. One man confessed that he had planned to retire after the coming year. With the skills to teach the Big6 in an integrated setting, he was reconsidering. Another, burned out in mid-career, had planned to leave the profession. She claimed that the institute changed her mind. Three years later, she is still teaching.

The students are quick to notice the differences in this new approach: all their teachers and library media teacher are speaking the same language—they are all talking about "The Big6."

Back at School

After the institute, teams return home with their unit, an implementation plan, and a timeline of events. The next step is to invite a community resource partner, perhaps a public or academic librarian, to join the team and help to assess local materials (print, non-print, and Web sites) available for teaching the unit. The relevant school library media materials are evaluated first, then the community partner's materials. When all team members know the availability and quality of resources, the library media teacher places an order for materials based on gaps in the collections. Team members contact additional resource partners such as biology professors, and other neighborhood experts on subjects related to the unit. One team brought in a student's grandmother who was a quilting specialist. The teams value the idea of a community resource partner and have expanded it beyond our original conception.

Once lessons are written to completion, community partners are in place, and materials assembled, the teachers introduce the units and students tackle the assignments. The students are quick to notice the differences in this new approach: all their teachers and library media teacher are speaking the same language—they are all talking about "The Big6." Lessons and assignments from one class to the next are related. In some schools, a composite grade will measure efforts and products in all integrated classes. Students see Big6 posters in each classroom beside the "Essential Questions" their teachers have posed. Just as the Big6 helps to organize student processes, "Essential Questions," a concept from the work of curriculum integration specialist **Dr. Heidi Hayes Jacobs**, Teachers College, Columbia University, help to organize the content the children will study (Jacobs, 1989). Finally, it is most likely that the students, at some point in the unit, will work in groups, similar to their teachers' team, and, as their teachers do, students will experience the highs and lows of collaboration.

If the students work in teams, they learn to cooperate by producing a group product, e.g., a multimedia program; a group-researched paper; a board game with its own rules, markers, and question-and-answer cards; a play written and performed by the team; a "claymation" video—all the results of collaborative efforts. In addition to group products, students also may be given choices for their individual work.

At the close of their unit, each team hosts a community open house. The first purpose of the open house is to celebrate student (and teacher) success. A second purpose is to provide the news media with positive school news. Third, the community open house is seen as a marketing piece for library media programs, our new curriculum, and the Big6. About four weeks prior to this celebratory event, team members attend an open house workshop. They discuss four areas:

- The content of the open house program to ensure that the school library media program, the state curriculum, and the project are a part of the evening's presentation

- The target audience, or the key civic and community leaders, to invite

- Publicity, emphasizing that multiple forms of publicity are most effective, and

- Evaluation, both formal and informal, including tips to help ensure success.

Despite the uniformity of the workshop agenda, each open house is distinctive and reflects the character of the school and community. Often children sing, dance, or dramatize a work related to the study. Short introductions are made, VIP guests are asked to speak, video clips are shown, and results or experiences from the project are shared. Then everyone is invited into the library media center to view student work. On the occasion of the first open house, a visitor from the State Office of Education approached the school, wondering if anyone would be out on such a dark, rainy night. She was in for a surprise. More than 100 parents, grandparents, and siblings crammed the library media center, and the district superintendent was there. The atmosphere, that would be the norm with forthcoming open houses, was one of excitement and celebration.

The real culmination of the Information Literacy Project takes place when the units are entered into the UtahLINK lesson database. For many teams, this is the hardest segment. After teaching the unit and hosting an open house, the task of reducing a full unit into the restrictive electronic template can be a chore. The task often falls into the hands of the most computer literate members of the team. In any case, this part of the project warrants special attention because sharing through UtahLINK gives these valuable units life beyond the originating individual school.

Benefits to Students and Teachers

The Big6 impacts students. Children benefit all along the spectrum of ability. For at-risk students, the

"I've never worked harder in my career! But then I've never had such great results..."

process can make a real difference in their attendance, participation in school assignments, and even in behavior. The process makes sense to them. With just six steps, it is hard for these students to get lost in the research process. On the night of the community open house, **Pam Bryner**, a fifth grade teacher at **Three Falls Elementary** exclaimed almost tearfully, "Even my special ed kids completed a project!" They never had before. Indeed, on the table beside pristine reports and carefully labeled displays of more able children were the special ed students' products. Unsure hands had lettered the titles, wrinkles marked the paper, but the assignments were complete. And the satisfaction of the students and their parents was immeasurable.

On the other end of spectrum, the gifted students are able to use the process fully, in every detail. The library media curriculum has the potential to challenge these talented students to raise the level of quality of their work. When the children in the middle of this ability range are asked, "Would you use the Big6 again?" the response comes quickly, "Oh, yeah! Before, my papers were a big mess. Now I know what to do!" They like the process because it helps them to organize and they like having choice in their assignments.

Hardly any teacher involved in the project would deny an increase in work. However, they are quick to say that the extra work pays off in terms of improved student achievement and, therefore, is worth the effort. Teachers realize, too, that while the integrated units demand a heavy "front-end" effort, once the units are taught, only minor editing is required in subsequent years. All in all, however, collaboration, if well organized, should divide the work, not multiply it.

What do the library media teachers have to say about workload? **JaDene Denniston**, veteran library media teacher whose article follows, exclaimed, "I've never worked harder in my career! But then I've never had such great results. Every single teacher in the school is teaming with me and together we plan and teach all the major units. Every teacher is doing the Big6!"

With the increased workload, institute participants need reminding that they are involved in real educational reform; this is not just another unit. With the combination of the Big6, integrated curriculum integration, and collaboration, this is a new way of doing business.

The original project plan used the concept of "supertrainers," i.e., each team would teach another team. After the successes of the first year, the project staff felt that it is nearly impossible to duplicate the experience of working with such national figures as

Mike Eisenberg and Bob Berkowitz. Furthermore, while some schools are successful in bringing one or two new members onboard after the institute, it is difficult to capture the excitement of the institute and transmit that to entirely new teams, especially in other schools.

Almost invariably, the enthusiasm of the institute prompts teams to want to expand either their units or their teams, or both. At the close of each institute, participants hear a cautionary tale, recommending that in the first year they keep their units contained and resist adding more subjects and teachers. If they create a "model" unit the first year, they can help to ensure success and be poised to expand the second year.

It was found that formal, regularly scheduled planning time with all the team members is a prerequisite to success. Efforts to secure this time are essential. Informal planning will take place among classroom teachers, on the fly, over lunch, between classes, so, with differing schedules, library media teachers must work hard to keep in the planning process and remain active members on the team.

Many teachers and principals are unaware of the changing roles of library media teachers. Although the institute places a recurring focus on these roles and their importance to the school's overall educational program, as always it is up to individual library media teachers to give action to these ideas in the schools on an ongoing basis.

Future Plans

In 1998, the Utah State Office of Education expanded from one to two institutes, one for elementary and one for secondary levels. Alumni teams represent more than half of Utah's 40 school districts. Although many schools have indicated an interest in sending additional teams for training, the goal of the project is to increase the number of new schools and school districts represented. Plans are well underway for this summer, and additional institutes are anticipated in the future.

The advent of the new library media curriculum prompts a need for a workshop just for library media teachers, an intensive in-service similar to the institute. A full day would be devoted to each of the three strands: information literacy, literature, and media literacy. Presenters and facilitators would focus on the new content and how to teach it. If a workshop is only as good as the "take-it-and-teach-it" materials one takes home, then planners must ensure plenty of practical applications. Within the "Information Literacy Across the Curriculum" institutes there is no

It was found that formal, regularly scheduled planning time with all the team members is a prerequisite to success.

time for attention to this level of detail about teaching the library media core curriculum.

Publicizing the successes of the project is important to the overall plan of advocating for school library media programs. In Utah, there is a fledgling friends group, PALS (Parents Advocating Libraries in Schools). Still in a formative stage, the members have not yet had a chance to make a difference in such issues as regular funding for school library media collections or staffing. The PALS vision is to organize regional chapters of parents and others who wish to support school library media programs. Once organized, they can function to help school libraries in many ways. Perhaps PALS, in promoting school library media programs, might become part of the effort to inform the general public about the positive impact that "Information Literacy Across the Curriculum" and the Big6 has had on their students.

Within three years there has been a quiet revolution in Utah. Quiet, not because it is taking place in libraries—the library media centers are noisy with activity. No, quiet because the Information Literacy Project is developing at a carefully measured rate. There are a number of reasons for this rate of development: the comprehensive training with lots of one-on-one consultation is possible only with smaller numbers; two post-institute visits to each school for further training and the open house; and the belief that the Utah model is being refined each year by working intensively with a manageable number of teams. Slowly, the Utah plan for implementing the new library media core curriculum and the Big6 is taking hold and making a difference in the way children manage information.

References

American Association of School Librarians, Association for Educational Technology. (1998). *Information power: Building partnerships for learning includes the information literacy standards for student learning.* Chicago: American Library Association.

Jacobs, H.H., (Ed.). (1989). *Interdisciplinary curriculum: Design and implementation.* Alexandria, VA: Association for Supervision and Curriculum Development.

Utah State Office of Education. (1996). Library media core curriculum standards. (**http://www.usoe.k12.ut.us/curr/library/core/**) [Online].

Begin at the Beginning: The Big6 in the K-2 School

v2 n4 p4-5, 16

By JaDene M. Denniston
Library Media Specialist,
Sunrise Elementary School

At the start of each new year, first graders come to school full of wonder and eager to learn. They have a natural appetite for knowledge, they are full of observations and of questions, and they want answers. "Look! I found a queen ant." "What's a queen ant?" "Does it bite?" "How many legs does it have?" "Those aren't queen ants." "Teacher, can fish really fly?"

These are just a few of the comments and questions that are heard during the first weeks of school. In the past, questions like these might have been given a cursory answer, or even dismissed in the rush of those beginning school days, but not this time. Fresh from statewide training in information literacy, the teachers listened with new understanding about questions and used them as the basis for the information problems that helped Sunrise Elementary first grade teachers begin to use the Big6.

Planning for Success

The Sunrise "Info Lit" team learned about the Big6 during four days at the 1997 "Information Literacy Across the Curriculum" summer institute at Solitude Resort near Salt Lake City. They traveled from a northern Utah university and agricultural town to learn about the new Utah Library Media Core Curriculum, about integrating this core curriculum with thematic units, and about how to collaborate to bring this about.

The Sunrise team, (comprised of **Nancy Bartelt**, principal, **JaDene Denniston**, library media teacher, and first grade teachers, **Anne Campbell**, **Jacqi McDowell**, and **Shelly Otte**), developed a unit on water using the state science core curriculum standards and the Big6. Before teaching the unit, however, the teachers wanted their students to feel comfortable with the Big6 and they planned ways to introduce the process.

Jacqi McDowell jumped right into Task Definition by teaching her students that they had an information problem about ants. She asked the students to brainstorm what it was that they already knew about ants and what they did not know. Then she moved into Information Seeking Strategies by instructing her students to brainstorm all the different

In the past, questions like these might have been given a cursory answer, or even dismissed in the rush of those beginning school days, but not this time.

places they could think of to find answers to their information problem. She was delighted that many of the students said "the library media center" or "Mrs. D," referring to Mrs. Denniston, their library media teacher.

In a neighboring classroom, Shelly Otte was just not sure how she would introduce the Big6. But while reading a picture book as a part of her math lesson, a student called out, "Fish don't fly!" and she knew just how to introduce the Big6. Mrs. Otte stopped reading to respond, "I think we have an information problem. Can fish fly?" This question led to a discussion on what the children knew, what they thought they knew, and what they needed to find out about fish. They brainstormed a list of many places where they could go for information and various ways in which they could solve their information problem.

Mrs. Otte was surprised when one student returned to school the next day with several pages of information his father had helped him find on the Internet. Mrs. Denniston joined the search, checking the library for books and electronic resources on flying fish. The students were well on their way to learning about their information problem.

Anne Campbell, another member of the team, introduced the Big6 with three charts called "KWL Charts." "K" represents information the students know already; "W," stands for what they want or need to know; and "L," is for the new information they are learning. She and the children examined what they needed or wanted to know and then focused on one of their questions. Next, for Information Seeking Strategies, the class made a fourth chart naming places they could go for information to answer their questions. Miss Campbell then told her students that she and Mrs. Denniston would help them use their ideas for information sources to solve their information problems about water. The class continued on their way through the Big6. When their research was completed, the students finished their KWL Charts with statements about new learning and whether or not they felt they had accomplished their task.

Launching the Projects

After the students had been introduced to the Big6 and were familiar with it, the first grade teachers began the water unit. Although the basic content of the unit remained unchanged from the past, there was a new twist: they added the Big6. To begin, the team planned a "Water Day" in the library for students to investigate many of the science core curriculum concepts about water. Stations were set up and parent volunteers helped with the rotations of small groups of students. Children from all seven first grades, not just the "Info Lit" team classes, participated in the hands-on water activities—one class at a time. Throughout these activities, the Big6 students were more proficient in choosing the water questions they wanted to personally investigate.

A key to the project's success was flexible scheduling that allowed additional class time in the library media center with Mrs. Denniston teaching and modeling the Big6.

Students from the three "Info Lit" classes were divided into 5 groups of 15 and scheduled into the library each Friday. The groups brainstormed information problems about water that they were keen to solve themselves. These first graders came up with some very useful questions to study: "What is water?" "Why do we need water?" "Where does water go underground?" "Why do animals need water to live?"

The one question that impressed the teachers the most came from Mrs. Otte's class. Amber, a seven-year-old, said that the one thing she really wanted to know about water was, "How does the Great Salt Lake get salty?" The teachers were amazed at the depth of this question. Acting on some Information Seeking Strategies of her own, Mrs. Denniston enlisted the help of a graduate student from nearby Utah State University for accurate information to answer Amber's query.

They wanted to know what their next Big6 question would be and when could they start!

With their questions in mind, students brainstormed all the possible resources they could use to solve their water information problems. Teachers were fascinated to watch these young children discuss where and how they were going to answer their own questions. Some students came up with the idea of asking their parents for help. One boy claimed that his father knew everything about water. The teacher questioned him further and learned that his father sells water purification systems. The dad agreed to come to school to demonstrate to the class why clean water is important to people. The children were intrigued to learn that the Earth's water supply is limited and people must continue to reuse the water available.

Gathering Information

Materials for study were gathered and community resource partners, including experts on water, were scheduled to come to work with the students. In addition, parent volunteers were enlisted to help with reading, interpreting data, and writing. Each Friday, for two months, the students listened, viewed, experimented, and recorded information in journals. When their journals were finished and they felt their infor-

mation problem on water had been answered or solved, the teachers asked students, in groups of three, to devise an experiment to show what they had learned. The experiments would be featured at the Big6 Water Night, an open house for parents and other community members.

Reviewing the Results

The school auditorium was crowded on the night of the open house. Almost all of the students hosted at least one family member. Other invited guests were also there in number. The program opened with a short multi-media presentation describing the project, from summer training to the unit's end. The team felt that it was important that parents understand the Big6 and why the team was teaching the process to their children. Next, guests visited classrooms where the students performed their experiments and taught their visitors concepts about water. Parents were surprised and delighted by what their first graders were able to do.

Tamara Grange, a school board member who attended the open house, commented, "I am amazed that first graders are capable of understanding such in-depth ideas." District Superintendent Steve Norton responded to the presentation, "The Big6 approach to teaching research skills has enabled our students, even in the early grades, to conduct research and then use the information to develop projects that help them to realize that subjects are connected. The night of presentations at Sunrise Elementary was an outstanding example of excellence in education." Assistant Superintendent Chad Downs added, "This has been a wonderful opportunity for Cache County students." Every comment heard that evening was very positive and, later, many appreciative parents wrote thank you notes. As much as the team welcomed this praise, the highlight of the event was the students' reactions. They wanted to know what their next Big6 question would be and when could they start!

When the three first grade teachers were asked if they would continue to incorporate the Big6 process in their lessons, all three exclaimed, "Yes!" because it helps students to understand the importance of solving information problems and provides critical thinking and other life-long learning skills. Shelly Otte summarized her feelings about the Big6, "I have seen genuine increased and sustained interest and excitement within the children wanting to learn new things. I never thought I would see this sustained interest in such young children. Their excitement is contagious and makes me want to engage in more and more research with them. The Big6 process really stays with the children. I couldn't teach any other way now."

Implementing Big6 information problem-solving into the three classrooms last year was such a positive experience that when Sunrise Elementary had the opportunity to send a second team to the 1998 institute, the faculty had to draw names because so many of the teachers were eager to attend. Of the second "Info Lit" project team, Helen Hellstern and Judy Merkley represented kindergarten; Jason Sokol, first grade; Mona Schenavar and Andria McCaul, second grade; and Peggy Escobar the reading specialist and JaDene Denniston, the library media teacher, completed group. After the institute, the new team returned to school so excited about acting on their training experience that the entire school is now implementing the Big6 process in their teaching.

Nancy Bartelt, principal of this kindergarten-through-second-grade school, reflected, "The Big6 has the power to energize an entire school. Sunrise teachers are enthusiastically embracing the concept that all of our children can benefit from the Big6 method of teaching. While those who attended the "Information Literacy Across the Curriculum" institute are approaching Big6 with a greater level of confidence, ALL of our teachers have attended our own Big6 in-service held here at school, and they are learning how to be Big6 teachers with the assistance of Mrs. Denniston. As a principal, when a new method of teaching is presented that has great promise for children, you hope that a systemic change will occur. I see that happening and I'm encouraged that, with the intense focus that we have committed to the implementation of the Big6, our children will benefit from the method for years to come."

JaDene Denniston shared her thoughts, "One of the elements in the water unit was to help students, parents, and other teachers see the importance of using the school library media center as an information learning center. Another was to empower Sunrise students with skills to help them solve any information problem and to help them become life-long learners. Sunrise Elementary is becoming a Big6 information problem-solving school. We believe that through teaching the Big6 Process and through the collaboration of all our teachers—classroom, speech, reading, resource, and school library media—we will empower our students to become life-long learners."

From all reports, it would seem that Sunrise students are on their way to fulfilling the school mission of "providing students with a love of learning in a quality early childhood setting, allowing them to become productive, responsible citizens of a technological and multicultural society." Certainly word about the Big6 is out and has even reached this year's new crop of kindergartners who came to school with their own unique questions. But, now it's different. Now, in addition to these questions, they ask "So, what information problem do we get to solve today?!"

"So, what information problem do we get to solve today?!"

The Big6 Goes to Middle School: Teaching an Integrated Unit

v2 n4 p6-7, 14-15

**By Roy Kanno,
Science Teacher, Dixon Middle School,
Dixon, Utah**

The students are noisy, even boisterous, as they move from class to class. One girl calls to another in Spanish. They jostle for position beside their best friends. Down the hallway, in a heated discussion about last night's game, a cluster of boys seems destined for tardiness. The walls surrounding these lively students are old, built in 1930, but the ideas that propel the instruction of the young people are new, on the edge of educational reform.

Dixon Middle School's involvement with collaborative teaching and integrated curriculum dates back to 1990 and, as one of five pilot schools for the state library media core curriculum, Dixon, in Provo, Utah, added the Big6 in 1995. Few realized at the time the potential for student impact held within these six steps, especially when taught with other subjects.

Background

In the summer of 1996, a team of Dixon teachers and their principal attended the Utah State Office of Education's "Information Literacy Across the Curriculum," a week-long workshop on integrated curriculum and the Big6. One of many teams on the school's faculty, this one was designated "The Odyssey" team. Members included principal, **Bob Gentry**, and teachers **Cheryl Duerden**, English; **Jeannette King**, library media; **Sherri Pack**, math; and **Roy Kanno**, science. **Deanne Lewis**, special education; **Kim Atkin**, history; and student teacher, **Brooke Jones** later joined the Odyssey team. This diverse group met with 14 other teams in the southwestern Utah town of Moab where they learned techniques for using the Big6 research skills to integrate interdisciplinary curricula.

One goal of the institute was for each team to develop an integrated unit of instruction, based on a theme. Dixon chose a topic of great local interest, traffic problems along the Wasatch Front. Utah's most concentrated area of population stretches from Salt Lake City, along the western foothills of the Wasatch Mountains, north to Ogden and south to Provo. This corridor lies in the relatively narrow land mass between the mountains and the Great Salt Lake and Utah Lake, and is known as "The Wasatch Front." During rush hour, the current volume of traffic clogs the corridor. A continuation of the state's high growth rate, coupled with anticipated large numbers of visitors during the 2002 Winter Olympics, makes traffic one of the most urgent problems of the Wasatch Front. Highly relevant, this theme integrates several subjects and suggests numerous, varied activities.

Implementation Calendar

The team spent time in August and September bringing the new members, Lewis, Atkin, and Jones, up to speed on the Big6 and attending a half-day in-service workshop on assessment techniques. A second workshop, held later in the fall, featured hypermedia instruction to help team members create a multimedia presentation for their end-of-unit open house. By the end of September, all teachers on the Odyssey Team, in collaboration with library media teacher Jeannette King, began integrating Big6 skills into their subject areas. For example, Mr. Kanno showed the students how the steps of the Big6 relate to the scientific method; Miss Pack made the connection to problem-solving skills in math.

In October, teachers began student team-building activities. For the major unit project, i.e., a collaboratively researched and written position paper proposing a solution to Wasatch Front traffic problems, the teachers thoughtfully put together student teams. Each team included an advanced English student, an advanced math student, a special needs or Chapter One student, a peer tutor, and a student familiar with the Internet. Near the end of October, English teacher Cheryl Duerden taught interview skills and assigned students to interview local drivers about traffic problems along the Wasatch Front. Kim Atkin, in history, taught classes about primary and secondary sources of information and the reliability of sources. As part of their lesson, the students watched a debate between gubernatorial candidates and evaluated their statements on traffic solutions.

From the end of October through the beginning of November, Mrs. King, the library media specialist, coordinated the students' efforts in searching the Internet for information about solutions to traffic

problems in other areas of the country. She did so using the Big6 as a framework thereby reinforcing the instruction the students had been receiving in the classrooms.

During November, Mr. Kanno's science classes learned how to take field notes and began gathering data on local traffic patterns. One assignment sent students throughout the neighborhood to tally traffic use on main thoroughfares and side streets. Equipped with mechanical counters and clipboards, the young people stood on curbsides, even during a snowstorm on one day. In Miss Pack's math class, the students organized and evaluated the data they had collected and entered it on 3-D graphs. Much to their delight, the graphs were on cakes and baking the cakes and representing the data in sugar frosting was a part of the assignment.

In December, Mrs. Duerden and Mrs. Lewis team-taught the skills for writing persuasive papers. First, the groups brainstormed ideas for their papers, a task allowing those without strong writing skills to come up with as many ideas and participate as actively as the better writers did. After establishing a focus for their work, the teams moved on to deal with Information Seeking Strategies, Location & Access, and Use of Information. A spirit of cooperation prevailed; if one team found information beneficial to another, they shared. As the teams began the Synthesis step, the more verbal students on each team took a greater part in finalizing their persuasive paper on traffic solutions. Also in December, Miss Atkin instructed the students to design, create, and evaluate a board game with a transportation theme as a part of their social studies assignment.

A spirit of cooperation prevailed; if one team found information beneficial to another, they shared.

With all assignments completed, the Odyssey Team held a community open house in February. Well over 100 parents and guests, including the school district's superintendent, **Dr. Michael Jacobsen**, attended the open house. The persuasive papers, colorful and clever transportation games, and samples of the students' frosted cake graphs were on display for all to see. The evening's program featured a hypertext presentation on the whole "Information Literacy Across the Curriculum" project. Several teacher and student pairs spoke from different viewpoints and reflected on their experiences with the Big6.

At the beginning of March, the students and teachers evaluated the project. The teachers were eager to learn how their students perceived the assigned tasks and the work they had accomplished. They wanted to know how students felt about their own levels of effort and the relevance of the skills they had acquired. To accomplish this task, the team created a survey to gather student opinion.

The Results

The Odyssey Team was pleased with the students' results. Teachers noted increased numbers of completed assignments, improved performance, and, in some cases, improved attendance. Figure 1 (below) summarizes the findings by linking:

- Components of the project
- Relevant Big6 skills
- Assessment tools
- Percent of the grade, and
- The average grade result.

Following the completion of the project, students completed a survey instrument to evaluate the project. An analysis of the surveys found a positive correlation among the perceived level of difficulty of a task, the perceived usefulness of a skill, and the degree of learning. In other words, the harder the task, the harder the students worked, and the more the students felt they learned. Also, the more useful or relevant they perceived the skill, the more willing the students were to put effort into learning that skill.

Project Support: Organizing for Success

The success of any undertaking with the complexity of this interdisciplinary project is based on well planned organization of time, resources, and people. Organizing the students into teams that would work well presented challenges. The Odyssey Team was comprised of a diverse group of 138 students. Of these young people, about 30 were Chapter One or "special needs" students; about 30 were advanced English students; and about 30 were advanced math, i.e., geometry, students. Ten percent of the Odyssey Team were ESL, or English-as-a-Second Language students. The teachers created 28 research teams of five or six members. In each group, the students took the jobs of leader,

recorder, computer technician, taskmaster, or cheerleader. Training assured each student of what was expected of him or her in the group roles.

As for arranging time and schedules, the Odyssey Team had a block of 230 minutes in which to teach the 138 students English, math, science, U.S. history, and an advisory class. The teachers were given complete freedom to arrange the time block into any configuration in order to meet the instructional needs of the students. For example, to accommodate the position paper assignment, the teachers divided the block into three 90-minute periods.

Organizing sufficient planning time is a common problem for almost any faculty. At Dixon, however, strong administrative support for team teaching allows the teachers a common preparation period in addition to their individual prep periods. The importance of this time together cannot be overstated. The Odyssey teachers found that the team prep time was critical for planning and organizing the project. This time gave teachers an opportunity to assess individual student's progress in all subjects and to brainstorm strategies for helping those who might otherwise have been lost among so many classmates.

Figure 1: Compiled Results of the Middle School Project				
COMPONENT	**BIG6 RELATED SKILL**	**ASSESSMENT TOOL**	**% OF GRADE**	**AVERAGE GRADE**
Interview	**1. Task Definition** asking pertinent questions	a rubric	10%	82%
Internet Notes	**3. Location & Access** **4. Use of Information** finding and evaluating sites, taking notes	a rubric	7.5%	100%
Field Notes	**4. Use of Information** observing, measuring, and recording	a rubric	7.5%	97%
3-D Graph	**5. Synthesis** organizing and presenting data	product guide	10%	98%
Persuasive Paper	**5. Synthesis** writing in persuasive mode	a rubric	35%	97%
Transportation Game	**5. Synthesis** **6. Evaluation** decision-making, and evaluating	product guide	15%	87%
Collaborative Learning	**1. Task Definition** **6. Evaluation**	rubric	15%	85%

Project Outcomes

Teachers Cheryl Duerden and Deanne Lewis discussed the social ramifications of students of differing abilities working together on teacher-selected teams. Mrs. Lewis, the special education teacher on the team, commented, "The students with disabilities reacted quite well within the group. Perhaps, for the first time, they had the opportunity to work closely with students who had abilities they didn't have. Completing assignments with the rest of the group raised the level of the abilities and skills of the special education students. The final products were not the products of just the higher-level students, everyone worked together."

Cheryl Duerden reflected on the impact to the advanced students. "It was really interesting to watch how the high achieving students, who were used to succeeding easily and independently, worked with their classmates who were not as academically advanced. These advanced students had the hardest time adjusting to the group dynamics. They were frustrated, even going home in tears in some cases, because the slower students were not performing at the level they were accustomed to, or were not finishing the assignments quickly enough. So we had to work with them, teaching delegation skills, and teaching them that they had to model certain school behavior that these other students hadn't ever done before. And as these students began really working together, they found that it wasn't as stressful as they thought it would be. It was pretty exciting for them most of the time, once they got past worrying that someone else, not as capable, was doing a part of the group assignment."

Principal Bob Gentry, who fielded phone calls and visits of the parents who voiced criticism of the project, notes "At first some parents were concerned about this new group approach, but as they began to come in and sit with the team, to see what the students were doing, the parents began to realize that this was a very valuable thing to do, and they began to appreciate the social skills their children were learning."

New friendships formed as a result of students having the opportunity to work with many classmates. This was an unexpected outcome of the project. Mrs. Duerden observed, "We would see the students walking down the hall at the beginning of the year and there were very definite social groups. Later those social groups crossed over and you would see kids walking together who never did before—they hadn't had enough in common to hang around together. At this age, they didn't see their common interests. But by working together, they saw one another's strengths and made new friends."

Insights

As the Odyssey Team reflected on the project, they shared their insights about the library media program, the teachers' role, and the students' performance.

ABOUT STUDENT PERFORMANCE

- All students can be successful if instruction and assignments are modified for their special needs.
- When students see the relevance of a task they will work hard to complete that task.
- Peer tutors are a good resource in helping to mainstream special needs students.
- Working in groups will help ESL students learn to speak and understand English and learn math and science content.

ABOUT THE LIBRARY MEDIA PROGRAM

- The Big6 is a very effective way for students to solve information problems.
- The project helped to clarify for students and staff the roles of the library media teacher as teacher, curriculum planning partner, and information specialist with extensive knowledge of resources in the library and on the Internet.
- With the clearest vision of the Big6, the library media teacher helps to give direction to the project.
- The library media teacher is a great resource to aid in research projects, especially when classroom teachers plan with her or him, from the start, not just before bringing a class to the library media center.

ABOUT THE TEACHER'S ROLE

- Integrated units require a great deal of work to set-up instruction, but the results are worth the effort.
- It takes a lot of planning, effort, and training for students to work effectively in groups; however, a group can produce work that is at a higher level of skill than the level of skill of the highest member of the group.

Conclusion

Bob Gentry, principal, summarized the "Information Literacy Across the Curriculum" project in this way: "What the project caused was more thinking and better thinking, better work on the part of the students where they actually worked on the production of things that made sense. This is all new, basically, and it's harder, and it's rigorous. But it's all applicable and valuable. The results shown by the team demonstrate that the harder the students worked, the more they enjoyed it." What more could educators ask?

The Big6 and Electronics: Research in the Rockies

v2 n4 p8-9, 13

By Patti Harrington, Assistant Superintendent, Provo School District

Kathy Luke, Director of Elementary Education

Ann Tidwell, Library Media Teacher, Sunset View Elementary

Suzanne Blakesley, Library Media Teacher, Timpview High School

Sandra Davis, Library Media Teacher, Wasatch

In Provo, Utah, a city nestled along the western slope of the Wasatch Range of the Rocky Mountains, a fifth grader listens to her elementary school library media teacher describe the research process. The final project will be due in three weeks, and she will learn to access the Internet, take pictures with a digital camera, utilize CD-ROM resources, look up information in online catalogs, and get help with research questions through KidsConnect, all as a part of her project. This student will choose to present a multimedia show about animals in their habitats while her best friend will decide to create a poster illustrating a variety of habitats. Another student will write a report that will include online graphics and digitized photos.

Research in the 1990s is fun, exciting, multimodal, and individualized! The days of note cards, a set number of pages for a paper, and uniform final products are fast disappearing. Now kids are copying and pasting, paraphrasing, reorganizing information from many sources, and producing a new product, unique to each child. Students in Provo are learning that it is fun to use electronic tools for research and for synthesizing and producing information. As students work on their final project, they use the Big6 as an organizer. Teachers recognize the Big6 as a conceptual framework for information literacy—one that provides students with a process that helps them

define a problem, brainstorm possible sources of information, locate information within sources, extract relevant data, organize and produce a product, and judge the effectiveness and efficiency of their work.

Background

When the Big6 was incorporated into the Utah Library Media Core Curriculum, the Provo School District was ready, willing, and able. Provo is one of 12 districts in the state that employs certificated library media teachers for their elementary schools. In Provo, every school has a library media teacher who is responsible for implementation of the Big6 and other library media content across the curriculum. As a result, the library media teachers are directly teaching information access strategies via technology, in addition to the traditional library role of engendering a love of literature.

"We believe that our library media centers should be the hub of information for our schools," says **Dr. Patti Harrington.** "That means that we continue to need experienced teachers in our libraries, and those library media teachers must be thoroughly acquainted with the latest technology, given the volume of information and the speed with which information can be transferred to learners through computers." Therefore, the Provo School District is working feverishly to provide in-service training to library media teachers in order to create the necessary level of proficiency. Since in-service programs are under the direction of Dr. Harrington and Dr. Kathy Luke, director of elementary education, there is clear emphasis and support from district administration.

Getting Ready with Meaningful In-Service Training

The Provo School District has combined a $68,000 grant from the Utah State Office of Education with matching district funds to provide 19 library media teachers with in-service training. Through this training, the library media teachers are learning the uses of desktop conferencing, web navigation and search tools, digitized photo and voice capabilities, databases, spreadsheets, graphics, and hypermedia. The intended outcome of the in-service training is for the library media teachers to learn these tools well enough to help students with research in the library and to offer direct instruction to teachers and students throughout the building. This is an ambitious project because some of the library media teachers, by their own admission, are not yet fully computer literate. Nonetheless, they are enthusiastic about this new opportunity. As one librarian commented, "We haven't had the technology until recently. How wonderful to get the training along with it."

"I am excited about this," says **Suzanne Blakesley**, library media teacher at **Timpview High School**. A former English teacher, Blakesley has long understood "book research," but claims to be "somewhat of a novice" with computers.

She now will be expected to add online services to her teaching abilities. Blakesley sees the Big6 as an integral part of her job. "The Big6 breaks down the research process into sizable chunks and integrates with technology so naturally that even I can learn to access electronic information with ease," she states. "As library media teachers, we need to take the lead in helping students access information and prepare final projects for whatever classroom assignments they have."

Taking a leadership role in integrating technology with the Big6 this year requires technical, "hands-on" in-service for library media teachers. The framework for this in-service features the Big6 and related technological concepts at meetings which are scheduled monthly. For example, in September, the library media specialists focused on the Big6 steps, Use of Information and Synthesis and learned ClarisWorks, a program suitable for word processing and multimedia presentations. **Ann Tidwell**, the lead facilitator for the group, notes, "The buy-in is total because the library media teachers finally have funding to support technology acquisition and a framework for instruction in the Big6 that is second to none in quality." To make learning these technical and intellectual skills possible, the district purchased a Macintosh G3 computer for each library media teacher to use for practicing and using the new concepts. In turn, the librarians instruct their own teachers on the concepts and software programs of the month.

To learn more about information literacy and further prepare for the district project, many of Provo's library media teachers and their classroom teachers have attended the Utah State Office of Education library media training institutes, "Information Literacy Across the Curriculum." At these institutes, the library media and classroom teachers studied the Big6 with Bob Berkowitz and Mike Eisenberg and planned for its implementation. As a result of the training, there is now a multi-disciplinary cadre of educators in many of the district's schools. These educators provide leadership in integrating the Big6 throughout the curriculum.

These are not stand-alone skills that can be mastered in isolation.

District-Wide Implementation

Information literacy and technology are two of the half-dozen concepts that are integrated throughout the curriculum in the Provo School District. "These are not stand-alone skills that can be mastered in isolation," Assistant Superintendent Patti Harrington notes. "Rather, they inform and refine the work of every student in the District and can be applied to subject-area adoptions and revisions district-wide." The Big6 is an essential component because it helps to organize learning in all disciplines.

Under this philosophy, Provo's social studies teachers have recently adopted the Big6 as the framework for teaching information processing to students. As the social studies curriculum undergoes a district-wide review, the Big6 will play a role in the choice of materials, the scope and sequence of work, and the development of product and project requirements. Teaming among the social studies and library media teachers will become a natural partnership. Dr. Harrington is hopeful that the Provo District may be one of the first in the state to provide, in every school, social studies instruction emphasizing the use of direct online resources in tandem with print resources and, in the words of Ann Tidwell, "a framework for instruction in the Big6 that is second to none in quality."

Just ask first grader Abish Purcell about using Big6. At Sunset View, where the Big6 is integrated with the curriculum, Abish and his brother and sisters developed a multimedia presentation for the school's "Heritage Days." The children brought pictures from home, scanned them into the computer, and arranged text and graphics to illustrate their Polynesian heritage. Abish and his siblings stunned the audience with their presentation of pictures of their parents dancing Polynesian style and with pictures of erupting volcanoes that are common on the islands. Their work has been transferred from computer to video and the Purcell family now has a cherished memory, all of which started in the context of the Big6.

From this year on, other library media teachers in Provo will be anxious to provide similar experiences to students throughout the district as they match electronics to the Big6.

Going For the Gold

v2 n5 p8-9, 16

By Elayne Finlinson
Library Media Specialist
Davis High School, Kaysville, Utah

Last but certainly not least! Here's one more article on the exciting Big6 activities taking place in the State of Utah. With all the bad press that the Olympics have been receiving, it's good to see how they can be a very positive force for developing critical thinking—in content and in the Big6 Skills.

"The important thing in the Olympic Games is not winning but taking part. Just as in life, the aim is not to conquer but to struggle well."

—Pierre de Coubertin, founder of
the modern Olympics

With this quote as a motto, and with the Big6 as a guide, 90 sophomores from **Davis High School in Kaysville, Utah**, spent six weeks going for the gold—Olympic Gold. These students were placed in an integrated curriculum project combining English, history, science, and the Big6 information problem-solving process to study the 2002 Olympics and its impact on the state and residents of Utah.

"How will the upcoming Olympics affect you?" was the question posed to students. The immediate relevance of the topic caught the interest of most students who would research and create a presentation in answer to this question.

Davis High administrators **Scott Greenwell**, principal, and **Corine Sayler**, vice-principal, supported the project by arranging students' schedules so that all 90 sophomores had the same teachers for English, history and biology—a near-Olympian feat in itself! To help facilitate cooperative planning, these teachers were given common prep periods. The idea for the Olympic Gold project was the result of the teachers' and administrators' attendance at the Information Literacy Across the Curriculum Institute in August 1998. At that time, **Ruth Barker** (English), **Shawnda Stevens** (biology), **Wendy Jensen** (history), **Elayne Finlinson** (library media teacher), along with administrators Greenwell and Sayler learned about the Big6 from Dr. Mike Eisenberg and wrote the integrated curriculum unit.

After the Institute, the four teachers used the Big6 information problem-solving process themselves to plan and implement the unit of study. As a part of Task Definition, teachers designed a rubric for grading students' final presentations. Information Seeking Strategies (Big6 #2) were used to identify all the people, athletes, places, books, videos, organizations and sources students might use to locate information. After information was gathered (Big6 #3), guest speakers were scheduled, a field study arranged, and books brought in from several city and county libraries. The team invited the Salt Lake Olympic Committee to participate and they accepted! "A Night of Academic Excellence" was scheduled so that students could showcase their findings. For Synthesis (Big6 #5), the teachers finished their lessons and, after a final review, prepared to teach them.

Catching Olympic Fever

First, students learned about the "Magic of the Big6" from Mrs. Finlinson, who used a multimedia presentation about Houdini to introduce the process steps. Just as Houdini performed magic to complete his marvelous feats, students were given a magical formula called the Big6 to help them create their presentations. They were taught that the process is as important as the product.

Next, working in groups of three, students were taught in-depth about Task Definition. The task for all groups was to research and present their findings about a chosen aspect of the Olympic Games. The project required students to investigate their chosen aspect through research supported by citations from a variety of sources. Students had to create an outline of their topic and prepare an oral presentation. Their choice of projects should encourage students with different learning styles and interests to participate. A few of the suggested options for a final product were multimedia presentations, artwork, oral demonstrations, videos, and Web pages. The Salt Lake Olympic Committee asked that one group help publish a brochure with a collection of newspaper articles for and against Salt Lake City hosting the Olympics.

During the initial three weeks, students learned how the historical, social, and environmental issues of the past have shaped the Olympic movement. In history class, students studied the history of the Olympics; the pros and cons of the Olympics coming to Utah; and the actual events comprising the Winter Olympics. Economic, gender, and political issues were also debated. In English class, outlining, note-taking, citing sources, editing, and supporting thesis statements became the focus of study. In biology class, students examined the critical issues related to preserving the natural resources surrounding the venues; preventing air pollution; conserving the renowned natural habitats of Utah; solving the transportation problem; and forecasting Utah's winter climate and weather. The library media specialist taught students how to use the online catalog to locate books and other materials; how to use search engines; how to evaluate a Web page; how to use CD-ROMS for effective research; and how to use specialized software to create a multimedia presentation.

Students were encouraged to use a variety of sources including human sources. They learned firsthand from a panel of Salt Lake Olympics experts. These experts included a journalist from KSL-TV, a representative from the legislature, the director from the Utah Department of Transportation for the 2002 Olympics, an economist from the Governor's office; and, from the Salt Lake Olympic Committee, a vice-president for human resources and volunteers. Also, panel members remained after the program to accommodate student interviews. Students put into practice the interviewing skills they had gained from an earlier unit lesson involving Big6#4, Use of Information.

Students visited the Utah Winter Sports Park in Park City, Utah, the venue for several of the Olympic events. While there, students toured the bobsled and luge run. They watched while athletes competed for final positions on the U.S. Olympic Luge Team. They saw the jumps where the freestyle skiers train and practice in the summer and listened to an athlete telling about the rigorous training necessary to compete. They heard lectures about the construction of the venues, the economics of building and maintaining these facilities, and the politics of surviving the dream of the 2002 Olympics. In the beauty of a crisp October day, students lined the luge and bobsled track from top to bottom as they watched Erin Warren, a member of the U. S. luge team, break her track record at the Utah Winter Sports Park.

The enthusiasm of these students cheering the athletes caused one teacher to reflect wistfully that, although the Games will be held so near to their homes, many of these students will not be able to afford to attend the Olympics in the year 2002. Would their "inside" experience today be remembered and compensate for missing the real event in four years? The answer might lie in their personal attitudes toward the Games, attitudes that, in some cases, changed during the course of the research project.

"For me, learning will never be the same. I just feel different about learning about new things."

Realism Sets In

As the unit drew to a close and knowledge about the Olympic Games increased, the students became more passionate about issues they now recognized might directly affect them and their environment. No longer were the classes in agreement about sponsoring the Olympic dream. The problems of hosting the games became real to students as they learned about the issues of terrorism, drugs, security, etc. However, the Big6 process had given them tools for problem solving and the outcome of the project was a knowledgeable body of voices ready for an audience.

These voices took form as each group converted the outline of their research paper into a multimedia presentation or other form of expression, e.g., demonstrations about nutrition, an Olympic game, a live mascot and torch bearer, a choreographed dance for an opening ceremony, and a brochure promoting the natural resources of Utah. Teachers were amazed at the creativity and quality of the students' projects and diverse thinking that they exhibited. The projects combined graphics, music, imagination and new knowledge. Not one group failed to turn in a product. Grading the projects became a pleasure, not a chore. Best of all, the lifelong benefit to the students was the information skills they had gained. One student, Michelle Johnson, typical of those involved in this interdisciplinary project, stated, "For me, learning will never be the same. I just feel different about learning about new things."

Olympic Gold

The Open House marking the end of the project took place on November 4, 1998. Proud students beamed as they presented their research to parents, fellow classmates, teachers, a county official, state and district educators, and the press. A local newspaper reporter caught the excitement of the evening, writing, "It was a performance fit for any senior honors project." The students, all sophomores, were pleased. For their teachers, the best part of the evening was watching the students, professionally attired, express what they had unearthed and created about the Olympics. The students had discovered the gold! They had given an Olympic-sized effort and, in the process, had caught the exhilarating feeling that comes from struggling and doing well. Paraphrasing Coubertin's Olympic motto,

"They had learned that the important thing is not winning but taking part. The aim is not to conquer but to struggle well."

They had struggled well.

CHAPTER 19

The BIG 6

Reports from the Front Lines–Integrating Big6 into the Curriculum

Reports from the Front Lines

v1 n1 p3, 15

By Carrie A. Lowe

*Big6™ in Action will be a regular feature of this newsletter. The purpose is to share ways in which educators are successfully implementing and using the Big6™ in their classrooms and library media centers. To share your own success stories, please e-mail them to **big6@ericir.syr.edu** or snail mail to Big6™ Newsletter, 4-194, CST, Syracuse University, Syracuse, NY 13244-4100.*

Donald Pedley, a teacher at The Ravensbourne School in the suburbs of London devised an effective lesson to help his 7th graders learn the skill of note-taking. He wanted to really grab their attention as well as help them learn note-taking skills—Big6™ #4. Pedley began the lesson with a traditional (somewhat dull) lecture on note-taking. Partway through the lesson, he had his assistant call him on his cellular phone, posing as a friend asking Pedley to join him for dinner. Pedley engaged the class in the conversation, asking them to help him take notes of the conversation to insure that he had all of the important

information. Pedley also took his own notes, which were disorganized and filled with superfluous (and downright wrong) information. After his phone conversation ended, Pedley enlisted the class (working in groups) to evaluate his notes and provide feedback on them. The students took great pleasure in pointing out their teacher's mistakes. Pedley found that this fostered fruitful discussions of styles of note-taking and short cuts. Another call from his "friend" a few minutes later allowed the class to practice their new note-taking skills. This was an excellent real-life scenario which led to new awareness and specific skills development in context.

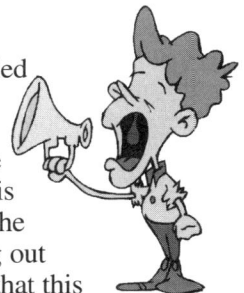

Ann Gray, a Library Media Specialist in Pittsburg, New Hampshire, found that a good way to teach the Big6™ is to reinforce formal lessons with spur-of-the-moment teaching. She recently shared a story on the Big6 listserv about an opportunity she had to do just that. Not long ago, third-graders began to trickle in to her library media center with an assignment to identify continents on a blank map. Rather than simply pointing them toward the correct source, Gray identified this as "a gold mine of opportunity" to teach the Big6™! She spent time with each student leading them through the

Big6™ steps, first asking them to identify their task and then to brainstorm possible sources. Atlases, of course, became the primary resource of choice. The students then located the atlases (print and electronic) and worked on finding the relevant maps in each atlas. The students, who were delighted with all of the "cool" information they discovered in atlases, were enthusiastic learners of the Big6 Skills™.

From the land of Green Bay Packermania, **Fort Atkinson, Wisconsin, Phyllis Schicker** discovered another excellent real-life application for the Big6 Skills™. In the weeks before the 1997 Superbowl, Schicker's school was increasingly dominated by football talk. Schicker used this topic as an opportunity to reinforce the importance of the Big6™ with a fourth grade class. The class discussed ways that the Packers could use the Big6™ to beat their opponent in an upcoming game. Schicker was pleased to be able to move the discussion past the level of, "we really hope the Packers win," to "what are the things that the Pack need to do to win?" (Task Definition) and "what information do they need in order to do so?" (Information Seeking Strategies) and "what should their game plan be?" (Synthesis). This focus was so successful that it even inspired a bulletin board — labeled "Winning with the Big Six," showing each of the steps on a football, and of course, proudly emblazoned "Go Packers!" Whether the Big6™ discussion in Schicker's class led directly to Green Bay's victory in the Superbowl last year has not yet been confirmed.

A third grade teacher in the state of Washington reported her recent conversion to the Big6 Skills" approach to information problem-solving. Apparently the new library media specialist in her school had been teaching the Big6 Skills™ to the students without really explaining the process to the faculty. The teacher began to hear her students using Big6™ terms when discussing lessons and projects, for example, "let's define the task—what do we need to do?" and "where should we look for information?" She asked the students about it. The students showed her some of the materials they had received during library time, and they taught her the Big6™! Needless to say, the teacher was impressed. Later that day, she approached the library media specialist to get more information on the Big6™ and to talk about how it might be used in her upcoming unit on "insects in the backyard."

To close, here's one from **Mike Eisenberg** (paraphrased from the recent *Helping With Homework* book). In a visit to middle school class to discuss the importance of Task Definition, Mike asked the class what they were working on. The

class reported that they would be taking an exam the following Monday (it was Friday). Mike then asked the class whether it would be a major test or a quiz. To everyone's surprise (especially the teacher), half of the class responded that it would be a test, while the other half of the class thought it would be a quiz. Mike, who knew that the exam was to be a test on the current chapter of the text, asked the class whether or not the test would be comprehensive. Again, half of the class reported that the test would be comprehensive, while the other half was certain that it would only cover the current chapter. Finally, Mike asked whether the test would be short answer or essay. The class was again divided on this issue. Mike asked the teacher not to look as he questioned how many of them planned to study for the exam that weekend. About three quarters of the students raised their hands. Mike then urged them to take responsibility for their own learning. "Never go into a test or assignment without knowing exactly what's going to be covered. Know what it's going to look like, and how it is going to be graded. You've got to do 'brain surgery' on your teachers—get into their heads and figure out what they want. Why waste time and effort studying the wrong materials or expecting the wrong style of test? Take control—make sure you define the task."

> *"Whether the Big6™ discussion in Schicker's class led directly to Green Bay's victory in the Superbowl last year has not yet been confirmed."*

Carrie Lowe, Masters of Library Science, School of Information Studies, Syracuse University. She holds a Bachelors in Education from the University of Wisconsin, Madison.

Big6 in Action: Reports from the Front Lines

v1 n2 p3,14

By Carrie Lowe

Big6 in Action is a regular feature of this newsletter. The purpose is to share ways in which educators are successfully implementing and using the Big6 in their classrooms and library media centers. To share your own success stories, please e-mail them to Big6@ericir.syr.edu or snailmail to Big6 Newsletter, 4-194, CST, Syracuse University, Syracuse, NY 13244-4100

On the Big6 listserv (big6@listserv.syr.edu), **Janice Wright, of Clifton Springs, New York** and **Kay Hudson, of Ashland, Ohio** recently brainstormed ways that the Big6 can be used to study planets (particularly Mars). Wright began the discussion by asking if anyone on the listserv had ideas for a unit combining the study of planets with the Big6 skills, to help her to plan a collaborative unit on Mars with a fifth-grade teacher. Hudson responded by describing a planetary Big6 project a fifth grade class in her elementary school had recently done. The class used the Big6 as a guide to research planets, using data charts for research questions and notes. The class created postcards as its final project, drawing a picture of the planet on one side and writing a message about their experiences on the planet on the other side. The project allowed for a great deal of creativity in the students' writing; "Dear Mom, Today we landed on Mars. It was quite cold…".

Barbara Jansen, Round Rock, Texas, offered another approach: present the objective to students as a problem to be solved, such as *"NASA has modified the Pathfinder so that humans can use it to travel to Mars. You have been chosen to head the mission, but you and your crew know nothing about Mars. What is the solution to this problem? Use the Big6 as a model to help the 'crew' solve this problem. The task to be identified is something like, 'Learn about Mars in order to prepare myself and the crew for the trip.'"* Then the students can brainstorm the specific questions they need to answer in groups and later search for the answers (Big6 #2, #3, and #4). The final product (Big6 #5) they create can be a manual to help the crew members survive the trip. They can then evaluate their process and product (Big6 #6) in terms of whether or not the crew members are well-prepared for the trip.

Both of these are all timely and imaginative tasks that require students to go well beyond traditional "planet reports."

Jennifer Merchant, Library Media Specialist at the Taipei American School in Taiwan, and John Daulton (formerly at Taipei but now in **Poland at the American School of Warsaw**) had a great deal of success working with Big6 #1 (Task Definition) with their middle and high school students. They found that stage #1.2 of Task Definition (identify the information needed) is too-often neglected so they chose to stress it to their students. This question is central to the research process, and creates an important foundation for information problem-solving.

Daulton and Merchant approach question 1.2 by having the students write out the answer to the question, "What information am I looking for?" They have found that having their list in-hand helps the students as they begin to search for information. Having a written record of what they are looking for

can also help students if they get stuck in Location & Access. The list provides a guide for finding the appropriate types of sources, as well as the information within the sources.

They also found that the list can guide the students as they begin to organize and prepare the information for a rough draft (step 5.1). The list can help students to see the main ideas in their project, and can even provide topic sentences for their written product.

One project that Daulton and Merchant designed to directly emphasize the importance of step 1.2 is a seventh grade science project. The list that the students create in step 1.2 will become the main elements for their project outline. Students can then put the information they find under these main elements. Once the outline is completed, the students need only add an introduction and a conclusion, and their rough draft will be well under way.

Daulton and Merchant also found that stressing 1.2 has an added benefit; it keeps easily-distracted middle schoolers on task. Previously, a great deal of instructional time was wasted assisting teachers in keeping students on task. Daulton and Merchant noted that, "As soon as we started taking the time to assist students in formulating the questions needed to complete the task, focus ceased being a problem." As anyone who has worked with middle school students knows, a strategy which keeps students on-task is a valuable one, indeed.

Another success story: **Claire Simpson** from **Moorestown, New Jersey,** uses a lesson to teach note-taking (Big6 #4.2) to her fourth-graders which is similar to that described by **Donald Pedley,** who was featured in the last *Reports from the Front Lines* (page 165). As you may remember, this lesson involved a skit in which the library media specialist plays a teenager who must take a very complicated, very important phone message, and learns note-taking skills through trial-and-error. In Simpson's version of the lesson, another teacher standing across the room plays the "grown-up," who calls to leave a message. The "teenager" tries fruitlessly to remember the message; fortunately the caller calls back to add something to the message. This time the message-taker jots down some notes, but only the most important things.

At this point, Simpson copies on the board the "key words" she wrote down while taking the message. She and the class then reconstruct the entire message using the key words as a guide. In this way, Simpson shows the class that it is not necessary to write down every word to get a complete message; only the *important* ones need to be there.

> *"As soon as we started taking the time to assist students in formulating the questions needed to complete the task, focus ceased being the problem."*

The positive outcomes from this activity were numerous. Simpson was able to get—and keep—the students' attention. They were able to understand the lesson and apply it to their classroom activities, as well as understand its real-world applications. Equally exciting was the fact that the teacher who assisted with the lesson got excited about the topic and stayed for the rest of the lesson. Another step toward team teaching!

File under: "I Guess You Had To Be There" – a couple of cute stories from sixth grade classes.

Kay Hudson's (Ashland, Ohio) students have devised a true "Hollywood" style of citing their sources. In a recent class, Hudson reminded her students that they need to "give credit" to their sources. One boy, who had written a standard citation for a reference work (title, volume, page number, etc.) asked for assistance in crediting his source. When Hudson pointed out that he had already done that, he replied, "No. Should I say, 'I'd like to thank the New Book of Knowledge for this information'?" Too many awards shows on television, perhaps?

And…, **Tami Little** from **Iowa** recently asked her students what they liked about the Big6. Besides the more predictable responses, one student piped up, "Well, the Big6 works because we are in sixth grade."

Who knows? Might be true.

Big6 in Action: Reports from the Front Lines

v1 n3 p3

By Carrie Lowe

Big6 in Action *is a regular feature of this newsletter. The purpose is to share ways in which educators are successfully implementing and using the Big6 in their classrooms and library media centers. To share your own success stories, please e-mail them to **Big6@ ericir.syr.edu** or snail mail to Big6 Newsletter, 4-194 CST, Syracuse University, Syracuse, NY 13244-4100.*

Greetings, Big6ers! Just when you thought that the holidays were over, we are heading into another season of special days. Fortunately, holidays provide the perfect opportunity for teaching information problem-solving skills, as noted in recent letters and postings to the listserv.

Black History Month

Black History Month (February) is one important observance which is usually met with a flurry of activities and assignments. **Kathryn Lafferty**, a library media specialist from Pennsylvania, reported that she has been working with a third-grade teacher to design a Black History Month-related assignment using the Big6. Her students are to research a famous African American and present their findings in an oral report and a four-page book. An interesting twist: when presenting the report (Big6 #5—Synthesis), the students become "living portraits"—standing behind a large empty picture frame and acting as the persons, they describe the African-Americans' lives and significant contributions.

Kathryn also designed a useful tool to teach note-taking. She created worksheets around terms such as "childhood" and "why famous" with lines coming out from the terms like a web. Students take notes on these "note webs." This technique helps students learn to take concise notes in their own words. Great idea, Kathryn!

Another creative idea for teaching the Big6 in the context of Black History Month comes from **Rob Darrow**, from **Clovis, California**. Rob and his students created a Bio Board featuring famous African Americans. Students search for information on particular individuals (Big6 #2 through #4). They search out contributions, biographical information, timelines, and photographs or pictures. Rob reports that these Bio Boards make wonderful decorations for a classroom, the library media center, or a school display case.

Valentine's Day

Another holiday, which is quickly approaching, is Valentine's Day. Mike Eisenberg reminds me that he has worked with middle school and early high school students on the task of "finding out if someone likes you." You can go through the entire Big6 process, but brainstorming Information Seeking Strategies (Big6 #2) is particularly fun. What are possible sources? Should you ask the person straight out? If not, how else could you gather information—from the person's friends, or maybe from observing how they act around you in the cafeteria? How does someone act if they like you? Also, in terms of Use of Information (Big6 #4), how do you know if the information is accurate and reliable? Finally, what sort of Synthesis (Big6 #5) and Evaluation (Big6 #6) does this kind of information problem necessitate? Mike reports that not only does this activity generate a great deal of excitement, but students quickly grasp the wide applicability of the Big6.

Travel

Another popular context for teaching the Big6 is travel. **Reuven Werber**, a library media specialist in

Israel, uses the concept of travel to teach information problem-solving skills to his ninth and tenth graders. Reuven introduces his students to the concept of information problem-solving with the following scenario: You have just received a request from relatives living abroad. They will be coming to Israel for a vacation and would like you to plan and guide them on a one-day tour of Jerusalem. The class then uses the Big6 to brainstorm some ideas and create a travel guide for their adventurous relatives.

The Big6 has also allowed our students to enter the mysterious world of international finance and strategic intelligence. Kay Hudson from Ohio reports that her high school students used the Big6 in their geography class to learn about Eastern Europe. Students worked for a public relations firm that had been hired by a wealthy investor. The young consultants were to choose an Eastern European nation, research it, and create a product that would convince their client to invest in the country in some way. Students created real estate advertisements, a business prospectus, and travel brochures. Our own inside sources tell us that the folks at Dean Witter are watching their backs—they may have some stiff competition for customers!

Keep those great ideas and stories coming! Until next time…

Big6 in Action: Reports from the Front Lines

v1 n4 p3,15

By Carrie Lowe

Greetings, Big6ers! In recent months, "Reports from the Front Lines" has focused on creative ways to integrate the Big6 into your classroom and library media curricula. For this column, I want to focus on an equally pressing issue for many Big6ers—how to "sell" the Big6 to fellow faculty members and administrators.

This topic has been discussed quite a bit recently on the Big6 listserv (**big6@listserv.syr.edu**). Not long ago, Mike responded to a listserv inquiry by a teacher facing the daunting task of introducing the Big6 to a school on a block-scheduling system. First, Mike considers block scheduling an asset in a school interested in integrating the Big6, since it can give teachers more time to work together. Mike advises teachers and library media specialists interested in introducing the Big6 recruit a "Big6 spokesperson." Begin by teaching fellow faculty members the Big6 in a faculty meeting, or discuss Big6 benefits one-on-one, stressing the importance of integrating information problem-solving skills into the curriculum.

Continue to emphasize the Big6 with other faculty or students by labeling your work in terms of the Big6. That is, if you teach a lesson on constructing a bibliography for a research paper, frame it in terms of Big6 #5—Synthesis; if you teach note-taking, make sure you present it in the context of the process—Big6 #4.2. Another key to making the Big6 approach usable is to present it to students and fellow teachers using a personal example, for instance, buying a gift for a family member. To assist fellow teachers in integrating the Big6 into their own curriculum, get involved. Find out what other teachers are doing in their classrooms, and suggest ways that you can team up to teach students the Big6 in context. These strategies should get you well on your way to persuading everyone in your school to use the Big6 strategy.

Kathy Spitzer, from **Cicero-North Syracuse, New York,** is the person who first suggested using the *I Love Lucy* video of Lucy and Ethel on the candy factory line as a metaphor for information overload and the need for teaching information problem-solving ("Job Switching," The I Love Lucy Collection, CBS/Fox Video, 2302, c1989). Wrapping the chocolates is just like processing information, and as the chocolates come by faster and faster, Lucy and Ethel are more and more frustrated. This really brings home the message that we can't just focus on content—packing in more and more. At one point, Lucy says to Ethel, "I think we're fighting a losing battle." Without Big6 process skills, students often are.

Anne Symons, from **Dawson Creek, British Columbia, Canada,** concurs that sharing a personal story is a great way to teach pupils (of all ages!) how to use the Big6 approach. She has used the problem of planning a Thanksgiving dinner for 12 people, with three vegetarian guests and one vegan guest. When presenting this problem to students and fellow educators, Anne fields suggestions and classifies them under the appropriate Big6 step. This allows people to see that, in many ways, they already use the Big6. It also allows them to see which steps they are missing in their information problem-solving strategy.

Since not every teacher has the flexibility that block scheduling can provide, it is necessary to consider some ways teachers with more rigid schedules can introduce the Big6 to colleagues. **Dr. Audrey Irene Daigneault** from **Groton, Connecticut,** has a suggestion—let fellow teachers spread the word! Audrey introduced the Big6 at a faculty meeting and then distributed Big6 bookmarks, enough for each student to have two. She then asked teachers to tape one bookmark to each student's desk, and give students the other bookmark to use at home. Teachers can direct students' attention to the bookmark on their desk and review the Big6 steps when homework is distributed.

Audrey reports, "Teachers like it because more of the homework comes back finished."

Dedicated Big6ers were given an opportunity to demonstrate their loyalty on the listserv recently when a new subscriber, **Elizabeth Bentley** of the **United Kingdom** wrote to the list asking, "What made you choose the Big6?" **Rob Darrow**, a library media teacher from **Clovis, California,** showed his true Big6 colors in his quick reply to Elizabeth's inquiry. Rob believes that one major strength of the Big6 is that it is easily understood by all ages. Rob begins the school year with a quick, basic introduction to the Big6 for all students. He then spends the rest of the year strengthens students' understanding of the Big6 by using it to solve information problems in context with the class. Rob also reports that because of the Big6, teachers and students look at librarians in a different light. The school librarian is viewed as an exciting teacher, not someone who simply stamps out books. The Big6 gives a face to information literacy and links the librarian to this important and interesting part of education. Finally, Rob believes that the Big6 is the best because it is so easily integrated into all curricula—teaching this to fellow teachers can make a Big6er of everyone at your school!

Anne Symons also responded to Elizabeth's question by further extolling the virtues of the Big6. Anne chose the Big6 for her information literacy curriculum because teaching the Big6 allows her to create assignments which "involve students in problem-solving or decision-making." She feels that the Big6 is an excellent choice since it brings important skills to existing lessons and units of the classroom.

Tami Little from **Hinton Community School, Hinton, Iowa** mentioned an idea from **Joanne Wolf** from **Topeka, Kansas,** who used a Big6 Burger to present to her faculty. Joanne gave each piece of the burger a Big6 Skill, the bottom bun, meat, cheese, tomato, lettuce, and a top bun each represented a skill. She actually sewed a soft, pillow version of the burger so the pieces could be added. The pillow became a display in her library.

Until next time….

Big6 in Action Reports from the Front Lines

v1 n5 p3, 5

By Carrie Lowe

Greetings, Big6ers! How can we use the Big6 to teach our students math and science skills? Once again, our colleagues have some great ideas!

Deborah Stafford, a library media specialist in **Wiesbaden, Germany**, wrote to the Big6 listserv (**big6@listserv. syr.edu**) recently about a math research project that she and a geometry teacher have been working on. For this project, students must choose two structures, one built before 1800 and one after. Students are given a list of facts to uncover about the structures, such as when the building was built, what it is, what its measurements are, where it is, and what are some of the geometric figures used in its construction. Rather than give students a list of specific structures, Deborah gives them a list of types of structures, such as castles, temples, statues, bridges, dams, stadiums, and skyscrapers. Armed with these lists, students choose two structures and find out about them. Impossible task? Not with the Big6!

Deborah helps students untangle the research problem by reviewing the Big6 with them and applying it specifically to this assignment. There are several ways to use the Big6 in this information problem: Students could brainstorm possible sources of information (Big6 #2, Information Seeking Strategies), study architectural models to find geometric patterns (Big6 #3, Location and Access), or consult sources (such as their geometry teacher) on how to figure out the measurements of the building (Big6 #4, Use of Information). Deborah reports that the teacher was very pleased with the project and with the students' abilities to find information.

A similar idea also focuses on geometry. Have students use magazines or books to locate a picture of a building. Next have student create an outline drawing of the building including all the architectural details. Identify the various geometric shapes that formed the components of the building, and create a key for identifying the geometric figures. This project focuses on Big6 #5, Synthesis. The teacher or library media specialist could demonstrate various methods for presenting information by using a key with color shadings or different patterns or by using different colors to outline the geometric figures within the building itself. Students can judge which presentation method best suits their building.

Pat Wilson of **Syracuse, New York,** contributed another idea to the listserv to integrate the Big6 and math concepts. This idea would be excellent to use during Black History Month or any month. Pat proposed a research project focusing on African-American inventors throughout history. There have been many: Garret Morgan (the inventor of traffic lights and gas masks), Madame C.J. Walker (inventor of very popular hair products, and the first female self-made million-

Teaching students how to use the new technology.

aire of any race), Edmond Berger (inventor of spark plugs), Ellen Eglin (inventor of the clothes wringer), and Elijah McCoy (inventor of a mechanism for oiling machinery while it is running), among others. Students could create a product that would explain the mathematical concepts involved in the inventions. It is unlikely that a research source will specifically state how mathematics played a role in the inventions. The teacher can help students use inference and logic to discover how math would have been used in the inventive process. This discovery process could lead students to further research on specific principles of mathematics. A similar process could be applied to scientific concepts, making this idea great for both math and science!

Many Big6ers, whether library media specialists or teachers, have become vocal advocates for the implementation of technology in schools. A side effect of this is that sometimes those who are most vocal are put in charge of the new technology when it arrives. Often, this includes teaching students how to use the new technology. **Sue Taylor of Holland, Michigan,** wrote recently to the list that she has found herself in just that situation at the grade school where she teaches. She asked advice from her colleagues who were in similar situations, and got several helpful responses. Pat Wilson, true to one of the central ideas of the Big6, advised Sue to always teach technology skills in context. For example, when students are ready to write up their research, she teaches them *ClarisWorks*. When they need to gather information, she teaches them to use the online catalog. Pat reports, "[this] ensures that the final product will not only stretch their research skills but also their technical skills." **Sandy Kelly from Westford, Massachusetts**, agreed with Pat's ideas and added a couple of other good examples of how to integrate the Big6 when teaching technology skills in context. For instance, using search engines to locate information on the World Wide Web or using Boolean searching to find information on a CD-ROM are part of Big6 #3, Location and Access.

If you have ideas for using the Big6 Skills to teach math and science concepts, technology skills, or anything else, share them with your colleagues by sending them to the Big6 listserv (**big6@listserv.syr.edu**) or directly to me (**calowe@mailbox.syr.edu**). Keep those great ideas coming!

Until next time.

Pat Wilson, true to one of the central ideas of the Big6, advised Sue to always teach technology skills in context.

Big6 in Action: Big6 Web Sites

v2 n2 p8, 14

By Carrie A. Lowe

Greetings, Big6ers! "Netting the Big6" which appeared in the September/October 1998 issue has sparked requests from our readers for more information on Big6 Web sites. In this column, we deliver!

Many of you are already aware of our Big6 Web site, "The Big6," which is located at *www.big6.com.* This evolving site contains lesson plans, information on Big6 resources, and links to schools implementing the Big6. But did you know that there is a whole world of other Big6 resources on the Web? Surf by these sites, and you'll see!

"The Big6—Dig It!" was created by **Shayne Russell,** a library media specialist in **Mt. Laurel, New Jersey.** This Web site is based on a lesson that Shayne did with her students before they began an archaeology research project in the media center. Shayne uses pictures from the Casa Malpais/Earthwatch archaeological expedition in Springerville, Arizona, to show students the process that archaeologists use to learn about the past through exploration. She cleverly compares the steps of the excavation process to the steps in the Big6. This lesson could easily be modified to use with students from fourth-grade on up. You can uncover "The Big6 - Dig It!" at: *www.voicenet.com/~srussell/ bigsixdigit.html.*

Verna LaBounty of **Kindred, North Dakota** has also developed a great online Big6 resource. You can find this Web site, "Big Six," by pointing your browser to: *www.kindred.k12.nd.us/CyLib/B6.html.*

"Big Six" is a great Web site for teachers unsure of how to approach the Big6 in the classroom. This resource gives a detailed overview of each step in the Big6, including questions teachers should ask themselves and their students. It also includes links to Web sites that can deepen students' and teachers' understanding of the steps of the Big6 process. "Big Six" also showcases Big6 projects from Kindred Public School. "Exploring Alaska" in "Big6 Examples" is a great project for fourth-graders and is a good example of a collaborative lesson.

File this one under: "Tools You Can Use." **Pam Barney** at the **University of Central Florida** has designed a useful Big6 tutorial for teachers. "Teaching Information Literacy: The Big Six Skills Approach to Information Problem Solving" can be found at *www.itrc.ucf.edu/webcamp/final_projects/ barney/big6.html.* This site is focused on information

Figure 1: Information Literacy Adventure Web Site

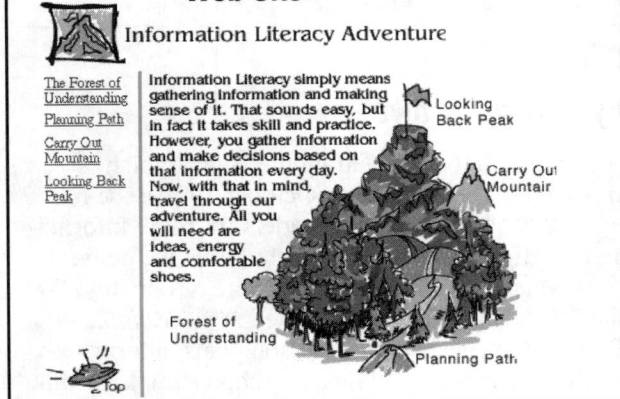

Information Literacy Adventure

The Forest of Understanding
Planning Path
Carry Out Mountain
Looking Back Peak

Information Literacy simply means gathering information and making sense of it. That sounds easy, but in fact it takes skill and practice. However, you gather information and make decisions based on that information every day. Now, with that in mind, travel through our adventure. All you will need are ideas, energy and comfortable shoes.

Looking Back Peak

Carry Out Mountain

Forest of Understanding

Planning Path

literacy and teaching information technology using the Big6. Pam breaks the Big6 into its component parts, and within each step, includes links to assignments and useful Web sites teachers can use with their students to reinforce Big6 skills. This is a great resource for teachers who want examples of how to integrate the Big6 with a number of curricular areas.

Supercool Web site alert! **Marlene Lazarra** (library media specialist) and **Aimee Heinzel** (technology facilitator), both at **Pleasant Ridge School** in **Glenview, Illinois,** have created an outstanding activity for teaching the Big6. Their Web site, "Information Literacy Adventure," approaches solving information problems using the Big6 like a journey. By clicking on different parts of the clever mountain picture (see Figure 1) they devised, students begin at the "Forest of Understanding," continue on to the "Planning Path," then move to "Carry Out Mountain," and end their journey at "Looking Back Peak." At each step of the way, students learn about important Big6 skills, and get tips on how to solve information problems. This site also includes an open letter to parents, stressing the importance of information literacy and teaching kids to solve information problems. Take a trek to prwww.ncook.k12.il.us and click on "Information Literacy Adventure" to see this project for yourself.

Do you have fabulous Big6 resources that you want to share with the world? Have you created a great Big6 Web site? If so, we'd love to hear from you. Send your ideas to: *big6@ericir.syr.edu.*

Big6 in Action: Reports from the Front Lines

v2 n3 p3, 15

By Carrie A. Lowe

Greetings, Big6ers! One response that we hear quite a bit from people first learning about the Big6 is, "This stuff would be great for teaching high school students about the research process. But I am an elementary school teacher. How can I use the Big6 with my students?"

"Big6 Believers" know that one of the great things about the Big6 is that it can be used with any grade level and applied to any information problem. For the youngest students, the Big6 terms can be translated into the Super3: Plan, Do, and Review (see *The Big6 Newsletter*, Vol. 1, No. 1). This information problem-solving motto is easy to remember, fun to say, and helps young students get a handle on information problem-solving.

Even our youngest students can think in terms of process. Here's one idea to try. Tell your students to imagine that they are characters in a story. What does every story have in common? They all have a beginning, a middle, and an end! Students should be able to relate their actions in the information problem-solving process to the place in the story. Let's take an example of an assignment given to a Kindergarten class. Students are to work with a partner to draw a picture showing five winter activities. Let's see how the Super3 could be applied. Are partners talking about which winter activities to include? (Plan). What about actually working on the project? (Do). How about looking over their picture before they turn it in? (Review). The Super3 is super easy and will put your little ones on the road to success!

Of course, there are lots of great activities that you can do with elementary students using the Big6 Skills. This is always a lively topic of conversation on the Big6 List, **big6@listserv.syr.edu**. Here's what some of the experts have been saying.

Debbie Mitchell is a library media specialist in her first year on the job at an elementary school. Debbie has been busy "spreading the word" about the Big6 to the teachers at her school. She has found the teachers to be receptive, particularly to ideas like collaborative planning. Debbie has found that convincing the Kindergarten teachers to use the Big6 is a bit more difficult. Kindergarten teachers believe that their students' library time should be more devoted to reading than to information skills. Debbie wrote to the list looking for ideas that could convince the Kindergarten teachers that their students are not too young to learn information problem solving skills. As usual, a team of Big6 experts was ready with some solutions to Debbie's dilemma.

Rob Darrow, of Clovis, CA, has been putting the Super3 to work with his daughter's third grade class. He offered Debbie some expert advice for proving to the Kindergarten teachers that even the youngest students need more than just story time in the library. Rob encouraged Debbie to start teaching her students the Super3 by creating some knockout posters or bookmarks for these kids. Then, she could mix her story telling with stories of the Super3, and have the students identify the steps of the Super3 within the context of every story she reads. (See pages 44-49 for some great ideas on using stories and the Big6). Once students learn to identify the Super3 in stories, the teacher or library media specialist will be able to prompt students to identify situations when they have used the Super3 in their own lives. Students (and teachers) will soon become aware of just how important information skills are, and what a powerful tool they can be for solving problems!

Rob ended his message to Debbie by waxing philosophical. He encouraged her to tell her students the same thing he does: "If you become a better information user, you will get a better job in the future. The people who will have the best jobs are the ones who know how to use the information the best! The earlier kids learn how to manage information, the better the world will be!" How true that is, Rob.

Other list members also offered advice about using the Big6 with younger students. **Dale Lyles, of Newnan, GA,** uses the Big6 for all elementary students instead of starting with the Super3 and working up to the Big6. Her advice to the list was to translate the Big6 into simpler statements and questions that even the youngest students would be able to understand. For instance, instead of 1.1— Define the problem and 1.2— Identify the information needed, try: 1. Task Definition: What do I need to do? Also, rather than insisting that her students memorize the Big6, Dale makes sure that the Big6 is posted so that students can see it and refer to it easily. Students will know the Big6 like the back of their hand before long!

Barbara Jansen also offered some great advice for using the Big6 with younger students. She revealed to the list that when she teaches the Big6 to teachers, she urges them to stress three things with their students. The first is awareness—it is important to point out to students when they use Big6 skills. For instance, a student is not just typing a paper in the computer lab—they are Synthesizing (Big6 #5)!

Once students learn to identify the Super3 in stories, the teacher or library media specialist will be able to prompt students to identify situations when they have used the Super3 in their own lives.

The second is developmental appropriateness—make sure that you are teaching the Big6 to students in a way that they can grasp. Finally, Barbara urges teachers to have fun with the Big6, so they can communicate to students that the information problem- solving process is an enjoyable one. Barbara has contributed lots of great ideas to The Big6 Newsletter about fun ways to teach the Big6 (see pages 42-45).

It is important to teach students information skills in the context of real-life needs and to fill students' "Big6 Toolbox" with skills that will help them solve information problems now and in the future. Location & Access skills are an important key to completing information problems successfully. **Mary Croix Ludwick, a library media specialist from The Colony, TX** has created a fantastic Location & Access unit for teaching third graders about the Dewey Decimal system, card catalogs, and electronic catalogs. This unit could be taught as a part of a major research project or literature project.

Mary begins the first unit by making her students be books. She gives her students posterboard "spines" with call numbers on them. Three students begin the activity by coming to the front of the room and arranging themselves on the "shelf." The rest of the class joins them in groups of three until the entire class is arranged on the shelf. The students then take these "books" to the library shelves to find where the book would have actually gone, had they been a real book.

Next, Mary teaches her students about card catalogs and electronic catalogs. Using Xeroxed catalog cards of actual books in the school library, Mary teaches her students to understand the information on the card. The students then use the cards to find the books, and compare the information on the card with that in the book. They then apply these same skills to the electronic card catalog. Is the information housed within the catalog a good description of the book? How can we use the catalog to find a book?

After Mary's students have learned all about classification, catalogs, and shelf placement, she has them actually shelve books. When they are able to shelve to her satisfaction, Mary pronounces them knowledgeable about shelf placement (imagine the wonderful crowns or other prizes that you could make for the students when you pronounce them Masters of the Dewey Decimal System!). From this point on, whenever Mary's students return a book to the library, they re-shelve it themselves. Sounds like a great idea to me!

Until next time,
Carrie

Big6 in Action: Reports from the Front Lines

v2 n5 p3, 11

By Carrie Lowe

Greetings, Big6'ers! In the last issue, we discussed Big6 lessons for elementary students. But of course, Big6 skills are important for students of all ages, from the youngest to the oldest. In this installment of the Big6 in Action, we focus on middle school mania. And if you've ever taught in a middle school, or even visited one, you know what we mean!

By now, Tami Little's "banana split" lesson is famous in Big6 circles and in schools all over the world. Although I have not had the opportunity to try the lesson with a class, I know it would be a big hit. Recently, **Melinda Miller-Widrick, from Colton, NY**, shared her answer to the banana split lesson on the Big6 mailing list. Instead of banana splits, Melinda and her students make their own trail mix or GORP (good old raisins and peanuts, for those of you who were never Scouts).

Melinda walks her students through the Big6 as they plan and make their trail mix. In Task Definition, the students decide to make trail mix. In Information Seeking Strategies, they decide on potential ingredients (cereal, raisins, nuts, M&Ms, sunflower seeds, etc.), and then decide which combination would mix well together. In the Location & Access step, students make a hypothetical trip to the grocery store, where they locate and access items (don't forget to make price a factor!). In Use of Information and Synthesis, students mix the ingredients to create their GORP. Melinda reports that her students' favorite step is, not surprisingly, Evaluation. This is where they taste their creation and discuss what they might do differently the next time they make trail mix.

Just like the Big6, making trail mix is a skill middle school students will use again and again. It is a snack they can prepare ahead of time and bring along to after-school activities and events.

Anyone who has ever worked with middle school students can attest to the fact that their stomachs are often their foremost concern. For this reason, food examples can work well to teach the Big6. Another great information problem to discuss with the class is, "I'm hungry for pizza. How can I get some for dinner?" Discuss different ways to get pizza, such as ordering it versus making it. Be sure to discuss your budget. If the class decides to make pizza, walk through the steps with them. What top-

pings should be on it? How much would it cost? If they decide to order it, be sure to discuss the index (phone book—a major Location & Access tool) they would use to get the restaurant's phone number. Or here's a great idea—why not collaborate with the home economics teacher and try making a pizza for lunch with your class? You could incorporate some math skills by having the students survey the class to find out what kind of toppings they prefer. Following this, they can turn the survey data into a chart and decide which toppings to include.

One of the great strengths of the Big6 mailing list is the ability to brainstorm curriculum ideas with other educators who are committed to teaching information problem-solving. **Debbie Stafford of Wiesbaden, Germany** learned this recently when she wrote to the list looking for advice. A teacher in Debbie's building was looking for good activities (something other than a poster or a writing assignment) with a strong Big6 component for a unit on the Golden Age of Greece. The Big6 list members suggested many good ideas. Some of these were:

- How about a talk show? She could have a host and have students play their character, dressed for the part.

- Have students create a newspaper from ancient Greece! Students can research and write articles on individuals and events. Special events could take the form of advertisements, as in, "Get your tickets for the 2nd annual Olympic Games now!"

- Stage a debate, following debate rules. Students can play the part of famous philosophers. Or, have the students debate aspects of Ancient Greek life that they research.

- Have the students compare a poem from the Golden Age with a modern poem of their own choosing. What things are different? What things never change?

- Present one of the great Greek plays, translated into modern English. Change the setting to the American inner city.

- Have the students create an entire radio network—talk show, sports and news broadcasts, interview, music, poetry reading, etc. Videotape the programs and give them to an elementary school class.

Does your middle school have a graduation party/dance? If you do, we're sure that this is a topic of discussion both inside and outside of school. So, how about using all this chatter to your advantage by engaging the class by using the Big6 to plan the end of the year party and handle the many different information problems? For example, there is the difficult decision of whether or not to bring a date, and if so, who to ask. . . not to mention how to ask. Another problem is what to wear. At this age, peers may be the best source of information to find out what is appropriate and what others are wearing. For the students who are planning the dance, there are issues of music, refreshments, and entertainment. We're sure that the school dance or party could lead to some very lively and fun discussions and would be a great way to demonstrate how the Big6 applies to real life.

Middle school students certainly have the enthusiasm and curiosity to make them naturally great problem solvers. We hope these suggestions will make it possible to channel this enthusiasm and curiosity to create assignments that interest and engage them. We'll bet that you will have a room full of excited problem-solvers before you know it!

Until next time,
Carrie

The Big6 Real-Life Problems

v2 n6 p8-9

By Carrie A. Lowe

What better way to demonstrate the usefulness of the Big6 than to apply the process to real-life situations?

"When will I ever use this?" moans a student referring to trigonometry, earth science, chemistry or any of a number of subjects. We've all heard this type of comment in our classrooms, the hallways, or at home. It is obvious that our students want to make a connection between what they are learning at school and real life. What better way to demonstrate the usefulness of the Big6 than to apply the process to real-life situations?

The following three very different examples illustrate how easy it can be to show students how the Big6 fits in with real life concerns. The first example is a space problem caused by to the emergency situation under which the Northernmost school in New Hampshire has been operating since last November. The second is an impromptu situation where a library media specialist's own need for a few prompts while storytelling showed students the importance of good note-taking skills. The third is a tale of a class fundraiser gone bad.

Space and the Big6

The K-12 Pittsburg School in Pittsburg, NH has been operating in a "crisis" situation since November of

Isn't that what good teaching is all about?

1997 when a severe air-quality problem forced the closing of the main building. As a result, the high school students have been sent to the elementary wing where, luckily, the library is located. The elementary students, however, were scattered to various locations across town, including the local church, a grocery store, and the town office. The art classes now take place on the stage, and the business classes take place in an empty restaurant. In addition, the principal, office staff, receptionist, nurse, special education teacher and a variety of classes have been set up in the library. The library has been unable to function as it should, and the library media specialist has had to take the library to the elementary classes—carrying boxes of books back and forth. It has been quite an undertaking.

All of these relocations presented a problem when it came time for the 1998 spring book fair. The book fairs are held twice a year and are major fundraisers for the library. The library staff did not want to cancel the bookfair despite the obstacles presented by all the relocations. Since the public is invited to the book fairs, the library media specialist was worried about how to find space for the book displays in the midst of a library that had already been rearranged to provide alternate spaces for classes and the office staff.

The library media specialist presented the problem to the sixth grade students. Their task was to figure out how to set everything up attractively and efficiently while still allowing all of the library's "guests" to function comfortably (Task Definition). The students brainstormed ideas (Information Seeking Strategies). These ideas were evaluated and synthesized into what was hoped to be a workable plan (Synthesis). Of course, the students were reminded that they would have to discuss the results of their plan after the book fair. One of the students was quick to label that as the Evaluation step of the Big6.

As it turned out, the suggestions that the students offered were much better than any that the library media specialist had thought of, and the practical use of the Big6 benefited not only the students but her as well. The library had a very good book fair in spite of the obstacles. Still, when the Evaluation step was carried out, the students identified some areas that needed to be improved for the fall book fair. By analyzing the book fair situation, the students learned a valuable lesson about how to successfully apply the Big6 to a real-life problem.

Storytelling as a Gateway to the Big6

Another way to make students aware of the applicability of the Big6 is to demonstrate how we as

teachers use the Big6 in our own lives. A library media specialist who was new to storytelling decided she would tell a story to the third grade. However, she found it necessary to use notes to jog her memory. This was a great way to demonstrate effective note-taking techniques (Use of Information).

After the library media specialist was finished telling the story, she confessed to students that she had jotted down a few notes in case she got stuck at one point or another. The following week when the library media specialist visited that same class, she reminded them of the storytelling experience and asked the class to tell her the characteristics of good notes. The students agreed that notes needed to be short, to the point, and carry the gist of the message.

To help the students practice the necessary techniques, the library media specialist repeated the same story. As the story was read, the students were asked to raise their hands if they thought they heard something that should be included in the notes. They then wrote on the board what they thought would be the simplest, clearest way to convey the information. The students did a good job and even had an added lesson because one of the students accidentally wrote something out of sequence. This was a perfect opportunity for the library media specialist to remind the students about how important it is to keep a semblance of order when taking notes so that they make sense later.

A Fundraising Opportunity

Finally, the library media specialist further demonstrated the applicability of the Big6 to real-life when the seventh graders held a fundraiser. These students put together "Halloween-grams" which are small bags of candy with messages attached. Students and staff purchase them to give out to friends. For some reason, the seventh graders were very unorganized. Because they had more orders than anticipated, they ran out of candy and bags several times and had to make numerous trips to the store. In addition to this difficulty, there was no system to keep track of who had received their candy-grams and as a result some orders were accidentally duplicated whereas others were never filled.

The seventh grade students were frustrated, but the teacher in charge wanted the "Halloween-grams" to be a learning experience and didn't want to step in and straighten things out for the students. When Friday arrived and students were desperately trying to finish things up and get the last bags out before the end of the day, one student said, "We're never selling candy-grams again!" Since they happened to be in the library filling the remaining orders, the library media specialist saw a perfect opportunity to jump in with a plug for the Big6—specifically the Evaluation stage. She suggested to the students that rather than giving up what could be a lucrative fund-raiser in future years, they should examine what went right as well as what went wrong so that the next time they tried to do this it would be a booming success.

Conclusion

These three situations are examples of how we, as teachers, can model the use of the Big6 in real-life situations. These skills will empower our students and they will begin to apply the Big6 to their own real life situations.

The BIG 6

Teaching Technology & Information Skills

PART VIII

Virtual Wisdom

AskA Services

v1 n3 p12

By Virtual Dave Lankes

QUESTION: "1000 Web sites, about a dozen news groups and a ton of listservs…am I missing anything?! The truth is in all this mass of information, can't I just talk to someone?"

It's easy when looking at the Internet to see only the World Wide Web. As URLs become as common as phone numbers, we are all guilty of assuming what we need can be found on the Web. However, students working on Information Seeking Strategies (Big6 #2), should also consider "people" as a source. And, the Internet can help here too. So, let's look at another type of Internet information service—AskA Services.

Ask-An-Expert services (such as Ask-A-Volcanologist or Ask-An-Astronaut) put the K-12 community (educators, students, and parents) in touch with experts. Often these experts can give a better answer than static Web pages. Experts are also aware of good Internet and non-Internet resources in the field.

I am currently working on a project called the Virtual Reference Desk that studies these AskA services. This project has located over 60 AskA services that seek to answer questions from the K-12 community. AskA services range in topics from the process of education (AskERIC), to mathematics (Ask Dr. Math), to the Amish (Ask an Amish Expert). Through e-mail or Web forms, a student or educator can ask a question. These services transfer the question to the best person to answer it. You'll generally get an e-mail reply that includes synthesis and resources.

Many AskA services also publish Web pages with information from previous responses. These archives of past question/answer sets known as FAQs (frequently answered questions), provide information in context. It is worthwhile to look at the FAQs before asking questions because someone else might have asked the same question before you. The Virtual Reference Desk has compiled a list of these AskA services, including their audiences, topic areas and location in an AskA Locator (http://www.vrd.org/locator).

Not all AskA services answer every question. Some services will take in thousands of questions and only answer a small representative subset (such as NASA's Ask-An-Astronaut). Other services will take a week or two to respond (such as MAD Scientist Network). Other services will answer all questions quickly (such as AskERIC and KidsConnect). In all cases, try to give the services as much context as possible. Grade level information, purpose of the question and extra information all help these services to give better responses. Again, be sure to check for FAQs or archives before asking questions…many of these services are in high demand.

In answer to the original question, there are people on the Internet waiting to talk to you and your students. If you're tired of looking through Web page after Web page, or can't find information you need in the form you need, give an AskA service a try. It might take a little longer than typing "www.killerwebsite.com," but chances are you'll get a lot more out of it.

Try the AskA Locator (http://www.vrd.org/locator), and let me know about other sites. Remember the true power of the Internet is not in the number of Web pages you can access, but your ability to get an answer. No Web page can answer a question better than an expert in the field.

Finding Lessons, Units, and Other Educational Material on the Web

v2 n1 p12-13

By Virtual Kathy Spitzer

Virtual Kathy? What gives? Just who is Virtual Kathy, and what happened to Virtual Dave? Well, Virtual Kathy is Kathy Spitzer, Assistant Editor for **The Big6 Newsletter***. Kathy is pinch hitting for Dave this issue because Dave has been just a little busy — with finishing his Ph.D., getting a new job as Assistant Professor at the School of Information Studies, Syracuse University, helping to write a funding proposal for the ERIC Clearinghouse on Information & Technology, and presenting his Virtual Reference Desk project at two national meetings. Way to go, Dave! Dave will be back next issue, but he better be careful—Kathy's "virtual wisdom" is pretty impressive.*

QUESTION: Isn't there an easy way to find lesson plans on the Web? I'm tired of sifting through so many different sites and coming up empty handed!

ANSWER: Yes—there is an easy way, and it will be getting even easier. Whether you're a classroom teacher looking for lesson plans and curriculum materials or a library media specialist locating materials for teachers, you're going to rave about the new Gateway to Education Materials (GEM) project site **www.thegateway.org.** Bookmark this one and tell all your friends!

GEM, The Gateway, is brought to you by your friends at the ERIC Clearinghouse on Information & Technology who also created AskERIC (**www.AskERIC.org**). GEM is sponsored by the U.S. Department of Education's National Library of Education and was developed in response to a call from the White House. In his April 19, 1997 NetDay address, President Clinton announced that his number one priority would be to make sure that all Americans have the best education in the world. He encouraged federal departments and agencies to support projects that would bring the power of the Information Age to all schools. GEM was one response to that call. The goal of GEM is simple—to provide the nation's educators with "one-stop, any-stop" access to substantial, but uncataloged, collections of Internet-based educational materials available on various federal, state, university, non-profit, and commercial Internet sites. These educational materials include lesson plans, activities, and projects that are searchable by grade, subject, or educational level.

As of August 1998, The Gateway contains more than 2,200 education resources from: Alphabet Superhighway; AskERIC; Computer Curriculum Corporation; Crossroads, A K-16 American History Curriculum; Eisenhower National Clearinghouse; Federal Resources for Educational Excellence; Library of Congress; Math Forum; Microsoft Encarta; Mid-continental Regional Educational Laboratory; Newton's Apple Lesson Plans; North Carolina Department of Public Instruction; School Library Media Activities Monthly; The Science Center; Virtual Reference Desk; and the U.S. Department of Education. And this is just the beginning. There are plans to add thousands more lessons from these and other organizations.

Best of all, The Gateway is easy to use. Several search mechanisms are available. By using the Simple Search (**www.thegateway.org/simple1.html**), you can conduct full-text, subject, keyword, or title searches and specify the desired grade or education level. You can also search by accessing a list of subjects or keywords. Retrieved records will link directly to the Internet resources they describe—it's that easy!

Sounds too good to be true, doesn't it? The Gateway sure worked for a teacher at Cicero-North Syracuse (New York) High School. She was looking for ideas to teach middle school students about accepting people of different races and ethnicities. She used the keyword search and clicked on "Racial Intolerance." This brought up two entries (**www.thegateway.org/index2/racialintolerance.html**). Analyzing the list of keywords for these entries led her to click on "Racial Attitudes." Bonanza! She found a multitude of entries—two of which were exactly the type of lesson she was looking for (**www.thegateway.org/index2/racialattitudes.html**).

For those of you who like to know the technical details, the Gateway is based on a meta-data standard developed by the GEM Consortium. Meta-data is "data about data," and makes it easier to represent the contents of large databases. For example, a card or online library catalog is filled with meta-data records about the books and other resources in the library. The GEM meta-data system is a massive virtual card catalog that enables educators to access educational materials of participating GEM consortium members via the Internet through The Gateway. What makes The Gateway a best bet is the human touch in creating the meta-data records. Sites are analyzed and categorized by subject and grade level prior to being added to the Gateway site. The cross indexing of subjects and keywords provides a value added service to educators! (For more information about the GEM meta-data effort or about how to become part of the GEM Consortium, check out **www.geminfo.org**). But, you don't have to know anything about meta-data or indexing or representation of information to use GEM. Just head for the Gateway. Try it, you'll like it!

A Hyperfiction Continuum (Interactive Documents)

v1 n6 p12-13, 15

By Virtual Dave Lankes

QUESTION: Aristotle told stories, Shakespeare told stories, I tell stories…isn't there anything new?

Katherine walked down the long, candle lit hallway. The corridor disappeared in the distance among flickering candlelight and oaken doors. Choosing a door, Katherine pushed hard as creaking hinges and the long dead tree gave way to a vast, cobalt blue interior. Light danced off a deep, illuminated pool of crystal water, sending veins of light and shadow over the leather bound books lining the walls. She selected a tome, set it on a nearby great table whose legs were gnarled and scarred by the engravings of long forgotten scholars. Opening the book, Katherine saw the odd symbols scattered upon the decaying parchment. With an indication, the letters reformed themselves into familiar words.

All right, I'll admit I am neither the most proficient or original storyteller. I give you the above passage not to enthrall you by the plight of Katherine, but rather as an example of a story. I'll use this example to demonstrate some of the new capabilities of hyperfiction—a new genre emerging from the digital age. Fiction is evolving into hyperfiction. This column explores some different levels of functionality you can achieve, and discusses the tools you'll need to create them.

Level 1: Electronic Documents

The first evolution of the story requires changing the medium from ideas to electrons. Once the story is digital it can be put in almost any format. It can be printed on paper, put on a Web site, pressed onto a CD-ROM, or even e-mailed. This column began as an electronic document. It is merely printed here for wider distribution.

There are a lot of options and possibilities when publishing a story in electronic form. The biggest advantage is the story can be put into almost any other format. The biggest problem with electronic documents is compatibility. Anyone working in an environment with Mac and Windows computers knows this problem. It may be digital, but the order of the digits does matter.

The problem is in the way word processors represent documents. Software tends to include the text of the story, the structure of the story, and the format of the story in a single document. When you read a book, all of these elements are part of the physical object. However, new printings may come with new covers and new typefaces.

In comparison, consider an electronic document's structure, and format as separate elements. This is the idea behind SGML (Standard Generalized Markup Language). Think about this article as a logical thing, not a physical one. It has content…words and an order—a rhetorical style and concepts. It has a structure—sub-sections, quotes, a title, and an author. And finally it has a format. By creating a story electronically using tools like HTML or the new XML (eXtensible Markup Language), an author can create content apart from structure, apart from format. In doing so, the reader can determine the format (Braille for the blind for example) apart from the publisher or author.

This concept becomes even more powerful when you think of structure in terms of concepts. Consider the following sentence:

Katherine walked down the long, candle lit hallway.

By structuring concepts by skill level, a reader could simply ask for more detail and get:

See Katherine walk down the hallway. The hallway is long. The hallway has candles.

The first sentence would be shown for more

With electronic documents, think of content, structure, and format as seperate elements

advanced readers and the latter for beginner readers (as determined by some sort of interface).

Using tools like HTML and XML, libraries and schools adapt to the whims of platforms and word processor writers. HTML allows users to move a file from computer to computer without regard to platform. HTML can be created with a simple text editor, more advanced HTML authoring software, recent versions of word processing programs (the next version of Microsoft Word is rumored to use HTML as its native file format).

The problem with HTML is that it may look different from browser to browser. If the author considers the format of the story to be essential, they might want to move to a tool like *Adobe Acrobat. Acrobat* software acts like a printer, but rather than printing to paper, it prints to an electronic document. The document can be viewed via a free reader application and it will retain all the formatting of the original document—graphics and all. You won't be able to edit it however, just share it.

Level 2: Linked Documents

Ok, so you've got your story in electronic form, HTML or Acrobat, why not jazz it up a little bit? The next level of hyperfiction is linking portions of the story. The links can be internal or external to the document. Like the "choose-your-own- adventure" books Mr. Stein of Goosebumps fame has brought back into vogue, hyperfiction stories can allow the reader more control over the course of events. The author can use links to either present a series of scenarios to the reader, or simply augment the linear narrative. For example, in the story above, the reader could click on Katherine's name to get background information about her. The doors in the long hallway could be a series of links. By clicking on different doors, different elements of the story might unfold.

HTML and *Acrobat* allow the author to embed links in their documents. Authors can link to other HTML or Acrobat documents, or any other media (including programs). HTML uses a tag that is embedded into a document. It looks like this:

Picking a door, <a href="Katherine.html"> Katherine</a> pushed hard as creaking hinges and the long dead tree gave way to a vast, cobalt blue interior.

This would display the word 'Katherine' in blue underlined text in most Web browsers. When a user clicked on the word 'Katherine' they would go to another HTML document named 'Katherine.html.' Pretty simple. Acrobat has an even easier interface that allows the user to select an area and then click through a series of dialog boxes to set the target of the link. Linking is what really puts the "hyper" in "hyperfiction." Other tools like HyperStudio and SuperCard create a series of screens (or cards) and link them together.

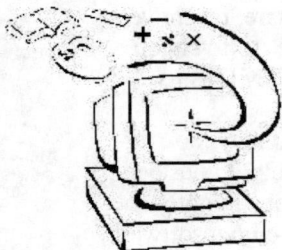

Level 3: Interactive Documents (Gaming)

On my first computer, a TRS80 Model III (hello fellow geeks), I played a game called *Pyramid*. There were no graphics, just small textual descriptions of the setting, and a simple command line interface that allowed you to use commands like 'N' for North, and 'look' to read the description of the setting. This early game was interactive, text-based storytelling. Some author took the time to develop a world and a story. The reader interacted with this story not in a linear way, but as a participant—discovering the story while being a part of writing it.

Computers have blurred the lines between fable and fantasy, recitation and recreation. In today's stories, the "reader" is often put in control of the story, and "authoring" has become more about setting a stage than acting the roles. Today's games, are really today's hyperfiction. In *Myst* the "reader" is placed on the dock of a strange island. There is no exposition, no three chapters of setting. Instead, the reader is creating the story of Myst through discovery. Only by the end of the game do the authors make clear their tale.

Tools such as *Quicktime VR* allow multimedia authors to create three-dimensional environments from photos or software. *Quicktime VR* movies can be linked together either via multimedia tools, or on the web. Other Internet protocols, such as Virtual Reality Modeling Language (VRML) allow hyperfiction authors to create full worlds with which users can interact.

In the story example, now the reader is Katherine! The Hallway and room are VRML code. The book a three-dimensional object.

Level 4: Collaborative Environments

Today's Internet allows many new possibilities for storytelling. Now readers can join each other in a common fable over the Internet. MOOs (Multiuser Object Oriented) and MUDs (MultiUser Domains) allow for role-playing fantasy storytelling. In MOOs and MUDs this collaborative authoring is all done through text, allowing the participants prose to create the images. Several schools have set up their own MUDs. Universities use these environments for foreign language training in virtual cities such as Madrid. Skyscrapers are created from code, and streets are paved with prose.

Microsoft has built a chat environment with VRML. "Readers" use avatars to interact with other "readers" in virtual worlds. Software such as the *Palace* takes software very similar to *HyperStudio* and allows multiple users to interact. Links take users from one "card" or screen to another. These screens can be on the same computer, or on any computer connected to the Internet. Schools can recreate themselves on the Internet, with students going from virtual classroom to virtual library to interact with other students, teachers and librarians online.

The world of hyperfiction is diverse and interesting. What we teach as storytelling with a linear structure and setting is changing dramatically. Today's stories are diverse, interactive, and different for every reader. Today, the author and the reader are becoming intimately tied together. Stories allow us to live outside of our experiences, isn't it time we let stories live outside their pages?

For more information about the items noted in this column check out:

- *Adobe Acrobat:* http://www.adobe.com
- HTML: http://www.w3c.org/MarkUp/
- *HyperStudio:* http://www.hyperstudio.com
- Microsoft *V-Chat:* http://beta.chat.msn.com/
- *Myst* and *Riven:* http://www.riven.com/
- *Palace:* http://www.thepalace.com/downloads/index.html
- *Quicktime VR:* http://www.apple.com/quicktime/
- VRML: http://vrml.org/
- XML: http://www.w3c.org/XML/

Intranets

v1 n1 p10, 15

By Virtual Dave Lankes

What's the latest in network and computing technologies? What's the Big6™ connection and how can new technologies be used for learning and teaching? These are the questions addressed in this column. The intent is to highlight cutting-edge developments from a use and users' perspective.

QUESTION: "What if I don't have fast, easy access to the Internet? Is there any way to still take advantage of Internet capabilities?"

Yes! In many cases you don't need a connection to the Internet to use Internet technologies. True you miss out on the huge amount of information provided on the World Wide Web, but you can still use software such as *Netscape* within the confines of your building or local area network. Both Windows 95 and Macintosh System 7.5 come with all the software you need to create your own small Internet, called an *intranet.*

Intranets are all the rage in business and the same tools and skills Fortune 500 companies are using to communicate with their employees are available for you and your students. By setting up intranets, students and faculty can create their own Web pages, get free building-wide e-mail, and teach and learn the skills businesses are eager for. You also have complete control of the information and resources provided on your own intranet.

An intranet is a local network that "looks and feels" like the Internet because it uses the same protocols and tools as the Internet.

For example, intranets use the TCP/IP protocol to get computers communicating with each other. A protocol is the "language" a computer uses to communicate over a network. For the Internet and intranets, that's TCP/IP. TCP/IP is usually already built into your operating system.

Both Windows 95 and the Macintosh OS include TCP/IP capabilities. Consult your documentation or systems person for details on how to hook up computers using TCP/IP.

Once you've wired and connected using TCP/IP, you are ready to build your intranet. Remember, the goal is to set up a local network that's not connected to the main Internet. You will be setting up a server—a computer that "serves" software functions to the other computers on your intranet. For example, you will add various Internet software programs that you want to provide, perhaps a browser, search engine, e-mail, ftp, even listserv or chat. Microsoft provides a free World Wide Server for both Macintosh and Windows95 operating systems directly from their Web site at http:// www.microsoft.com. Other free e-mail, listserv, gopher, ftp and chat servers are available through the WWW as well. Most of these programs come with ample documentation, and are relatively easy to set up.

While the above focuses on the technical side of setting up an intranet, the truly creative and interesting part is deciding what to offer on your intranet. This is the "information-side" of the effort and the Big6™ approach provides a useful guide to setting it up. For example, students can define the task of their intranet and part of their Information Seeking Strategies might be to survey the students and faculty in the school. Students might also scour the Internet for resources that would be appropriate (and legal) to include. Setting up the various systems is a major synthesis effort, and of course, they must evaluate the results. And, once the system is established, students

can use the intranet itself as a "Big6™ support system" because it could provide school-wide e-mail for ask definition, resources for information seeking, location & access, and information use, and a Web server to synthesize their own Web pages.

For more information on intranets check out:

- **Yahoo's Guide to intranets**

  http://www.yahoo.com/Computers_and_Internet/ Communications_and_Networking/ Intranet/

For a general overview of the Internet, consult:

- **Lankes, R. D. (1996). Bread and Butter of the Internet: A Primer and Presentation Packet for Educators.**

  Available (WWW): http://ericir.syr.edu/ithome/ monographs.html#bread.

Virtual Dave Lankes is Associate Director of the ERIC Clearinghouse on Information & Technology and the Information Institute of Syracuse.

Presenting a Good Image

v1 n5 p12-13

By Virtual Dave Lankes

QUESTION: I've created a great presentation, now how can I show it to my whole class?

Take a computer, a scanner, a graphics tablet; add software like *PhotoShop*, *PowerPoint*, and CD ROMs of clipart; and almost any individual can create an impressive presentation. There is, however, one small problem. Making things look good on a 15-inch monitor is a snap, but showing that image to an entire class can be a nightmare.

In this article, I look at some of the issues involved in presenting information (Big6 #5.2) to large groups. There are three basic options when you deliver a computer presentation to a large group:

- Printers,
- TVs and Monitors, and
- LCD Panels and Projectors.

Printers

One easy way to get a computer presentation off the screen is to print out your slides. You can print your computer-generated presentation on paper and use an opaque projector, or print the slides on transparencies and show them using an overhead projector. Or you can use a special printer (it's actually a high-resolution monitor in front of a camera) and create 35mm slides.

You can use almost any printer to create paper copies or transparencies. The question is, do you want color or black and white output. Laser printers provide better quality for black and white copies. If you want color, you could buy a color laser printer or a color ink-jet printer. The prices for these color printers range from $300 to $1000.

TVs and Monitors

Using a TV is another way to display computer output to an entire class. Many K-12 classrooms already have access to a TV. There is a difference, however, between a computer monitor and a TV monitor. TVs use a standard called NTSC (National Television Standard Code) that draws a picture in two passes (skipping a line on the first round, and filling it in on the second round). NTSC presents two main problems:

- It was never meant for fine detail, and
- It is not compatible with most computer output (VGA).

To overcome these two problems, you can buy hardware that converts computer output (VGA) to NTSC. These scan converter boxes cost less than $200. The image on the TV monitor is never quite as good as what you see on a computer display. Single point lines flicker, bright colors bleed into each other, and the colors never seem quite right. However, the TV is bright enough to be seen in full daylight or with the classroom lights on.

Using a large monitor is a better idea. Large monitors are available in 21 to 40 inch sizes for about $5,000 or less. Another great option is the new home theater PC. The *Gateway* Destination computer, for example, comes with a 36-inch monitor, a Pentium processor, a 4GB hard drive, DVD (Digital Video Display) player, and five channel surround sound— the works for under $4,000. The drawback: Large TVs and oversize monitors are not very portable when you want to take your show on the road.

LCD Panels and Projectors

Projecting the computer image is a great way to display a computer desktop so that students can work collaboratively on task definition, information seeking, and synthesis. When you use a projector or LCD panel, you can adjust the size of the image to meet your needs.

The quality of LCD panels has improved, but the clarity of projected images is still not very good. LCD panels cost less than $1,000, and can project most types of displays. However, you need to add the cost of a high-power overhead projector. These sys-

tems work best in a dark room. The larger you make the image, the lighter and fuzzier it gets (meaning it may be difficult to show your images to the whole school in the gymnasium).

LCD Projectors incorporate the light source and display unit. They may weigh as much as 10-20 pounds, but the image is superior to an LCD panel's image. You'll need to dim the lights, but you don't have to turn them off. While you can expect to pay between $3,000 to $8,000 for an LCD projector, there simply is no better option for high quality, portable projection. There are also combination projection units that can display a computer image or a VCR tape. Combination projection units can be used as an overhead projector, or as an opaque projector. They cost around $5,000.

When you are choosing any projection system (panel or projector) you may want to look for:

- **DISPLAY TYPE:** How many pixels and colors can the projection system send to the screen? The minimum resolution you need is 800 by 600 pixels at thousands of colors.
- **MEDIA TYPE:** In addition to displaying output from a computer, you can use projectors (and panels) to project video (from a VCR) and sound (from the computer, the VCR, or any other sound source). You'll need to check what kind of connectors the device has for video. (S-VHS is common, but some support NTSC output like a TV.)
- **LUMENS:** Look for a minimum of 250 lumens. A high quality built-in room projector may have up to 1,000 lumens.

The Future?

The new trend, something called DLP (Digital Light Processing), consists of several hundred thousand mirrors mounted on a microchip. When current is supplied to the chip, certain mirrors reflect the light of a certain color. Unlike LCD panels, where light passes through a semi-transparent membrane of liquid crystals (meaning some of the light is absorbed), DLP reflects all light so it provides a brighter image. Because DLP is a digital technology, images have a much higher resolution.

Conclusion

LCD Projection systems are less expensive, more portable, and more powerful than ever. Bottom line: If you have the money, buy high quality projectors. If not, buy a good ink-jet printer or use a TV.

For more information about the items noted in this column, see:

- *Presentations Online* for presentation technology and techniques
  www.presentations.com
- *InFocus* for information on their LCD panels and LCD projectors
  http://store.infocus.com/
- *PhotoShop*
  http://www.adobe.com/prodindex/photoshop/main.html
- *Hewlett Packard* for color printing information and products
  http://www.pandi.hp.com/pandi-db/home_page.show
- *Gateway* Destination
  http://www.gateway.com/
- *PC Magazine's* review of LCD Projectors
  http://www8.zdnet.com/pcmag/features/lcdprojectors/_open.htm
- Texas Instrument's Discussion on DLP
  http://www.ti.com/dlp/

Real Time Messaging for Collaboration

v1 n4 p12-13

By Virtual Dave Lankes

QUESTION: "Okay, e-mail is great—but what's next?"

In the newest James Bond film "Tomorrow Never Dies," Bond has an incredible, intelligent telephone. This telephone does the normal phone stuff (i.e., calling people, delivering 10,000-volt shocks), but it also drives his car! I mean it turns the thing on, turns the wheel, and shoots rocket launchers—the whole thing. I can't tell you how many cold mornings I wish I could launch my car's rockets from my phone.

What does this have to do with education, learning, and the Big6? That phone represents what we all long for—a simple device that combines all of our communications activities. From a Big6 perspective, we use telephones and other communications technologies:

- to discuss our tasks and collaborate on solutions with others (Big6 #1 and #5)
- to locate and access information sources such as other people (Big6 #3), and
- to interact with those other people (Big6 #4).

Today, many of us use cellular phones, pagers, date books and laptops to seek, locate and engage information. But having to use all these is still too cumbersome. The good news is that computers are finally starting to live up to their promise to converge all of these technologies. So, let's get started with an Internet-based system for fast, real-time, information gathering and synthesis.

First you need a computer hooked up to the Internet with at least a 14.4 modem (although 28.8 or faster is preferred). Next we want to load ICQ for Windows or Mac. ICQ (think "I seek you") is free software that allows you to set up an account, and then create a "buddy" list of other ICQ users. Once set up, you can see who is online at any given time, send each other quick messages, engage in text-based chats and a lot more. You can tell people you are ready to talk, away from your desk, or just ask people not to disturb you. Once you are on someone's contact list, they can send you quick short notes that pop on your screen as soon as the messages are sent—in real time. It's great for phone messages or quickly sending someone a file or a URL.

There are other Internet paging software packages as well. IPage works well, and AOL has freely distributed their Instant Messenger on the Internet (in fact they are distributing it for free with the newest *Netscape Navigator*).

The next piece of software you'll need is conferencing software. I recommend NetMeeting, but it is only available for Windows95. If you check out ICQ's web page you'll find a list of other conferencing software. Once you have a conferencing package installed on your machine, you can see if someone is on, page them to see if they want to talk, then link seamlessly into a conference call. When I say a conference call, I mean it—hook up a microphone and it is almost (almost, but not quite) as good as talking on the phone.

In addition, with Internet-based conferencing, you can share a white board for sketching ideas and even applications on either machine. For example, recently Mike Eisenberg and I were in two different cities, but we were able to work jointly on a *PowerPoint* presentation—in real-time. We made an initial contact via ICQ and launched NetMeeting to speak and hear each other. I then brought up *PowerPoint* on my computer, and was able to share it with Mike—through the "collaboration" function of NetMeeting. We could talk to each other over the Internet while sharing a mouse to make real-time changes to the PowerPoint presentation.

To improve audio conferencing, I recommend using a combination headset/microphone, which costs about $24 dollars at an electronic store. With this device, you avoid feedback and ambient noise (both of which these computer conferencing packages are susceptible to).

Want to add video-like CU-SeeMe? No problem. Relatively inexpensive video cameras (like the Connectix QuickCam, costing between $100-$200) will allow you to send video with your voice as well.

Linking these software pieces with the old stand-bys (the Web and e-mail), you have a truly distributed work environment, combining the full range of communications and information capabilities.

What's next? Well, all of these features are quickly working their way into the handheld market. ICQ will soon be available for WindowsCE, Microsoft's handheld computer operating system. Hey, maybe next year I'll be able to launch my car's rockets from the comfort of my home AND surf the Web on my phone!

For more information about the capabilities noted in this column check out:

- ICQ http://www.mirabilis.com
- Page http://www.ichat.com
- Netscape Navigator http://www.netscape.com
- WindowsCE http://www.microsoft.com/products/default.asp
- NetMeeting http://www.microsoft.com/products/default.asp
- Connectix QuickCam http://www.connectix.com/
- CU-SeeMe http://www.cuseeme.com/
- PowerPoint http://www.microsoft.com/products/default.asp
- Tomorrow Never Dies http://www.tomorrowneverdies.com/

Synthesis Tools

v2 n2 p12-13

By Virtual Dave Lankes

QUESTION: "How do I turn all of this paper into something I can use on the computer?"

There's the information. It sits mocking you. Resources, data, knowledge, scattered about your desk, floor, or classroom. Reams of notes, index cards, printouts, pictures, a long forgotten lunch laughing at the task before you. Your computer's hard drive is plotting to crash as it bursts at its hermetically sealed seams. Folders hide in the file system with descriptive names like "data," "stuff," and "important." It's now time to synthesize!

In previous articles we tackled much of Big6 #5.2 in the discussion of projectors and hardware to allow your presentation to escape the confines of your computer. In this article we'll target the 'minor' task of impounding all your research and information in your computer.

Scanners

Let's start with all those dead-tree (paper) resources you've accumulated in the course of your investigation. Scanners are a wonderful thing. These days you can get a good color scanner for under $1,000. Features to look for are resolution (600 dpi minimum), color capacity (32bit color), and a means to connect it to your computer. Most connections will be SCSI devices. For Mac users this is no problem, for Windows users this may require adding a separate hardware card to your computer. In the future the connection issue will be made easier with the introduction of the USB (Universal Serial Bus). USB is on both new Macs and Windows PCs and will allow you to hook up devices such as scanners, keyboards, cameras—almost anything.

You can scan documents into your computer as images or as text. Bringing in your document as text will allow you more flexibility since you will be able to manipulate that text in the future. To accomplish the task, you'll need some Optical Character Recognition (OCR) software. Software such as *OmniPage* and *Textbridge* look at the dots on a page and try to interpret them as letters and words. These software packages are very accurate although your output will depend on the quality of the original that is being scanned. Don't expect to be able to bring in handwritten notes as text. The OCR software can't recognize handwriting.

Digital Tablets

The *CrossPad* digital tablet, which costs about $350, is solving the "handwriting problem." It looks like a thick tablet holding a plain old legal pad. You write out your notes, sketches and ideas on the CrossPad electronic legal pad (with special pen), then attach the tablet to your computer and instantly upload them to your PC. You write on the legal pad with the provided pen in ink. You treat it just like another pad of paper. But, when you're done, you connect the tablet to your computer with a serial cable and upload all the data. The CrossPad has been recording the movement of the pen, and can now transfer those drawings digitally.

Handheld computers like the *PalmPilot* and Compaq's *PC Companions* also allow the user to keep notes and images electronically. Unlike the *CrossPad* where you write on paper, here you work directly with a small computer and computer screen. These devices also keep calendar information and contacts.

Digital Cameras

Do you need to store images? Digital cameras allow you to quickly create digital images. Gone are the days of wires and serial ports—most cameras now store images on PC Cards (also called PCMCIA cards). These small credit card size devices pop out of the camera and right into the PC card slot of your computer. Digital cameras cost around $300-$700 and take very good images (although the quality is not as good as regular film at the consumer level). For the ultimate in convenience, take a look at the Sony Mavica camera. This digital camera stores images directly to a standard 3.5 inch floppy disk. Just take the pictures, pop out the floppy disk, pop it into the drive of your computer and view the images stored as JPEG files.

Putting It All Together

OK, so now you've scanned in your notes and taken your pictures. We will address video and sound in an upcoming article. How can you put your notes and pictures together?

In previous articles, I've discussed Hyper Text Mark-up Language (HTML) and Portable Document Format (PDF) as file formats for presenting documents. However, each of these formats has associated synthesis tools. PDF has a program called Adobe *Exchange*. You create a base document in any piece of software that can print (like a word processor). When it is time to print the document, print it to a PDF file by selecting the "Acrobat PDF Writer" option instead of your normal printer. Open that PDF file in Exchange and you can add links, movies, and buttons.

In terms of HTML, there are several widely-available HTML authoring tools. Two good ones include SoftQuad's *HoTMetaL* and Macromedia's *Dream-weaver*. These programs make HTML markup automatic and allow you to easily combine text and images with links.

More advanced synthesis tools include *PowerPoint* and MacroMedia *Director*. These tools let you combine media (text, sounds, pictures, animation) with special effects and interactive controls. *PowerPoint* is the easier of the two programs, but is pretty linear. It was built around the concept of a slide show and while you can do some linking it is

best for linear presentations. Director is more complicated, but can do a lot more. Director is a full multimedia authoring environment that can create animations and sophisticated programs. You can also save Director movies into standalone programs to be distributed on CD-ROM or save them as Shockwave movies to use on the Web.

In next month's article we'll take a look at movies, sound, and other ways to present information on the Web.

Helpful Links

Look here for more information and free demos:

- CrossPad **http://www.cross-pcg.com/products/crosspad/index.html**
- Mavica Digital Camera: **http://www.ita.sel.sony.com/products/imaging/mvcfd7.html**
- Macromedia Director and Dreamweaver: **http://www.macromedia.com**
- SoftQuad's HoTMetaL: **http://www.softquad.com**
- OmniPage:**http://www.caere.com/products/omnipage/suite/**
- TextBridge: **http://www.scansoft.com/**
- Acrobat: **http://www.adobe.com**
- PalmPilot: **http://palmpilot.3com.com/home.html**

Web Authoring

v1 n2 p12

By Virtual Dave Lankes

QUESTION: "I know how to use the Web to locate and engage information. Now I want to synthesize—to create my own Web pages. Are there any easy ways to do this?

Repeat after me: HTML is my friend. Of course, just because it's your friend doesn't mean you have to, you know, hang out together. HTML stands for HyperText Mark-up Language and serves as the foundation of the web. By embedding certain keywords between the symbols < > you can tell a web browser how to display text and images on the screen.

Here's a simple example of how HTML works: The keywords, or tags, you use affect how text and graphics are displayed on the screen. For example, to write:

This is a really neat thing!

You would have to tell the browser using HTML what text is bold, italics and so on. So in HTML this sentence would look like:

This is a really <i>neat</i> thing!

The "" tells the browser to make every thing after that tag bold, the "" tells it to stop making text bold.

You can do very sophisticated formatting in HTML. You can create tables, make frames on the screen, and format pictures. However, you need to be very specific about how text and graphs are formatted. This process of tagging text by hand can be very time consuming. To get a feel for the effort involved, save your favorite Web page in source (HTML) format and open the saved file in a text editor—you should see a lot of codes (browsers will also let you look at the source directly as well).

By using HTML, you can mark-up links, images, and text and share your findings with the world. You've probably already created an HTML file without even realizing it. For example, if you "surf the Web" and save bookmarks using Netscape, you are actually creating an HTML file (bookmark.htm—try to find this file on your hard disk; you can view it using a word processing program). You can even save the file onto a floppy disk and distribute it to others.

However, this doesn't really answer the question about easily creating your own web pages. The bookmark file doesn't allow you to add more detailed information such as analysis, pictures and other things needed to truly synthesize information. And, creating HTML from scratch can be tedious.

One alternative is to use one of the numerous HTML authoring tools available. Some of the best are: *Claris Home Page, Microsoft's Front Page* and *Netscape's Composer* (built into Netscape's newest browser release). You can create a document just as you would in a word processor, and the program will output to an HTML file. Any of these tools will allow you to drag links, pictures and text from your favorite browser into your document of your making.[1] These tools will even upload and download HTML pages to a web server automatically.

Still, these tools are fairly complicated for the average computer user. That's why it is still much simpler for most people to present their information in print form using word processing or various works (i.e., Claris or Microsoft) software packages.

But—good news! You can do both—create documents for printing and the Web at the same time! Increasingly, synthesis software (e.g., word processing, spreadsheets, presentation software) allows you to output documents for printing and in HTML. The

That's right—most of your favorite word processors are now HTML editors.

resulting HTML documents can be shared through the Internet or your own intranet (please see page 182 for a discussion of intranets).

That's right—most of your favorite word processors are now HTML editors. *Word Perfect, Microsoft Word*, and *Claris Works* all include the ability to save files to HTML simply by choosing "Save as…" from the file menu and setting the file type to HTML. Word Perfect has the best implementation in my opinion; Word's HTML is a bit clunky and makes some odd formatting decisions. Also, note that HTML is not as full featured as what you are used to with print word processing documents. That is, the resulting Web pages may not look as good as your printed output—expect to loose columns and some of the "fancier" formatting options.

Finally, if you really want a synthesizing treat with the web, try Microsoft Office 97 (for Windows 95). Every application in Office (Word, PowerPoint, Excel and Access) is HTML aware. That is, you can create HTML pages from any of these programs, for example in:

ACCESS: create a database of annotated Web sites organized by subjects resulting in reports and tables in HTML. You can even, with a little more work, set it up so the database is built dynamically on the Web—able to accept input remotely from others.

EXCEL: make a spreadsheet and charts of local weather information, and then save the resulting worksheets and charts in HTML and post on your Web site or intranet.

POWER POINT: create classroom presentations combining text and graphics—even record a narrative to go along with the presentation. When you're finished, save the entire presentation and upload to the Web for anyone to view. The narration can be heard using RealAudio format.

WORD: combine text and graphics in reports, flyers, newsletters and save them in HTML and then move the files to the Web. Instant Web site!

In using these programs, we're not talking about scripting and a lot of obscure commands. All of these options are simple menu items within the programs. Microsoft has even provided wizards to walk you through the process. These programs even allow you to save to and open files directly from an FTP site as if it were your local hard drive. And, if you don't have Office 97, hang on a little longer—HTML capabilities are already or will be built into almost all software products in the near future.

---

[1] Of course there are some serious copyright and intellectua property questions here. I'll leave those for you to ponder on your own.

So, it's time to get on the web—not as a surfer, but as an author/publisher. With HTML tools and HTML capabilities within various packages, it is just as easy to synthesize information for the Web as it is to do so in print or on disk.

It's time to share your work and that of your students with the world!

(For more information and free demo):

- Microsoft Office 97:
  http://www.microsoft.com/office/
- Microsoft Front Page:
  http://www.microsoft.com/frontpage/
- Netscape: http://www.netscape.com
- Claris Home Page:
  http://www.claris.com/products/

Web Portals - Make Them Work For You

v2 n5 p10-11

By Brian D. Eisenberg

QUESTION: "I'm confused with all the talk about Portals. So, just what is a Portal and how can I benefit from using one?"

If you use the World Wide Web, chances are you've already been to a Portal, though you may not have realized it at the time. After all, everyone's been to Yahoo—right? Do you remember in 1994 when Yahoo introduced its searchable directory on the Web? They were one of the first companies to capitalize on the search engine concept. It didn't take long for others to catch on, and soon companies like *Altavista, Lycos, Infoseek,* and a host of other search engines entered into this emerging market.

As time progressed, these Web sites established large user populations and soon became some of the most popular sites on the Web. To keep up with the changing needs of growing user populations, many of these companies realized the need to expand and modify their services; not only to maintain the loyalty of their existing users but to attract new users to their sites. This spawned fierce competition. In the course of several short years, the competition resulted in the evolution of what we now call the "Web Portal."

As previously mentioned, *Yahoo* first pioneered the Portal concept in 1994. You might be thinking, "But wait a minute, if Portals have been around since 1994, why all the recent hype?" Well, it has to do with the rapid growth and expansion of the Web as well as advancements in Web technologies and E-commerce. When compared to the search engines of the past, today's Web Portals offer many new and exciting information resources and services. Portals are everywhere these days—we read about them in the news and we watch their stocks skyrocket up and down and back up again.

Now that you've got some background information, it's time to learn what Portals are and how you, your students, and your colleagues can use them. Portals are sites that provide one-stop access to popular Web resources and services. A Portal is a centralized location that provides access to everything you need. Portals are the first place you go when you access the Web; that is, the first page that loads when you launch your Web browser.

Most Portals allow you to customize sections for news, sports, stocks, weather, health, education, and technology. Some Portal sites have the capability to automatically customize a Portal for you by compiling information based on your zip code. All you do is enter your zip code and the Portal will add various information content and links that relate to where you live. For example, my Portal is configured to give me the latest weather and traffic information for the Seattle metro area.

In addition to customized information content, many Portals offer services such as Web-based e-mail, a personal homepage, calendar and scheduling programs, address books, TV listings, maps and driving directions, chat rooms, discussion boards, yellow pages, local news, classifieds, and of course, online shopping. When used properly, these services can really help make life easier by filtering information. Sounds like Big6 #5, Synthesis to me! That's right! Portals help organize information from multiple sources and present the result.

So how do you maximize the many resources and services that Portals offer? Most Portals offer "Site Tours" and provide detailed instructions to help guide you through the many options. Review what each Portal offers and then decide which Portal will best suit your needs. Then go to the Portal and click "Personalize" or "Customize" and follow the instructions.

To illustrate how you might customize a Portal, here's how I do it. I use the *Microsoft Network* (MSN) Portal as my homepage. I customized several sections for news, weather, education, technology, stocks, and my personal links. My personal links are URLs for sites that I frequently use but are not found anywhere else on my MSN Portal. For example, the first site I added to my personal links section is a link to *My Yahoo* portal. That's right, *"My Yahoo."* I rely on both Portals to help meet my daily information needs. I use my MSN Portal for customized information content and Microsoft Network services like *Expedia* for real estate and loan information,

Sidewalk to find information such as local restaurants, special events, or recreation, and *Expedia* for booking airline tickets, hotels, and car rentals, etc.

I use *Yahoo's* Portal in combination with the MSN Portal because it allows me to customize and synchronize my *Outlook* calendar, schedule, and contacts—something I can't do with my *MSN* Portal. I use Yahoo's Yellow and White pages to find restaurants, business addresses, etc. I rely on *Yahoo's* mapping services to get driving directions to any location I need. In doing so, I automatically add each address to my personal address book, so I can find it quickly later. *Yahoo* stores the address as well as the driving instructions and related information. When I want to return to an address I can save time by just retrieving this information. Granted, the scenario I just described might seem fairly complex, but the resources and services available on today's Portals can be used in many useful and helpful ways.

Not only can Portals work well in our personal lives, but they also can be incorporated into lessons at school. For example, teachers can help their students incorporate Portals into the Information Seeking Strategies process by having the students customize a Portal for classroom use. An effectively designed Portal can give students an interface they can use during Location & Access. Or how about a lesson on how to manage information overload? Demonstrate to your students how they can sort the information they need for daily living by having them make their own Portals. I'll bet the relevance of this lesson will guarantee that they'll pay attention.

Below is a list of Portals. Check them out to get a first-hand look at some popular Web Portals that can help you organize and synthesize your important information. Who knows? Portals just might make your day a little less hectic!

Selected Portal Links:

- AOL: http://www.aol.com
- Microsoft Network (MSN): http://www.microsoft.com
- Netscape: http://home.netscape.com
- Excite: http://www.excite.com
- Altavista: http://www.altavista.com
- Infoseek: http://www.infoseek.com
- Go: http://www.go.com
- Snap: http://www.snap.com
- Lycos: http://www.lycos.com
- Goto.com: http://www.goto.com

MP3 - The Future of Audio?

v2 n6 p10-11

By Virtual Kathy Spitzer

QUESTION: "What is the future of audio on the net?"

Now that it's summer and you have some time to learn and experiment (and read and relax, of course), how would you like to learn about MP3, the newest technology for sound files on the Internet? If you'd like to try it out for yourself, you'll need access to a computer running Windows 95, 98, or NT or a Macintosh computer with Internet access and the ability to download files. A speedy Internet connection will help.

About MP3

Before I describe the how to's, let's learn about MP3 and what it can do. MP3 is shorthand for MPEG 1 Layer 3 (that is the first version of the MPEG standard and the specific part of the standard dealing with audio). MPEG was developed in 1988 by the Moving Pictures Experts Group (MPEG), a committee that was formed under the auspices of the International Standards Organization. Some of the first uses included video disc players and video on the Internet. Subsequent versions of the standard have improved format and found their way into cable systems and satellite TV. MP3 is quickly becoming the medium of choice for distributing music on the Internet—often without the permission of the creators of the music.

MP3 works by employing a compression algorithm (similar to that of zip compression with which you may already be familiar) that can convert music, video, or spoken words (think audio books) into a file format that can be read on a computer. Let me give you an example.

With software, such as *Audiograbber* on a PC or *MacAmp* on a Mac, I can capture a song from a CD and create a standard, *uncompressed* sound file such as a WAV (Waveform Audio File Format) file. This WAV file of a 3-minute song takes up about 35 megabytes of storage space. By using the MP3 compression standard, that same 35 MB WAV file can be saved as an MP3 file that will only be about 1 megabyte! I can play it with an MP3 player on my computer or on a portable MP3 player which is similar to a walkman. And the sound quality is good—maybe not good enough for those of you real audiophiles who want to tweak the bass and treble; but, so good that some listeners can't tell the difference between MP3 and CD.

For you *Star Wars* fans out there, here is the **dark side**. Copyright. Yes, at the present time, there are lots and lots of Web sites featuring pirated songs in the MP3 format. And, unbeknownst to us, our students might very well be downloading illegal songs from these very Web sites in our schools or libraries. It is our responsibility to teach our students about copyright and about respecting intellectual property rights.

Another negative is that MP3 is only now getting support in most popular software packages. MP3 is not as easy to use in presentations as Quick Time files. You can't cut and paste an MP3 file into PowerPoint or a word processor. You'll need to download special MP3 encoders and players from the Web. However, despite these down sides, I think you'll see real support for MP3 in standard software packages this year.

MP3 in Schools and Libraries

Okay. I can hear you now. You're saying, "Kathy, how am I going to use MP3 in school or in my library? Let's connect MP3 to the Big6. The MP3.com web site features a free 45-minute summary of the news created by the editorial staff at The *New York Times*. (Available at: **http://www.mp3.com/audible/**). On this same page, you can also access free MP3 files developed by the staff at *The New York Times* for the following sections:

- **FRONT PAGE:** covers all of the New York Times front page stories
- **INTERNATIONAL:** features the top three international stories
- **UNITED STATES:** includes the top stories from around the United States
- **BUSINESS:** presents a summary of market activity and trends
- **JOURNAL:** allows you to listen to an article on culture, science, or food
- **SPORTS:** features the top stories in sports and
- **COMMENTARY:** presents the "Editorial of the Times" and such columnists as William Safire, Maureen Dowd, and Frank Rich.

I don't know about you, but I'm just about salivating at the rich assignments that students could be given to use the above features. How about having students listen to the top stories each day and produce their own newspaper or newscast? You could have different groups work on different sections of the project. Through such an assignment, students would practice their listening skills (Big 6 #4, Use of Information) and Synthesis skills (Big6 #5).

While not offering a collection of freebies like the MP3.com site, another site that is worth knowing about is Audible.com (**http://www.audible.com**). This site is marketing MP3 files in hopes of capturing an audience of those people who currently listen to "books on tape." It offers a collection featuring business programming, and general programming including education, fiction and nonfiction, humor, spirituality, sports, and time-shifted radio programming. Audible.com is banking on the availability of portable walkman-like MP3 players that are coming on the market.

Here are just a few other potential uses of MP3:

- Providing listening comprehension exercises on disk for foreign language or English as a Second Language students
- Putting important announcements on the school's web site
- Making a demonstration disk for music students (after necessary copyright permissions are secured, of course).

Getting Started with MP3

I can tell you want to try MP3 for yourself, so here's what you need to know to get started. If you are going to play MP3's that you download from the Internet, you need a player. You can either download one or buy a portable one. For about $200 you can purchase a Diamond Rio MP3 player. This is a portable MP3 player that you can hook up to your computer via the parallel port. It allows you to download 60-minutes of MP3 audio, and you use it like you would any other portable stereo. There are no moving parts so there is no skipping. You can even add extra memory through flash cards for even more capacity.

If you want to download an MP3 player to your

Selected links for more information and free demos:

GENERAL MPEG INFORMATION
- http://www.rcc.ryerson.ca/rta/brd038/papers/1996/mpeg1.htm
- http://www.mpeg.org/MPEG/

PLAYERS
- Audiograbber http://www.audiograbber.com-us.net/
- MacAmp http://mac.org/audio-video/macamp/
- WinAmp http://www.winamp.com/
- Diamond Rio http://www.diamondmm.com/products/current/rio.cfm

computer, check the MPEG.org site for a good selection— available at ***http://www.mpeg.org/MPEG/MPE-audio-player.html.*** Some players are freeware while others are shareware that needs to be registered after a trial period, and still others include those that you must purchase.

After you've chosen and downloaded a player, you'll also need to configure your browser. The previously referenced MPEG.org site has links about configuring your browser as well. If you choose a player that is capable of streaming, you may be able to configure your browser to stream the MP3. Streaming will play the MP3 file while it is downloading so that you don't have to wait to hear what you're getting.

Now you can try out your newly installed player. Visit ***http://www.mpeg.org/MPEG/mp3.html#music*** and choose a site that features free and legal music. Or you can visit www.audible.com and listen to a selection from a book or a news story. And don't forget about the free New York Times selections I mentioned above. Happy listening!

PART **IX**

Parent Connection

Helping With Homework

v1 n1 p4-5

By Mike Eisenberg

So, I'm at breakfast this morning (June 6, 1997) at the bagel place with my son Brian. Instead of reading our usual local newspaper, we pick up the *Wall Street Journal*. Big shot investors–that's us. Brian grabs the front page and says, "Hey, Dad—that's you!" Right on the front page, there's a story about homework and kids and parents. "Homework Should Be a Critical Assignment for Mom and Dads." (*Wall Street Journal*, June 6, 1997, p. 1).

Wow! What an opportunity! But, as I read on, I become more and more uneasy. The article is talking about an effort to get people to re-meet their kids, says Deb Carr, Reading Supervisor for the Hazelton, Pennsylvania Schools. So far so good. But, what's being proposed is for parents and kids to meet over homework. And not just the homework they currently have, they are talking about new interactive homework—playing math games, recording weather and other local information, surfing the Web for information about animals or whatever.

Apparently, there are a number of these kids-parents homework-school programs being promoted in various communities. The programs seek to involve parents into their kids' learning by having them work together on curriculum-oriented projects. For example, Skeen Elementary School in Leesburg, Florida sends home a weekly 'contract' telling parents what to expect—reading, worksheets, and projects. The parents sign the contract and agree to help. Bells Middle School in Potomac, Maryland began offering bonus homework in response to parents' requests for more. The common element in these and other programs seems to be students working with their parents on new subject area content.

And that's what makes me uneasy. Bob and I certainly support parents and children working together on homework. After all, that's what the *Helping with Homework* book is all about! But, it's not about adding new homework. Students have plenty to do already! And teachers are overburdened by curriculum to cover. Adding new tasks for kids and their parents to do—and for the teachers to grade—only adds to the burden of content, to information and task overload.

The article talks about homework coming in and out of fashion, and it's certainly in style now according to Harris Cooper, a University of Missouri psychologist. One of the reasons given is the infor-

> *"Adding new tasks for kids, parents, and teachers only adds to the burden of content, to information and task overload."*

mation explosion itself. William Stixrud, a Washington psychologist, laments that his high school biology textbook was 300 pages while his daughter's is 1,000. This is something that I've often talked about: information is exploding and we all have to deal with more and more everyday.

But—BUT—the solution is not to cram in more, or work faster, or work more. The solution is to work smarter—not to try and learn and remember content, but to focus on the process of dealing with all this information. That means information processes, information literacy-the Big6™ (ta da!). The new interactive homework programs that are mentioned in the *Wall Street Journal* article seem to be missing the boat. They are focusing on new content, not applying processes to existing content. Parents and kids—being asked to work together interviewing neighbors about changes in the community or coming together to a math magic night at school? Sorry, but wrong.

These additional activities only add to the content burden. It adds new material to the curriculum (oh boy, just what the teachers need). It gives parents more to learn and do themselves (because they've got so much time on their hands). And, adding more content misses the target in terms of what kids really need. Kids need to learn how to do. This means how to solve information problems, wherever they may find them. That's using the Big6™ to:

- size up a problem (Task Definition)
- figure out alternative information resources and choosing the best one given the nature (and importance) of the task, and the time (Information Seeking Strategies)
- get to the information in the resources as quickly as possible (Location & Access)
- determine what information in the resource is relevant to the task (Use of Information)
- combine and present the information in a logical way using an appropriate medium (Synthesis)
- determine whether they've done a good job and how they might improve next time (Evaluation).

Parents can play a major role in helping students to learn these skills. As stated in our *Helping with Homework* book, parents can help with an assignment at three different points in time:

- before their children actually start their homework—by talking the students through the process
- during the work—by troubleshooting with their children if they get stuck
- after their children are finished—by checking their work.

In this way, parents act as guides, coaches, and helpers. The parent is not being asked to teach—as that usually leads to their children exclaiming "that's not the way my teacher does it." The parents are guiding their children on teacher-determined, established goals and curriculum. This curriculum is not an add-on, it's not additional homework to "enrich" the "real" curriculum. The parents are helping their children in relation to their central concerns, the very things that they will be evaluated on.

So, yes—involve parents in a homework partnership. That's great. But not by putting more of a content and time burden on parents, the kids, or on teachers themselves. Focus on having parents guide and advise their children as they work through their existing work. Help them help—with the Big6™.

Parents and the Big6 - It's Time!

V2 n3 p8-9

By Marlene Lazarra

Ask parents about the Big6 and most will say they know about the Big Six consulting firms or the Big 10 and Big 8 college sports conferences, but most have never heard of the Big6 approach to information problem-solving. However, that's not the answer you'd get from parents who attended a recent evening presentation I gave at Pleasant Ridge School, Glenview, IL. I spoke on information and technology literacy, and the Big6 figured very prominently in my presentation.

Introducing the Big6

Since its introduction over the past two years, the Big6 has been just that—"big"—at Pleasant Ridge School. Fourth- through sixth graders at the suburban school use the Big6 when they're in math class, when they plan presentations for their classmates, and when they're researching all kinds of topics. I work together with teachers to help students learn about this information literacy process and provide opportunities to use it whenever an information problem arises.

For example, earlier this year, a fifth grade teacher brought her class to my Learning Center to begin a social studies unit. I began a discussion about the Big6 with the class, and a student said, "Oh, we just talked about that in math this morning." As the teachers and students discussed how they had used the Big6 in math, they talked about applying the Big6 to their research project.

I also co-taught a sixth grade health education unit with the physical education teacher. We grouped students according to learning styles, and the students relied on the Big6 as the framework for their projects. Students were asked to research a particular health-related topic, write a paper on it, and teach their classmates about it by using technology in their presentations. Students created videos, used spreadsheets to create charts, etc. One group's presentation on the heart can be seen at their Web site:

http://prwww.ncook.k12.il.us/StaffStudents/ stuwork/peprojects/PEhome.html

Teachers used the Big6 to plan more effective projects. Before the Big6, students would typically stop with Skill #4, Use of Information. As one sixth grader said, "I took information from at least three sources, put it in my own words, and wrote my paper." The Big6 helps teachers and students to continue their learning by focusing on Big6 Skill #5, Synthesis and Big6 Skill #6, Evaluation. This had a dramatic impact on student (and teacher) learning—particularly in terms of student self-evaluation. In many classrooms, teachers now allow time for students to reflect on and assess their progress. Students now go beyond writing a traditional paper or report to applying their new knowledge of the information process in a variety of exciting ways.

Missing Piece

I was pleased to see teachers and students use the Big6. However, I realized a necessary component was missing when I read the responses of Pleasant Ridge parents to a PTA survey—information literacy was not mentioned. I therefore approached the PTA President and offered to do a presentation for parents to teach them about information literacy. The PTA president agreed, and asked me to also give the presentation to parents of students from the cluster school (K-3).

In planning the presentation, I used the Big6 myself. For example, I defined my task as follows: to make parents aware of the information explosion and the need for information literacy. I decided that the presentation should answer the questions:

- What is information literacy?
- Why do we teach this?
- How do we teach it?
- When do we teach it?
- How can parents help?
- How can good teaching strategies be modeled within the presentation?

After defining the task, I continued using the Big6 framework as I gathered and sorted through resources to select the materials I would need to do an effective presentation. I decided that I would begin with a video, demonstrate the thinking processes used with the Big6, incorporate a slide show presentation, and follow up with a brief discussion period.

Presenting the Big6 to Parents

I began my presentation by showing parents a portion of the "Job Switching" segment from an old *I Love Lucy* show (this idea came from Mike Eisenberg who got it from Kathy Spitzer), and asked them to think about why I was showing this, and what the video had to do with information literacy. Thus, I modeled a strategy for helping students to focus as they watch a video (or TV show).

Because I wanted parents to see a real life application of the Big6 process, I demonstrated how I used the Big6 stages to plan and create the presentation for parents. Prior to the presentation, I had written the Big6 stages on a large whiteboard. I described my thoughts as I determined the task and identified questions that needed to be answered. As I described Big6 Skill #2, Information Seeking Strategies, I held up the various resources available, including books and printouts downloaded from various electronic resources. When I got to Big6 Skill #6, Evaluation, I told them I knew I was efficient because I was there with everything I needed; however, I wouldn't know if I was effective until they filled out the parent feedback forms.

Following this demonstration, parents were shown a slide show presentation. Each slide highlighted the questions I had generated when planning, and I discussed each in turn. As parents watched the large-screen television, I elaborated on each point, describing actual classroom scenarios to explain how the Big6 process works.

When I got to Big6 Skill #6, Evaluation, I told them I knew I was efficient because I was there with everything I needed; however, I wouldn't know if I was effective until they filled out the parent feedback forms.

Parents joined in a lively discussion and when one parent asked where she could learn more about computers, I told her to "use the Big6" and think about her particular needs, available resources, etc. This was a great way to demonstrate that the Big6 is useful for any information problem.

The parent feedback form was distributed and I invited parents to pick up copies of several articles I had photocopied. Feedback was overwhelmingly positive. I followed up by sending home copies of articles and Web site URLs to those who asked for more information. As further evidence of the effectiveness of the presentation, I can report that Eisenberg and Berkowitz's book Helping with Homework: A Parent's Guide to Information Problem-Solving (1996) has been checked out by parents almost continuously since that evening.

Conclusion

There's still much more learning and sharing to do. Parents have asked for more information on search engines, evaluating Web sites, and how to effectively do online searching. I am now wondering how to get parents to look at and use the school's Web-based Big6 Information Literacy Adventure (see The Big6 Newsletter, "Big6 In Action," Vol. 2, No. 2). Perhaps a weekly note in the school newsletter might also help. The bottom line is—the Big6 works and parents know it. This is an important opportunity for the entire educational community to work together to help students succeed.

About the Author

Marlene Lazarra is the Learning Center Director for Pleasant Ridge School, Glenview, Illinois. She has 18 years experience as a library media specialist. "The Big6 has given me a whole new focus and has actually helped 'recharge my batteries,'" says Lazarra. (lazarra@ncook.k12.il.us)

The BIG 6 — Teaching Technology & Information Skills

PART X

Final Notes

Questions? Ask Mike and Bob

v2 n1 p8-9

We've recently received a number of questions related to information, technology, learning and teaching, and the Big6. So, we thought we'd share a few of these with you—along with our responses, of course. If you have additional questions, please e-mail them to: big6@ericir.syr.edu.

Q: As a classroom teacher, I am so overwhelmed by the amount of information on the Web that I don't know what to do to help students begin to make sense of it?

A: Yes, the Web is a good news-bad news story. There's so much out there, but how do you really use it effectively and efficiently? Making sense of the Web involves most of the Big6 process—from Task Definition to Evaluation.

TASK DEFINITION: Don't start with the Web; start with the problem. Discuss what the students are trying to accomplish and what the result might look like.

INFORMATION SEEKING STRATEGIES: Consider options and alternatives – even within the Web. Big6 #2.1 involves brainstorming possibilities while #2.2 involves choosing the best sources given the situation. That means applying criteria, such as closeness to the problem, accuracy, currency, and authority. Students should be able to explain why they chose to use a particular Web site based on one or more of these criteria.

LOCATION & ACCESS: Search tools are a key! Discuss how the various search systems differ. Students should be able to explain why they prefer one over another.

USE OF INFORMATION: This stage involves selecting good information, again based on applying relevant criteria such as accuracy, authority, preciseness (close to the need), and ease of understanding. Discuss criteria and how to make choices based on criteria.

SYNTHESIS: Ease of use is the primary concern in Synthesis. How easy is it to find information on a Web site? Is it logical, easy-to-understand, and simple to navigate.

Evaluation: One aspect to focus on is efficiency— saving time and effort while maintaining quality. This relates directly to the original concern of not being overwhelmed by information. What are some strategies for using the Web for a purpose, but doing so without wasting considerable time?

We suggest working on some of these Big6/Web issues in context—that is, when students are working on a project or assignment that lends itself to using the Web. And, you don't have to cover all Big6 in each context. The first time, discuss the Web and Task Definition, later cover Information Seeking Strategies or Evaluation. The key is to link students' learning about the Web into a relevant Big6 and curricular context.

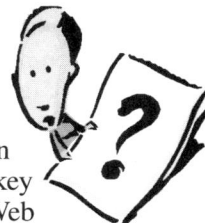

As a teacher, it's your decision how to structure instruction in relation to the Web. If you think the Web provides information to support students' learning, then the challenge is to structure Web use both from a Big6 perspective as well as an instructional design perspective. For example, you may be more interested in having students gain experience in using Web resources than in having them select Web resources. To do this, create folders and pre-select materials for students by setting bookmarks. This narrows the scope of Big6 instruction to Big6 #4, Use of Information. Pre-selecting helps students get off to a good start and focuses their efforts on using Web information and recognizing the characteristics of valuable sites. Instruction at another time may emphasize efficient search strategies for Web use, Big6 #2 – Information Seeking Strategies and #3, Location & Access.

Q: I'm a library media specialist. With information becoming available in places other than the library, how will I be able to reach out to students and teachers? I'm afraid they will no longer need to come to the library.

A: This question is arising more and more frequently. And, we have a ready answer: the LIBRARY is not a place – it's a concept. The LIBRARY is everywhere. So, if students and teachers are using information resources, systems, and networks in their classrooms, homes, or even shopping malls, that's LIBRARY! If we help our students use information more effectively and efficiently, we are doing our job. If the school is wired, and students are using resources in their classrooms—go to the classrooms. If they are using the Web from home, discuss how to maximize their Web skills when working at home. As far as coming to the central library, that's where we should provide special resources (for example, stand-alone CD-ROMs, a high-quality, high-interest fiction collection) or high-end systems (for example, multimedia production hardware and software) that make it desirable for students to come to the library. The bottom line is remember that wherever students interact with information—that's LIBRARY.

Here is also where curriculum mapping becomes essential (see *The Big6 Newsletter,* March/April, 1998, p. 8-9, 14-15). Curriculum maps allow library media specialists to know what is going on in the classroom so that they can respond with relevant instruction, resources, reading guidance, and other services in a timely, contextual way. Curriculum mapping helps the LIBRARY meet the needs of its users regardless of location.

Q: **I try to keep up with technology, but I feel so inadequate. With the card catalog there were certain rules that we followed, and they didn't change as rapidly as technology does these days. Now I feel that even though I try to learn new technologies as fast as I can, I am never on top of it. I guess what I'm trying to say is that I'm not an expert anymore.**

A: Yep, technology does change—and frequently. According to Moore's Law, technological capability doubles every 18 months! That means that my new computer is 400 percent more powerful than your three-year-old model or eight times more powerful than a six-year-old machine. And, no matter how much you know, there is always something else to learn. So, what do you do? First, realize that no one is an expert on all things anymore. We all narrow our focus—one person is a graphics person, another does superior Web-based searching. Second, networking,

cooperating and collaborating with others—and sharing expertise is a good model for accomplishing work. In school, this means classroom teachers working closely with library media specialists and technology teachers and with the students themselves.

Computers and the Internet represent new forms of technology. Overhead projectors and film projectors are teacher-oriented technologies, and most teachers are comfortable using technology in this way. But computers and the Internet are learner-oriented technologies, and teachers are less experienced and comfortable using technologies in this way. Recognizing these differences is part of the process of mastering these technologies.

Finally, look at your desire to keep up with new technologies as your own Big6 problem to solve. Define the task—what aspects of technology do you want to stay up on and what are the information requirements (amount of information, format, quality)? Then move on to Information Seeking Strategies and the rest until you have developed a personal system for staying up-to-date on the areas you feel are most essential.

*That's all for this time. Again, if you have additional questions, please e-mail them to Mike & Bob at **big6@ericir.syr.edu***

Index By Blythe A. Bennett

relevance 115, 159
reluctant teachers 42
Research Buddy 88-89
responsibility 96, 119, 122
review books 108
rubric 23, 63, 122, 163
Russell, Shayne 171

S

satisfaction 115, 153
scanners 186
SCANS (Secretary's Commission on
     Achieving Necessary Skills) 5, 6
Schicker, Phyllis 166
science 170
scoring guides 122, 123-126
self assessment 119-122, 126, 196
self evaluation 24, 44
SGML 181
Shannon, George 47
Sharmat, Marjorie Weinman 49
Simpson, Claire 167
Small, Ruth 115
Smith, Sharyl 149, 150
social responsibility 8, 12
song 42-43, 45, 145
special needs 65-70, 153, 159-160
Spencer, Lynn 49
Spitzer, Kathy 3, 8, 9, 59, 94, 169, 179, 190
sports 71-74, 74-75, 100
spreadsheet 72
Stafford, Debbie 170, 174
state-wide implementation 149
states and information literacy 9
story strips 45
storytelling 44-49, 52, 173, 175, 176
Stripling, Barbara 16
student achievement 21, 153
study tips 131-132
summative assessment 123
summer institute 151
Super3 20, 41, 172-173
Symons, Anne 169, 170
synthesis 58, 109-110, 168
synthesis tools 186-189

T

Tait, Sunnie 139
task definition 57, 95-97, 166, 167
task definition log 97
Taylor, Sue 171
TCP/IP 183

teaching information literacy skills 11
team teaching 168
technology 60-63, 74, 75, 77-81, 84, 107, 201
technology skills 29
television 184
Tepe, Ann 22
textbook 107-108
Thanksgiving dinner 169
Thomas, Nancy 139
Tidwell, Ann 161
toad, a home for 44-47
Todd, Ross 21-22
trash-n-treasure 43, 86, 103-104
travel 168-169
Tredennick, Diane 50
triads 97
use of information 57, 103-108

U

Utah 149-164
UtahLINK 152, 153

V

vague assignment 96
Valentine's Day 168
Venn diagram 50
Virtual Reference Desk 179
virtual wisdom 179-192
visual organizers 23
VRML 182

W

Washington, George 51
web authoring 187-189
Web sites (Big6) 171
Werber, Reuven 168
Wilson, Pat 170, 171
Wolf, Joanne 170
Workshop Planning 61
Wright, Janice 166
WWW *see Internet*

X

XML 181

Z

Zurkowski, Paul 3